Contents

Introduction (v)

Study Guide (vii)

Part A: Financial Systems and Auditing

1 Accounting systems 3

2 Management control 19

3 The role of the auditor and the auditing environment 43

4 Planning the audit 55

5 Recording audit work 71

6 Audit evidence and audit procedures 91

7 Audit reports and auditors' liability 115

Part B: Taxation (Finance Act 2009)

8 The tax practitioner and the UK tax environment 143

9 The personal tax computation 151

10 Taxation of employment 169

11 Income from investments and property 201

12 Tax documentation and payment of tax 211

13 The taxation of businesses 229

14 Trade profits – basis periods and losses 275

15 Corporation tax 301

16 Corporation tax administration 325

17 Capital gains tax 335

Tax Rates and Allowances 347

Appendix: Edexcel Guidelines 351

Index 359

Review form

LEARNING MEDIA

Introduction

BPP Learning Media's **Business Essentials** range is the ideal learning solution for all students studying for business-related qualifications and degrees. The range provides concise and comprehensive coverage of the key areas that are essential to the business student.

Qualifications in business are traditionally very demanding. Students therefore need learning resources which go straight to the core of the topics involved, and which build upon students' pre-existing knowledge and experience. The BPP Learning Media Business Essentials range has been designed to meet exactly that need.

Features include:

- In-depth coverage of essential topics within business-related subjects

- Plenty of activities, quizzes and topics for discussion to help retain the interest of students and ensure progress

- Up-to-date practical illustrations and case studies that really bring the material to life

- A glossary of terms and full index

In addition, the contents of the chapters are comprehensively mapped to the **Edexcel Guidelines**, providing full coverage of all topics specified in the HND/HNC qualifications in Business.

Each chapter contains:

- An introduction and a list of specific study objectives
- Summary diagrams and signposts to guide you through the chapter
- A chapter roundup, quick quiz with answers and answers to activities

Other titles in this series:

Generic titles

Economics

Accounts

Business Maths

Mandatory units for the Edexcel HND/HNC in Business qualification

Unit 1	Business Environment
Unit 2	Managing Finance
Unit 3	Organisations and Behaviour
Unit 4	Marketing Principles
Unit 5	Business Law
Unit 6	Business Decision Making
Unit 7	Business Strategy
Unit 8	Research Project

Pathways for the Edexcel HND/HNC in Business qualification

Units 9 and 10	Finance: Management Accounting and Financial Reporting
Units 11 and 12	Finance: Auditing and Financial Systems and Taxation
Units 13 and 14	Management: Leading People and Professional Development
Units 15 and 16	Management: Communications and Achieving Results
Units 17 and 19	Marketing and Promotion
Units 18 and 20	Marketing and Sales Strategy
Units 21 and 22	Human Resource Management
Units 23 and 24	Human Resource Development and Employee Relations
Units 25-28	Company and Commercial Law

For more information, or to place an order, please call 0845 0751 100 (for orders within the UK) or +44(0)20 8740 2211 (from overseas), e-mail learningmedia@bpp.com, or visit our website at www.bpp.com/learningmedia.

If you would like to send in your comments on this Course Book, please turn to the review form at the back of this book.

Study Guide

This Course Book includes features designed specifically to make learning effective and efficient.

- Each chapter begins with a summary diagram which maps out the areas covered by the chapter. There are detailed summary diagrams at the start of each main section of the chapter. You can use the diagrams during revision as a basis for your notes.

- After the main summary diagram there is an introduction, which sets the chapter in context. This is followed by learning objectives, which show you what you will learn as you work through the chapter.

- Throughout the Course Book, there are special aids to learning. These are indicated by symbols in the margin:

Signposts guide you through the book, showing how each section connects with the next.

Definitions give the meanings of key terms. The *glossary* at the end of the book summarises these.

Activities help you to test how much you have learned. An indication of the time you should take on each is given. Answers are given at the end of each chapter.

Topics for discussion are for use in seminars. They give you a chance to share your views with your fellow students. They allow you to highlight holes in your knowledge and to see how others understand concepts. If you have time, try 'teaching' someone the concepts you have learned in a session. This helps you to remember key points and answering their questions will consolidate your knowledge.

Examples relate what you have learned to the outside world. Try to think up your own examples as you work through the Course Book.

Chapter roundups present the key information from the chapter in a concise format. Useful for revision.

- The wide **margin** on each page is for your notes. You will get the best out of this book if you interact with it. Write down your thoughts and ideas. Record examples, question theories, add references to other pages in the Course Book and rephrase key points in your own words.

- At the end of each chapter, there is a **chapter roundup** and a **quick quiz** with answers. Use these to revise and consolidate your knowledge. The chapter roundup summarises the chapter. The quick quiz tests what you have learned (the answers often refer you back to the chapter so you can look over subjects again).

- At the end of the Course Book, there is an index of key terms.

Part A

Financial Systems and Auditing

Chapter 1
ACCOUNTING SYSTEMS

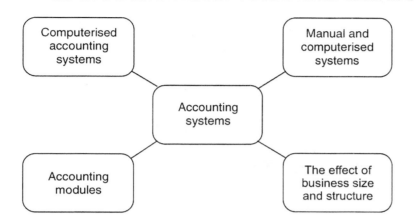

Introduction

These days most accounting systems are computerised. Hence, a sound knowledge of computer applications in accounting is very important, even for a beginner. While using a computer package does require a certain level of specialist knowledge about the unique characteristics of the system, the good news is that the principles of computerised accounting are the same as those of manual accounting. Even the accounting functions retain the same names in computerised systems as in more traditional written records.

This chapter starts by introducing you to accounting packages and then it takes a somewhat detailed look at the operation of the programs available to deal individually with the various parts of the accounting system such as the sales ledger, purchase ledger etc. Such programs are called modules and are discussed in Section 3.

A modern computer generally consists of a keyboard, a television-like screen, a box-like disk drive which contains all the necessary electronic components for data processing, and a printer. This is the computer hardware. Computer programs are the instructions that tell the electronics how to process data. The general term used for these is software. Software is what we are concerned with in this Course Book.

Your objectives

In this chapter you will learn about the following.

(a) The major features of accounting packages
(b) The functioning of the sales, purchase and nominal ledger modules
(c) The effect of business size and structure on the accounting system.

1 MANUAL AND COMPUTERISED SYSTEMS

FOR DISCUSSION

As most accounting systems are computerised, why do you think we learn bookkeeping as though they were manual? Do we really need to learn bookkeeping at all when the computer does so much of the work?

In this chapter, we focus on computerised accounting systems and the functioning of the sales, purchases and nominal ledger modules. However, you should not lose sight of the fact that both manual and computerised systems are intended to achieve the same results: the recording of transactions and the production of accurate accounts.

2 COMPUTERISED ACCOUNTING SYSTEMS

2.1 What are accounting packages?

'Software' can be defined as computer programs that tell the hardware what to do.

Definitions

> **Accounting packages** are collections of computer programs or software designed to carry out specific accounting tasks. They may be customised or bought 'off-the-shelf'.
>
> An **accounting suite** is a set of accounting modules or programs.

Examples of accounting packages are packages for payroll, sales and purchase ledger packages and tangible non-current assets register. Small businesses are more likely to purchase 'off-the- shelf' packages as this is normally a more cost effective option. Larger organisations may develop 'bespoke' software.

FOR DISCUSSION

Which accounting packages are you familiar with? What are they used for? Are they 'off-the-shelf' or 'bespoke'?

One of the most important facts to remember about computerised accounting is that in principle, it is exactly the same as manual accounting. Even the accounting functions retain the same names in computerised systems as in more traditional written records. Computerised accounting still uses the familiar ideas of day books, ledger accounts, double entry, trial balance and financial statements. The principles of working with computerised sales, purchase and nominal ledgers are exactly what would be expected in the manual methods they replace. The only difference is that these various books of account have become invisible. Ledgers are now computer files which are held in a computer-sensible form, ready to be called upon.

2.2 Coding

Computers are used more efficiently if vital information is expressed in the form of codes. For example, nominal ledger accounts will be coded individually, perhaps by means of a two-digit code: eg

05   Profit and loss account
15   Purchases
22   Trade receivables ledger control account
41   Trade payables ledger control account
42   Interest

In the same way, individual accounts must be given a unique code number in the sales ledger and purchase ledger.

When an invoice is received from a supplier (code 1234) for £3,000 for the purchase of raw materials, the transaction might be coded for input to the computer as:

	Nominal ledger		Inventory		
Supplier code	*Debit*	*Credit*	*Value*	*Code*	*Quantity*
1234	15	41	£3,000	56742	150

Code 15 might represent purchases and code 41 the trade payables control account. This single input could be used to update the purchase ledger, the nominal ledger, and the inventory ledger. The inventory code may enable further analysis to be carried out, perhaps allocating the cost to a particular department or product. Thus the needs of both financial accounting and cost accounting can be fulfilled at once.

2.3 Using an accounting package

When a user begins to work with an accounting package he or she will usually be asked to key in a password. Separate passwords can be used for different parts of the system, for example for different ledgers if required. This prevents access by unauthorised personnel. The user will then be presented with a 'menu' of options such as 'enter new data' or 'print report'. By selecting and keying in the appropriate option number or letter the user will then be guided through the actions needed to enter the data or generate the report.

Activity 1   **(5 minutes)**

Give some examples, from your own experience, of the use of passwords.

Although accounting packages are, in principle, exactly the same as manual accounting, they do have certain distinctive advantages and disadvantages.

2.4 Advantages and disadvantages of accounting packages

The main advantages of accounting packages are as follows.

(a) The packages can be used by non-specialists as use of codes for input means that correct accounts will be updated.

(b) A large amount of data can be processed very quickly.

(c) Computerised systems are more accurate than manual systems.

(d) A computer is capable of handling and processing large volumes of data.

(e) The ability to integrate systems or modules prevents wasteful repetition as one entry may update several records.

(f) Once the data has been input, computerised systems can analyse data rapidly to present useful control information for managers such as a trial balance or a trade receivables schedule.

Although the advantages of computerised accounting systems far outweigh the disadvantages, particularly for large businesses, they still suffer from certain disadvantages. The main ones are as follows.

(a) The initial time and costs involved in installing the system, training personnel and so on.

(b) The need for security checks to make sure that unauthorised personnel do not gain access to data files.

(c) The necessity to develop a system of coding and checking.

(d) Lack of 'audit trail'. It is not always easy to see where a mistake has been made.

(e) Possible resistance on the part of staff to the introduction of the system.

We next look at the 'building blocks' of the accounting package namely, modules.

3 ACCOUNTING MODULES

3.1 What are they?

An accounting package will consist of several modules.

Definition

A **module** is a program which deals with one particular part of a business accounting system.

A simple accounting package might consist of only one module (in which case it is called a stand-alone module), but more often it will consist of several modules. The name given to a set of several modules is a suite. An accounting package, therefore, might have separate modules for:

(a)   invoicing
(b)   inventory
(c)   sales ledger
(d)   purchase ledger
(e)   nominal ledger
(f)   payroll
(g)   cash book
(h)   non-current asset register
(i)   report generator

and so on.

Linking modules in such a way that data input into one module can then be transferred automatically to all other relevant modules can increase efficiency and reduce errors.

3.2   Integrated software

Each module may be integrated with the others, so that data entered in one module will be passed automatically or by simple operator request through into any other module where the data is of some relevance to form an integrated accounting system. For example, if there is an input into the invoicing module authorising the despatch of an invoice to a customer, there might be automatic links:

(a)   to the sales ledger, to update the file by posting the invoice to the customer's account

(b)   to the inventory module, to update the inventory file by:

   (i)   reducing the quantity and value of inventory in hand
   (ii)   recording the inventory movement

(c)   to the nominal ledger, to update the file by posting the sale to the sales account

(d)   to the report generator, to update the sales analysis and sales totals which are on file and awaiting inclusion in management reports.

The advantages of integrated software are as follows.

(a)   It becomes possible to make just one entry in one of the ledgers which automatically updates the others.

(b)   Users can specify reports, and the software will automatically extract the required data from all the relevant files.

(c)   Both of the above simplify the workload of the user, and the irritating need to constantly load and unload disks is eliminated.

There are some disadvantages of integrated software as well. They are as follows.

(a)   Usually, it requires more computer memory than separate (stand-alone) systems – which means there is less space in which to store actual data.

(b)   Because one program is expected to do everything, the user will often find that an integrated package has fewer facilities than a set of specialised modules. In effect, an integrated package could be 'Jack of all trades but master of none'.

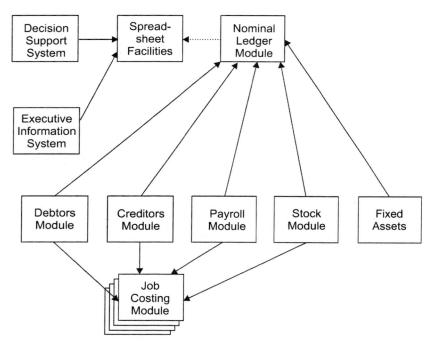

Figure 1.1: Integrated accounting system

FOR DISCUSSION

What are the benefits and disadvantages of different computer accounting packages you have used?

Now that you understand the general nature of accounting modules we look at some of the accounting modules in more detail, starting with the sales ledger.

3.3 Accounting for trade receivables

A computerised sales ledger will be expected to keep the sales ledger up to date, and also it should be able to produce certain output (eg statements, sales analysis reports, responses to file interrogations etc). The output might be produced daily (eg day book listings), monthly (eg statements), quarterly (eg sales analysis reports) or periodically (eg responses to file interrogations, or customer name and address lists printed on adhesive labels for despatching circulars or price lists).

What we need to do is to have a closer look at the form that input, output and processing take within a sales ledger. We will begin by thinking about what data we would expect to see in a sales ledger.

3.4 Data held on a sales ledger file

The sales ledger file will consist of individual records for each customer account. Some of the data held on the record will be standing data (ie it will change infrequently). Typical items of standing data are:

(a)   customer account number

(b) customer name

(c) address

(d) credit limit

(e) account sales analysis code

(f) account type (there are two different types of account – open item or balance forward – which we will look at shortly).

Each of these items is referred to as a field of information.

Other data held on a customer record will change as the sales ledger is updated. Such data is called variable data, and will include:

(a) transaction data
(b) transaction description (eg sale, credit note etc)
(c) transaction code (eg to identify payment period allowed)
(d) debits
(e) credits
(f) balance.

The file which contains these customer records – the sales ledger – is an example of a master file. If it is updated from another file containing various transactions, then that file is called a transactions file.

Activity 2 (5 minutes)

What is the relationship between a file, a field and a record?

3.5 Input to a sales ledger system

Bearing in mind what we expect to find in a sales ledger, we can say that typical data input into a sales ledger system is as follows.

(a) Amendments:

  (i) amendments to customer details, eg change of address, change of credit limit, etc

  (ii) insertion of new customers

  (iii) deletion of old 'non-active' customers.

(b) Transaction data relating to:

  (i) sales transactions, for invoicing
  (ii) customer payments
  (iii) credit notes
  (iv) adjustments (debit or credit items).

Some computerised sales ledgers produce invoices, so that basic sales data is input into the system. But other businesses might have a specialised invoicing module, so that the sales ledger package is not expected to produce invoices. The invoice details are already available (as output from the specialised module) and are input into the sales ledger system rather than basic sales data. So item (b)(i) of the list of typical data should read as follows.

> (b) (i) Sales transactions, for invoicing (if the sales ledger is expected to produce invoices) or invoice details (if already available from a specialised invoicing module).'

3.6 Processing in a sales ledger system

The primary action involved in updating the sales ledger is modifying the amount outstanding on the customer's account. How the amount is modified depends on what data is being input (ie whether it is an invoice, credit note, remittance etc).

When processing starts, the balance on an account is called the brought-forward balance. When processing has finished, the balance on the account is called the carried-forward balance. These terms are often abbreviated to b/f and c/f. What a computer does is to add or subtract whatever you tell it to from the b/f balance, and end up with a c/f balance. This is the same principle which applies to manual accounting.

	£	£
Brought forward account balance		X
Add:		
Invoice value	X	
Adjustments (+)	X	
		X
		X
Deduct:		
Credit note value	X	
Adjustments (–)	X	
Remittances	X	
		(X)
Carried forward account balance		X

This method of updating customer accounts is called the **balance forward method**.

Alternatively, the computer might use the **open item method** of processing the data. Under this method, the computer identifies specific invoices, and credits individual payments against specific invoices. Late payments of individual invoices can be identified and chased up. The customer's outstanding balance is the sum of the unpaid open items.

3.7 Outputs from a sales ledger system

Typical outputs in a computerised sales ledger are as follows.

> (a) Day book listing. A list of all transactions posted each day. This provides an audit trail – ie it is information which the auditors of the business can use when carrying out their work

> (b) Invoices (if the package is one which is expected to produce invoices)

> (c) Statements. End of month statements for customers

> (d) Sales analysis reports. These will analyse sales according to the sales analysis codes on the sales ledger file. They may be by customer or by the type of product sold. They may also do it by region or sales office

(e) Trade receivables reminder letters. Letters can be produced automatically to chase late payers when the due date for payment goes by without payment having been received

(f) Customer lists (or perhaps a selective list). The list might be printed on to adhesive labels, for sending out customer letters or marketing material

(g) Responses to enquiries, perhaps output on to a screen rather than as printed copy, for fast response to customer enquiries

(h) Output on to disk file for other modules – eg to the inventory control module and the nominal ledger module, if these are also used by the organisation, and the package is not an integrated one

3.8 The advantages of a computerised trade receivable system

The advantages of such a system, in addition to the advantages of computerised accounting generally, are its ability to assist in sales administration and marketing by means of outputs such as those listed above.

3.9 Purchase ledger

A computerised purchase ledger will certainly be expected to keep the purchase ledger up to date, and also it should be able to output various reports requested by the user. In fact, a computerised purchase ledger is much the same as a computerised sales ledger, except that it is a sort of mirror image as it deals with purchases rather than sales.

3.10 Inputs to a purchase ledger system

Bearing in mind what we expect to see held on a purchase ledger, typical data input into a purchase ledger system is:

(a) details of purchases recorded on invoices
(b) details of returns to suppliers for which credit notes are received
(c) details of payments to suppliers
(d) adjustments.

3.11 Processing in a purchase ledger system

The primary action involved in updating the purchase ledger is adjusting the amounts outstanding on the supplier accounts. These amounts will represent money owed to the suppliers. The computer will adjust the owed brought-forward balance by adding or deducting the value of transactions as you tell it to. The carried-forward balance becomes the new balance recorded on the suppliers account. This processing is identical to updating the accounts in the sales ledger, except that the sales ledger balances are debits (trade receivables) and the purchase ledger balances are credits (trade payables).

3.12 Outputs from a purchase ledger system

Typical outputs in a computerised purchase ledger are as follows.

(a) Lists of transactions posted – produced every time the system is run.

(b) An analysis of expenditure for nominal ledger purposes. This may be produced every time the system is run or at the end of each month.

(c) List of trade payables balances together with a reconciliation between the total balance brought forward, the transactions for the month and the total balance carried forward.

(d) Copies of trade payables' accounts. This may show merely the balance b/f, current transactions and the balance c/f. If complete details of all unsettled items are given, the ledger is known as an open-ended ledger. (This is similar to the open item or balance forward methods with a sales ledger system.)

(e) Any purchase ledger system can be used to produce details of payments to be made. For example:

(i) remittance advices (usually a copy of the ledger account)
(ii) cheques
(iii) credit transfer listings.

(f) Other special reports may be produced for:

(i) costing purposes
(ii) updating records about tangible non-current assets
(iii) comparisons with budget.

The last accounting module we will look at is the nominal ledger. This module enables a business's profit or loss to be calculated.

3.13 Nominal ledger

The nominal ledger (or general ledger) is an accounting record which summarises the financial affairs of a business. It is the nucleus of an accounting system. It contains details of assets, liabilities and capital, income and expenditure and thus enables the profit or loss to be calculated.

The nominal ledger consists of a large number of different accounts, each account having its own purpose or 'name' and an identity or code. Some nominal ledgers are separately structured, but others are posted automatically from related modules (eg sales ledger module, purchase ledger module). This difference in the types of computerised nominal ledger which exist has implications for what is input into the system, as we shall see.

A nominal ledger will consist of a large number of coded accounts. For example, part of a nominal ledger might be as follows:

Account code	Account name
100200	Plant and machinery (cost)
100300	Motor vehicles (cost)
100201	Plant and machinery depreciation
100301	Motor vehicles depreciation
300000	Total trade receivables
400000	Total trade payables

Account code	Account name
500130	Wages and salaries
500140	Rent and rates
500150	Advertising expenses
500160	Bank charges
500170	Motor expenses
500180	Telephone expenses
600000	Sales
700000	Cash

A business will, of course, choose its own codes for its nominal ledger accounts. The codes given in this table are purely for illustrative purposes.

It is important to remember that a computerised nominal ledger works in exactly the same way as a manual nominal ledger, although there are some differences in terminology. For instance, in a manual system, the sales and trade receivables accounts were posted from the sales day book (not the sales ledger). But in a computerised system, the sales day book is automatically produced as part of the 'sales ledger module'. So it may sound as if you are posting directly from the sales ledger, but in fact the day book is part of a computerised sales ledger.

3.14   Inputs to the nominal ledger

Inputs depend on whether the accounting system is integrated or not.

   (a)   If the system is integrated, then as soon as data is put into the sales ledger module (or anywhere else for that matter), the relevant nominal ledger accounts are updated. There is nothing more for the system user to do.

   (b)   If the system is not integrated then the output from the sales ledger module (and anywhere else) has to be input into the nominal ledger. This is done by using journal entries. For instance:

Accounts	Debit	Credit
	£	£
A/c 300000	3,000	
A/c 600000		3,000

Where 600000 is the nominal ledger code for sales, and 300000 is the code for trade receivables. However, regardless of whether the system is integrated or not, the actual data needed by the nominal ledger package to be able to update the ledger accounts includes:

   (a)   date
   (b)   description
   (c)   amount
   (d)   account codes (sometimes called distinction codes).

3.15 Outputs from the nominal ledger

The main outputs apart from listings of individual nominal ledger accounts are:

(a)   the trial balance

(b)   financial statements.

4   THE EFFECT OF BUSINESS SIZE AND STRUCTURE

The Edexcel Guidelines require you to assess the factors which influence the nature and structure of accounting systems. The main factors are the effect of the business size and structure.

The structure of businesses is covered in depth in Mandatory Unit 3, Organisations and Behaviour. You should refer back to your work for that unit in order to revise the main types of business structure.

We now turn to consider the finance function and authority within the organisation.

4.1   The finance function and authority

The finance function is part of the technostructure of an organisation and therefore we must consider how the authority of departments in the technostructure is exercised over the middle line and the operating core. The types of authority that a manager or a department may have are line authority, staff authority and functional authority.

Definitions

- **Line authority** is the authority a manager has over a subordinate.

- **Staff authority** is the authority one manager or department may have in giving specialist advice to another manager or department, over which there is no line authority. Staff authority does not entail the right to make or influence decisions in the advisee department.

- **Functional authority** is a hybrid of line and staff authority, whereby the technostructure manager or department has the authority, in certain circumstances, to direct, design or control activities or procedures of another department. An example is where a finance manager has authority to require timely reports from line managers.

> ### Activity 3 (10 minutes)
>
> What sort of authority is exercised:
>
> (a) by the financial controller over the chief accountant?
> (b) by the production manager over the production workforce?
> (c) by the financial controller over the production manager?

4.2 Problems with authority

Problem	Possible solution
The technostructure can **undermine** the **line managers**' authority, by empire building.	**Clear** demarcations of line, staff and functional authority should be created.
Lack of seniority: middle line managers may be more senior in the hierarchy than technostructure advisers.	Use **functional authority** (via procedures). Experts should be seen as a resource, not a threat.
Expert managers may **lack realism,** going for technically perfect, but commercially impractical, solutions.	Technostructure planners should **be fully aware** of **operations issues.**
Technostructure experts **lack responsibility** for the success of their ideas.	Technostructure experts should be involved in **implementing** their suggestions and should take responsibility for their success.

4.3 Dangers of a weak technostructure

(a) **Legal** restrictions such as the Companies Act might be broken by the line managers.

(b) **Increased risk**: expert advice might be ignored or not sought.

(c) **Important work** not directly involved with day-to-day operations, such as personnel planning, new technology and management techniques **might be ignored**.

4.4 Dangers of an over-strong technostructure

(a) Professional specialists sometimes have **divided loyalties** between their organisation and their profession. Computer specialists, for example, might want to introduce state of the art computer systems when these might not be the most appropriate for the organisation.

(b) **Instability.** Many professional specialists have skills which can be marketed to other organisations, so that their careers are not necessarily tied to one organisation.

(c) The technostructure **introduces rules and procedures** such as control systems, job evaluation and appraisal systems, and these tend to **hamper operations.**

(d) Different departments or levels in the technostructure might have **conflicting expertise**.

(e) It may be **difficult to measure the benefits** to the organisation of various aspects of technostructural work as these benefits are indirect.

4.5 The accountant's role

In many companies, the finance function is one of the most important expert roles in the organisation. The roles of the management accountant and financial accountant are technostructural roles but are different. The **financial accountant** is likely to play a less direct role in the operational running of the business than the **management accountant**, but is crucial to a company's effective boundary management with shareholders.

4.6 Information

The **financial accountant** classifies accounting information and is responsible for presenting this to **external shareholders**. The need to provide financial accounting information to shareholders has a necessary impact on the activities of the strategic apex, middle line and operating core.

(a) A business's performance is **measured in money terms**. Business decisions impact on the firm's financial results. 'What will shareholders think?'

(b) The **timing** of business transactions is important for financial reporting purposes.

Financial reporting is not an optional extra. The published accounts are an important source of communication with outsiders. Reported levels of profit determine the return that investors can receive. They also indirectly affect the company's cost of capital (although this is more determined by expectations of future benefits) by affecting the share price. Published financial information therefore affects the cost of one of the organisation's most important resources, money.

The **management accountant** is even nearer the policy making and management process. This is because the management accountant is not primarily interested in reporting to interested parties external to the organisation. After all, the requirements of external users of accounts may be different to those involved in managing and running the business in several respects.

- Level of detail
- Aggregation of information
- Classification of data
- The period covered

Internally, accountants therefore provide information for **planning and controlling** the business.

- Past cost information
- Product profitability
- Cost/profit centre performance
- Desirability of investments
- Competitors performance
- Sensitivity analysis
- Alternative options

The accountant provides information essential for the current management and decision-making of the business. If line decisions are assessed in accounting terms, even in part, then the accountant will be involved in them. Accountants assess the future financial consequences of certain decisions.

Activity 4 **(15 minutes)**

Hanbury Limited runs a chain of 10 hotels in various city centres across the UK. Each hotel offers customers accommodation, restaurant facilities, room service and each hotel has a bar. Both permanent and temporary staff are employed to work on reception, in the bar and restaurant and to service the bedrooms.

What information would you expect the management accountants to provide to the management of Hanbury in order to assist them in running the business?

4.7 Control and stewardship

The accounting staff's authority is generally expressed in procedures and rules. For example, capital investment is analysed in financial terms. People have formal expenditure limits. In many respects, money and funds are a business's lifeblood, and monitoring their flow is a necessary precaution. If the flow of funds dries up a business can fail very easily. Proper financial control ensures that the business is adequately financed to meet its obligations.

Chapter roundup

- Computer software used in accounting may be divided into two types:

    - dedicated accounting packages;

    - general software, the uses of which include accounting amongst many others.

- In principle, computerised accounting is the same as manual accounting, but a computerised approach has certain advantages, the principal one being improved efficiency.

- An accounting package consists of a number of 'modules' which perform all the tasks needed to maintain a normal accounting function like purchase ledger or payroll. The modules may or may not be integrated with each other.

- The size and structure of an organisation will have a considerable impact on the operation of the finance function.

Quick quiz

1   What is an accounting suite?

2   What is coding?

3   What are the advantages of integrated software?

4   What sort of data is input into a sales ledger system?

5   What is the open item method of processing?

6   What are the typical outputs from a purchase ledger system?

Answers to Quick quiz

1   A set of accounting modules or programs.

2   A way of labelling accounts for ease of recognition and posting.

3   One entry to an account will automatically update others; users can specify reports; work of the user is simplified.

4   Amendments to customer details. New customer information. Transaction data.

5   The computer identifies specific invoices, and credits specific payments against specific invoices allowing late payments of invoices to be identified and chased up.

6   List of transactions posted; analysis of expenditure; list of trade payable balances; copies of trade payable accounts; other information on payments; special reports

Answers to Activities

1   Some of the more common examples for using passwords are to prevent/limit access to:

   (i)   Personnel records
   (ii) Accounting records
   (iii) Future plans
   (iv) Product formulae.

2   A file is made up of records which are made up of fields. Make sure you learn any terminology like this, because it will make your answers far more convincing in an assessment.

3   (a) Line authority
    (b) Line authority
    (c) Functional authority

4   Some examples of the management information likely to be provided are below, you may have thought of others:

   •   Income statement for each hotel prepared on a monthly basis

   •   Comparisons of actual performance to budget

   •   Analysis of the profitablity of seperate income streams (rooms, bar, restaurant)

   •   Analysis of employee costs by function

   •   Comparison of monthly performance of each hotel against budget

   •   Key ratios such as profit per customer, profit per room

   •   Occupancy rates by hotel by month

   •   Sensitivity of restaurant performance to changes in customer numbers or cost of ingredients

Chapter 2
MANAGEMENT CONTROL

Introduction

The environment within which a business operates and the systems it adopts are critical in determining the degree of control exercised by management of the business over the accounting and other functions.

Management are usually keen to ensure that an adequate system of control is in place, to ensure that nothing should go wrong in the running of the business and there should be no scope for fraud.

Management control is closely related to business risk, in that management try to eliminate the impact of uncertainty in making business decisions. 'Risk' is sometimes used to describe situations where outcomes are not known, but their probabilities can be estimated.

Business risk is covered in the BPP Learning Media Business Essentials Course Book on Business Strategy.

Your objectives

In this chapter you will learn about the following.

- (a) Types of risk
- (b) Features of accounting and control systems
- (c) Types of internal control
- (d) The inherent limitations of internal control
- (e) Fraud
- (f) Value for money auditing
- (g) Corporate governance

1 TYPES OF RISK

There are three types of risk mentioned by the Edexcel Guidelines for Unit 11, being operational risk, financial risk and compliance risk. These make up business risk.

1.1 Operational, financial and compliance risk

Operating risk can be defined as the chances of errors or mistakes being made within the operations of the business. For example if no Board authority is required for the purchase of fixed assets, a major fixed asset that is not required by the business might be purchased, or if customer job specifications are not adequately checked, goods might be manufactured for a customer which are not entirely to the customers' specification.

Financial risk covers all of the risks of incorrect payments being made or not all due receipts being collected. For example if there are not adequate payroll control systems it might be possible for 'dummy' employees to be paid and the additional wages taken by a member of the payroll department.

Compliance risk is the overall risk that a company will not comply with all of the legal requirements laid out in the Companies Act. One key area here is the requirement for the directors of a company to keep proper accounting records.

Definition

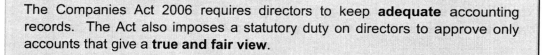

The Companies Act 2006 requires directors to keep **adequate** accounting records. The Act also imposes a statutory duty on directors to approve only accounts that give a **true and fair view**.

1.2 Accounting records: statutory requirements (s386-9 CA 2006)

Every company must keep adequate accounting records that are sufficient to:

1   Show and explain the company's transactions and to disclose with reasonable accuracy, at any time, the financial position of the company at that time and to enable the directors to ensure that any accounts required to be prepared comply with the requirements of the Act.

2   The records must contain entries from day to day of all sums of money received and expended by the company and the matters in respect of which the receipt and expenditure takes place.

3   A record of the assets and liabilities of the company.

4   Where the company's business involves dealing in goods, the accounting records must enable the company to establish the statement of inventory at the end of each financial year end including the stock taking records.

1.3 Business risk

Business risk cannot be eliminated, but must be **managed** by the company.

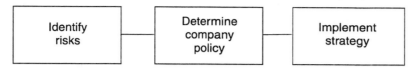

1.4 Responses to given risks

Broadly speaking, there are four potential responses a company can take to any given risk:

- Accept risk (ie live with it – only acceptable if it is a low risk)
- Reduce risk (by instituting a system of internal control or protection)
- Avoid risk (by not engaging in that activity or not accepting a contract)
- Transfer risk (by taking out insurance)

Risks to the business can exist on an individual department and individual level and also on a higher, strategic level. Employees at all levels should be involved in identifying risks.

Depending on the risk identified, company policy may be set at a department or at Board level.

Activity 1 **(10 minutes)**

For the following two departments, think of (a) a risk that the company might face and (b) what policy they might adopt in respect of it.

(i) Purchasing department
(ii) Human resources department

Designing and operating internal control systems is a key part of a company's risk management. This will often be done by employees in their various departments, although sometimes (particularly in the case of specialised computer systems) the company will hire external expertise to design systems.

NOTES

1.5 The role of internal audit

The internal audit department has a two-fold role in relation to risk management.

- Monitoring the company's overall risk management policy and ensuring it operates effectively.

- Monitoring the strategies implemented to ensure that they continue to operate effectively.

Going back to the diagram in Paragraph 1.3, this can be shown as:

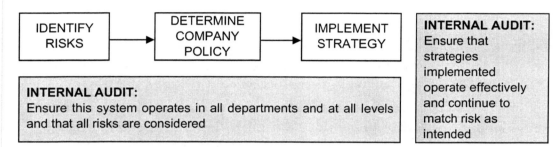

As a significant risk management policy in companies is to implement internal controls to reduce them, internal audit have a key role in assessing systems and testing controls.

Internal audit may assist in the development of systems. However, their key role will be in **monitoring the overall process** and in **providing assurance** that the **systems** which the departments have designed **meet objectives** and **operate effectively**.

It is important that the internal audit department retain their **objectivity** towards these aspects of their role, which is another reason why internal audit would generally not be involved in the assessment of risks and the design of the system.

2 FEATURES OF ACCOUNTING AND CONTROL SYSTEMS

Definition

An **internal control system** comprises the control environment and control procedures. It includes all the policies and procedures (internal controls) adopted by the directors and management of an entity to ensure, as far as practicable, the orderly and efficient conduct of its business, including adherence to internal policies, the safeguarding of assets, the prevention and detection of fraud and error, the accuracy and completeness of the accounting records, and the timely preparation of reliable financial information. Internal controls may be incorporated within computerised accounting systems. However the internal control system extends beyond those matters which relate directly to the accounting system.

International Standard on Auditing 315 (ISA 315) *Obtaining an Understanding of the Entity and its Environment and Assessing the Risks of Material Misstatement* covers the whole area of controls. ISAs are issued by the Auditing Practices Board on all aspects of auditing. You will become familiar with some of them while you are working on this Unit.

2.1 Control environment

The control environment is the framework within which controls operate. The control environment is very much determined by the management of a business.

Definition

> **Control environment** includes the governance and management functions and the attitudes, awareness and actions of those charged with governance and management concerning the entity's internal control and its importance in the entity.

The ISA adds to the definition of the control environment that a strong control environment does not, by itself, ensure the effectiveness of the overall internal control system. However, aspects of the control environment (such as management attitudes towards control) will be a significant factor in determining **how controls operate**. Controls are more likely to operate well in an environment where they are treated as being important. In addition consideration of the control environment will, as shown above, mean considering whether certain controls (internal audits, budgets) actually exist.

The following factors will be reflected in the control environment.

Communication and enforcement of integrity and ethical values	Control systems can only be effective where managers and staff have integrity and follow a system of ethics. The ethical system provides guidance on 'right' and 'wrong' – in other words it is ethically correct to follow control systems. Without ethics, controls may not be followed and managers/staff would not see this was incorrect.
Commitment to competence	Competence is the skills and knowledge necessary for each individual to carry out jobs. The company needs to ensure that each individual does have the necessary skill and knowledge so that the control system can be run effectively.
Participation by those charged with governance	The control system will be reviewed by staff independent of that system ie those charged with governance. In a large company this will be the audit committee and internal audit department; in a smaller company this may be a manager outside of the accounting department.
Management's philosophy and operating style	Management must show a pro-active approach to risk management. This provides a lead for the rest of the company to follow. If management appeared not to be interested in controls then staff would also be less inclined to follow control systems.

Organisational structure	The company's organisational structure provides the framework within which the control system works. The structure must therefore provide appropriate communication and reporting systems to enable the control system to be effective.
Assignment of authority and responsibility	Authority and responsibility are assigned appropriately within the company. This means staff know when they have to implement/follow controls and how to report control weaknesses to an appropriate manager.
Human resource policies and practices	These relate to the recruitment, training, evaluation, promoting and paying of staff. Basically, policies should be in place to ensure that appropriate staff are hired and that they are trained so that the control system can be operated effectively.

The ISA identifies five elements of an internal control system, as follows:

1. The control environment
2. The entity's risk assessment process
3. The information system
4. Control activities
5. Monitoring of controls

These elements are explained below.

2.2 Risk assessment process

Definition

Risk assessment process is the entity's process of identifying business risks relevant to the financial reporting objectives and deciding about the actions to address those risks and the results thereof.

The external auditor will enquire with management to ensure that risks that could affect the business have been identified and appropriate controls put into place to minimise the impact of those risks. The fact that management have carried out a risk assessment will provide the external auditor with some confidence that company systems will not have errors in them.

2.3 Information system

Definition

> **Information system** is the system that processes information within an organisation. It includes not only the processing of information but also the procedures to initiate, record, process and report on financial statements, both manual and computerised.

The external auditor will review the information system to ensure information can be processed completely and accurately. Where this takes place, then the external auditor gains confidence that the financial statements will also be complete and accurate.

2.4 Control activities

Definition

> **Control activities** are specific activities within an organisation which are designed to address risks and therefore help ensure that management directives are carried out.

Examples of specific controls include:

Authorisation controls

Transactions should be **approved** by an appropriate person (eg overtime being approved by departmental managers). Important aspects of documentation are:

(a) **Multi-part documents.** Copies are sent to everyone who needs to know about the event recorded in the document.

(b) **Pre-numbering of documents.** Missing numbers in a sequence may indicate that operations have not been **recorded** or have **not** been **processed** further, for example outstanding orders.

(c) **Standardisation of documents.** Each document should be in a standard format showing clearly the required information.

Performance reviews

Review of staff to ensure they have been operating the control system effectively.

Information processing

Controls over information processing systems to ensure that:

- All information is processed (completeness of processing)
- Information is accurately processed
- Appropriate authorisation is obtained for the processing of each item of information

Physical controls

Authorised personnel alone should have access to certain assets, particularly those which are valuable or portable. An example would be ensuring the inventory store is only open when the stores personnel are there, and is locked at other times.

Restricting access to records can be a particular problem in computerised systems as we shall discuss in the next chapter.

Segregation of duties

Segregation of duties is a vital aspect of the internal control system. Segregation of duties implies a **number of people** being involved in the accounting process. Hence it is more difficult for fraudulent transactions to be processed (since a number of people would have to collude in the fraud), and it is also more difficult for accidental errors to be processed (since the more people are involved, the more checking there can be). Segregation should take place in various ways:

(a)   **Segregation of function.** The key functions that should be assigned to different people are the **carrying out** of a transaction, **recording** that transaction in the accounting records and **maintaining custody** of assets that arise from the transaction.

(b)   The various **steps** in carrying out the transaction should also be segregated.

(c)   The **carrying out** of various **accounting operations** should be segregated. For example the same staff should not record transactions and carry out the reconciliations at the period-end.

For small businesses however, the possibility of segregating duties is not always practical, due to insufficient staff to divide responsibilities adequately. In this situation the business should look to compensate with alternative internal controls. For example, a small owner-managed business may only have one member of accounts staff, but the owner might monitor staff work more closely.

2.5   Monitoring of controls

Definition

> The external auditor should obtain an understanding of the major types of activities that the company uses to **monitor internal control** over financial reporting and how the entity initiates corrective actions to its controls.

Ongoing monitoring means that management is continually assessing the effectiveness of the company's internal control systems. Monitoring may be undertaken by the company's senior managers or in some situations by the internal audit department of the company. Where internal audit are involved, the external auditor will also carry out limited monitoring of the internal audit function.

BPP
LEARNING MEDIA

2.6 Limitations of internal control systems

Any internal control system can only provide the directors with **reasonable assurance** that their objectives are reached, because of **inherent limitations**. These include the following.

- The costs of control not outweighing their benefits
- The potential for human error
- Collusion between employees
- The possibility of controls being by-passed or overridden by management
- Controls being designed to cope with routine but not non-routine transactions

> **Activity 2** **(15 minutes)**
>
> Consider the accounting function of the organisation where you work, or any organisation of which you have had experience. Which of these types of internal control do you think have proved most effective?

3 FRAUD

3.1 What is fraud?

Give an employee responsibility, and he may manage the resources under his control dishonestly. The incidence of **financial fraud,** including fraud in a computer environment, appears to be increasing fast. This trend, together with the increasing sophistication of fraudsters, creates difficult problems for management and for **internal auditors.**

The mere presence of internal auditors will serve to discourage fraudsters for fear of being discovered, although the public's expectations tend to go much further. Everyone has their own idea of where an acceptable bending of the rules ends and fraud begins, so it is appropriate to start with a definition of fraud.

Definitions

> **Fraud** comprises both the use of deception to obtain an unjust or illegal financial advantage, and intentional misrepresentation by management, employees or third parties.
>
> An **error**, in contrast, is an unintentional mistake.

3.2 Types of fraud

Some of the most common methods of fraud are described briefly in the following paragraphs.

3.3 Ghost employees

These are imaginary employees for whom the wages department prepare wage packets which are distributed amongst the fraudsters. This type of fraud arises when there is extensive reliance on casual workers, and minimal record keeping for such workers. Inflated overtime claims can also result from poor time recording systems.

3.4 Miscasting of the payroll

This fraud often succeeds due to its simplicity. If there are twenty employees, each to be paid £100, then the computer program for the payroll could be adjusted so that an extra £50 is added to the total added up for the amounts to be paid. Thus management approve a payment of £2,050 for the period's wages, each employee gets his £100 and the fraudster collects his extra £50. Manual payroll systems can be manipulated in a similar way. When employees are paid in cash, this type of fraud can be hard to trace.

3.5 Stealing unclaimed wages

This is effectively confined to wages paid in cash and can occur when an employee leaves without notice or is away sick. In the case of a subsequent claim for unpaid wages, it could be claimed that the cash in the original pay packet was paid back into the bank.

3.6 Collusion with external parties

This could involve suppliers, customers or their staff. Possible frauds are overcharging on purchase invoices, undercharging on sales invoices or the sale of confidential information (eg customer lists, expansion plans) to a competitor. Management should watch out for unusual discounts or commissions being given or taken, or for an excessive zeal on the part of an employee to handle all business with a particular company.

3.7 Teeming and lading

This is a 'rolling' fraud rather than a 'one-off' fraud. It occurs when a clerk has the chance to misappropriate payments from trade receivables or to trade payables. Cash received by the company is 'borrowed' by the cashier rather than being kept as petty cash or banked. (It is also possible, although riskier and more difficult to organise, to misappropriate cheques made payable to the company.) When the cashier knows that a reconciliation is to be performed, or audit visit planned, he pays the money back so that everything appears satisfactory at that point, but after the audit the teeming and lading starts again. Surprise visits by internal auditors and independent checking of cash balances should discourage this fraud.

A common fraud, arising when one employee has sole control of the sales ledger and recording trade receivables' cheques, is to pay cheques into a separate bank account, either by forged endorsement or by opening an account in a name similar to the employer's.

The clerk has to allocate cheques or cash received from other trade receivables against the account of the trade receivable whose payment was misappropriated. This prevents other staff from asking why the account is still overdue or from sending statements etc to the trade receivables. However, the misallocation has to continue as long as the money is missing. This fraud, therefore, never really stops. It can be detected by independent verification of trade receivables balances (eg by circulation) and by looking at unallocated payments, if the sales ledger is organised to show this. In addition, sending out itemised monthly statements to trade receivables should act as a deterrent, although in a really elaborate fraud the clerk **may** be keeping two sets of books, so that the statements show the trade receivable's own **analysis** of amounts due and paid off in the month, but do not agree with the books.

FOR DISCUSSION

Discuss with your tutor and fellow learners which types of business you think might be more prone to frauds such as teeming and lading.

3.8 Altering cheques and inflating expense claims

These are self-explanatory.

3.9 Stealing assets

Using the company's assets for personal gain and stealing fully depreciated assets are both encountered in practice. Whether or not the private use of company telephones and photocopiers is a serious matter is up to the company to judge, but it may still be fraudulent. More serious examples include the sale by employees of unused time on the computer, which is a growing fraud.

3.10 Issuing false credit notes

Another way of avoiding detection when cash and cheques received from trade receivables have been misappropriated is to issue a credit note which is not sent to the customer (who has paid his account) but is recorded in the books. Again, the issue of itemised statements monthly should show this up, as the customer would query the credit note. A similar tactic is to write a debt off as bad to cover up the disappearance of the payment.

3.11 Failing to record all sales

A very elaborate fraud may be perpetrated in a business with extremely poor controls over sales recording and minimal segregation of duties. In such circumstances, a dishonest bookkeeper may invoice customers but fail to record the invoices so that the customer's payments never have to be recorded and the misappropriation is not missed.

3.12 The role of the internal auditors

The internal auditors should start their work by identifying the areas of the business most susceptible to fraud. These will include areas where cash is involved, and the other areas where the internal auditors' judgement is that the internal controls are insufficient to safeguard the assets. The existence of a properly functioning system of internal controls will diminish the incidence of frauds, so the internal auditors' opinion on the internal control system is of fundamental importance. Whenever a fraud is discovered, the internal auditors should judge whether a weakness in internal controls has been highlighted, and if so what changes are needed.

4 PREVENTION OF FRAUD

Fraud will only be prevented successfully if potential fraudsters perceive the risk of detection as being high, and if personnel are adequately screened before employment and given no incentive to turn against the company once employed. The following safeguards should therefore be implemented:

(a) A good internal control system
(b) Continuous supervision of all employees
(c) Surprise audit visits
(d) Thorough personnel procedures

4.1 Comparisons

The work of employees must be monitored as this will increase the perceived risk of being discovered. Actual results must regularly be compared against budgeted results, and employees should be asked to explain significant variances.

4.2 Surprise audit visits

Surprise audit visits are a valuable contribution to preventing fraud. If a cashier is carrying out a teeming and lading fraud and is told that an audit visit is due the following week, he may be able to square up the books before the visit so that the internal auditors will find nothing wrong. But if the threat of a surprise visit is constantly present, the cashier will not be able to carry out a teeming and lading fraud without the risk of being discovered, and this risk is usually sufficient to prevent the fraud. The internal auditors do not need to carry out any sophisticated audit tests during their surprise visit. The fraud deterrent effect on the employee is highly significant, because the employee thinks that every figure is being checked.

4.3 Personnel procedures

Finally, **personnel procedures** must be adequate to prevent the occurrence of frauds.

(a) Whenever a fraud is discovered, the fraudster should be dismissed and the police should be informed. Too often an employee is 'asked to resign' and then moves on to a similar job where the fraud is repeated, often because management fear loss of face or investor confidence. This is a self-defeating policy.

(b) All new employees should be required to produce adequate references from their previous employers.

(c) If an employee's lifestyle changes dramatically, explanations should be sought.

(d) Every employee must be made to take his annual holiday entitlement. Often in practice the employee who is 'so dedicated that he never takes a holiday'

is in fact not taking his leave for fear of his fraud being discovered by his replacement worker while he is away.

(e)   Pay levels should be adequate and working conditions of a reasonable standard. If employees feel that they are being paid an unfairly low amount or 'exploited', they may look for ways to supplement their pay dishonestly.

5   MANAGEMENT FRAUD

So far, we have concentrated on employee fraud. However, arguably more serious (and very much more difficult to prevent and detect) is the growing problem of **management fraud**.

5.1   Reasons for management fraud

While employee fraud is usually undertaken purely for the employee's financial gain, management fraud is often undertaken to improve the company's apparent performance, to reduce tax liabilities or to improve the manager's promotion prospects. Managers are often in a position to override internal controls and to intimidate their subordinates into collusion or turning a blind eye. This makes it difficult to detect such frauds. In addition, where the company is benefiting financially rather than the manager, it can be difficult to persuade staff that any dishonesty is involved.

This clash of interest between loyalty to an employer and professional integrity can be difficult to resolve and can compromise an internal auditor's independence. Management fraud often comes to light after a takeover or on a change of audit staff or practices. Its consequences can be far reaching for the employing company in damaging its reputation or because it results in legal action. Because management usually have access to much larger sums of money than more lowly employees, the financial loss to the company can be immense.

6   RESPONSIBILITY FOR REPORTING FRAUD TO MANAGEMENT

A company's **external auditors** are required to report all instances of fraud that they find to the company's management, unless they suspect management of being involved in the fraud. If they uncover fraud by management, they should report the matter to the appropriate **public authorities** or seek **legal advice**. The external auditors should also report to management any material (ie significant) **weakness in the company's systems of accounting and internal control.** You will cover external auditors' responsibilities, with respect to fraud, in more detail later in this chapter.

If **internal auditors** uncover instances of fraud, they should also report this to executive management. If they discover management fraud, they should make use of lines of communication to the company's **audit committee**, which should be in place as a matter of good corporate governance practice. The audit committee should have the authority to take appropriate action, which is likely to include discussion of the matter with the external auditors.

7 CONTROL PROCEDURES FOR REDUCING FRAUD RISK

Maintaining key control procedures reduces the risk of fraud occurring and increases the risk of detection. Controls over cash are particularly important. These procedures are summarised below.

7.1 Cash receipts

Segregation of duties between the various functions listed below is particularly important. In other words, more than one person should have responsibilities within each particular area.

Receipts by post

- Safeguards to prevent interception of mail between receipt and opening
- Appointment of responsible person to supervise mail
- Protection of cash and cheques (restrictive crossing)

Control over cash sales and collections

- **Restrictions** on **receipt of cash** (by cashiers only, or by salesmen etc)
- **Evidencing** of receipt of cash (numbered receipt forms/sealed till rolls)
- **Clearance** of cash offices and registers
- **Agreement** of **cash collections** with cash and sales records
- **Investigation** of cash shortages and surpluses

Recording

- Maintenance of records
- Limitation of duties of receiving cashiers
- Holiday arrangements
- Giving and recording of receipts

  - Retained copies
  - Serially numbered receipts books
  - Custody of receipt books
  - Comparisons with cash records and bank paying in slips

Paying into bank

- Daily bankings
- Make-up and comparison of paying-in slips against receipt records and cash book
- Banking of receipts intact/control of disbursements

Cash and bank balances

- Restrictions on opening new bank accounts
- Limitations on cash floats held
- Restrictions on payments out of cash received
- Restrictions on access to cash registers and offices
- Independent checks on cash floats
- Surprise cash counts
- Custody of cash outside office hours
- Safeguarding of IOUs, cash in transit
- Insurance arrangements
- Control of funds held in trust for employees

- Bank reconciliations
  - ○ Issue of bank statements
  - ○ Frequency of reconciliations by independent person
  - ○ Reconciliation procedures
  - ○ Treatment of longstanding unpresented cheques
  - ○ Stop payment notice
  - ○ Sequence of cheque numbers
  - ○ Comparison with cash books

7.2 Cash payments

The arrangements for controlling payments will depend to a great extent on the nature of business transacted, the volume of payments involved and the size of the company.

Cheque payments

- **Custody** over **supply** and issue of cheques
- **Preparation** of **cheques** restricted
- **Cheque requisitions**
  - (a) Presentation to cheque signatories
  - (b) Cancellation (crossing/recording cheque number)

- **Authority** to sign cheques
  - (a) Limitations on authority
  - (b) Number of signatories
  - (c) Prohibitions over signing of blank cheques

- Safeguards over **mechanically signed cheques**/cheques carrying printed signatures

- **Restrictions** on issue of **blank** or **bearer** cheques

- **Prompt despatch** of signed **cheques**

- **Obtaining** of paid **cheques** from **banks**

Cash payments

- Authorisation of expenditure
- Cancellation of vouchers to ensure cannot be paid twice
- Limits on disbursements
- Rules on cash advances to employees, IOUs and cheque cashing

7.3 Cheque and cash payments generally

The cashier should generally not be concerned with keeping or writing-up books of account other than those recording disbursements nor should he have access to, or be responsible for the custody of, securities, title deeds or negotiable instruments belonging to the company. (This is an example of **segregation of duties**.)

The person responsible for preparing cheques or traders' credit lists should not himself be a cheque signatory. Cheque signatories in turn should not be responsible for recording payments. (This is another example of **segregation of duties**.)

Activity 3   **(20 minutes)**

PCs (personal computers) have been marketed for small and medium sized businesses that have previously been using manual or mechanical systems for bookkeeping and accounting functions. In reviewing computer controls in this environment, the auditor is likely to find general control weaknesses which would not be anticipated in larger computer installations using for example an on-line, real-time system.

Why do you think the auditors are likely to find weaknesses in the controls over a PC-based accounting system in a small company?

---

8   ISA 240 ON FRAUD

ISA 240 *The Auditor's Responsibility to Consider Fraud in an Audit of Financial Statements*, emphasises that it is the responsibility of the directors to take reasonable steps to prevent and detect fraud. It is also their responsibility to prepare financial statements which give a true and fair view of the entity's affairs. The UK Combined Code on Corporate Governance has made a variety of suggestions to help directors fulfil their responsibilities.

ISA 240 distinguishes between **fraud** and **error**. Error refers to an unintentional misstatement in the financial statements, including the omission of an amount or a disclosure. In contrast fraud refers to an intentional act by one or more individuals involving the use of deception to obtain an unjust or illegal advantage.

There are two types of fraud that are relvant to external auditors in their audit of a company's financial statement:

- Fraudulent financial reporting
- Misappropriation of assets

Fraudulent financial reporting involves intentionally misstating the financial statements (including omissions of amounts or disclosures) in order to deceive the users of the financial statements.

Misappropriation of assets involves the theft of an entity's assets and is often accompanied by falsification of records in order to conceal the fact the assets are missing.

It is not the external auditor's responsibility to actively to search for fraud nor is it the primary purpose of an external audit. However the external auditor is responsible for reaching an opinion on the financial statements of the company and, as discussed above, the occruence of fraud could lead to material misstatmeents in the financial statements. An efficient and well-designed audit should detect a material fraud.

Where a fraud is identified it is the responsibility of the external auditor to report this to management, unless they suspect management of being involved in the fraud.

ISA 240 identifies examples of risk factors that might increase the likelihood of a fraud occurring (appendix 1) and also examples of circumstances that may indicate the possibility that the financial statements contain a material misstatement resulting from fraud.

8.1 Examples of fraud risk factors

- Incentives/Pressures

  For example, if the financial stability or profitability of a company is threatened by poor economic conditions or there is excessive pressure on management to meet expectations of third parties, such as investors or those charged with governance.

- Opportunities

  For example, if monitoring of employee activities by management is ineffective or internal control systems are inadequate.

- Attitudes/Rationalisations

  For example low morale among senior management or a known history of previous violations.

8.2 Examples of circumstances that may indicate the possibility that the financial statements may contain a material misstatement resulting from fraud.

Discrepancies in the accounting records	Transactions that are not recorded in a complete and timely manner.
	Unauthorised transactions.
	Last-minute adjustments.
	Evidence of employees' access to systems and records inconsistent with that necessary to perform their authorised duties.
	Tips or complaints to the auditor about alleged fraud.
Conflicting or missing evidence	Missing documents.
	Documents that appear to have been altered.
	Unavailablity of documents in original form (i.e. only photocopies available).
	Significant unexplained reconciling items.
	Inconsisten, vague or implausible responses from management arising from inquiries
	Inadequately explained differences between the accounts receivable ledger and the control account.
	Missing inventory or physical assets of significant magnitude

Problematic or unusual relationships between the external auditor and management	Denial of access to records.
	Undue time pressures imposed by management to resolve complex or contentious issues
	Unusual delays by the entity in providing requested information.
	Denial of access to key IT operations staff and facilities
	Unwillingness to address identified weaknesses in internal control on a timely basis

9 CORPORATE GOVERNANCE

9.1 Introduction

Definition

'**Corporate governance** is the system by which companies are directed and controlled'. *Cadbury Committee report*

'**Good governance** ensures that constituencies (stakeholders) with a relevant interest in the company's business are fully taken into account. ' *Hampel Committee report*

The issue of corporate governance has existed since companies began to be used commonly as part of business. However, in the late twentieth century, some high profile frauds and questionable business practices led to **public and government attention** being firmly fixed on **business management**. In the late 1990s, a series of committees were set up to consider the matter.

The key committees were:

- Cadbury Committee 1992 (corporate governance)
- Greenbury Committee 1995 (directors' remuneration)
- Hampel Committee 1995 (corporate governance)
- Turnbull Committee 1999 (corporate governance)
- Higgs report and new Combined Code – 2004

Each committee made various **recommendations** about how companies should be run and monitored to provide **safeguards** to shareholders.

Activity 4 (5 minutes)

Based on your knowledge of company law, which type of company do you think is most likely to be affected by the need for good corporate governance measures?

LEARNING MEDIA

Although the issues raised in considering the answer to the activity above are generalisations, corporate governance issues have **historically** tended to be **directed** at **listed, public limited companies.**

In 2004, the Stock Exchange issued a revised **Combined Code** (updating the 1998 code) of corporate governance requirements drawn from the recommendations of the Higgs report. Following this Code is **mandatory** for **companies listed on the Stock Exchange** (who have to disclose their reasoning for any non-compliance) but can be seen as **good practice** for **any UK company.**

The combined code is continually being updated and was last updated in June 2008 for accounting periods beginning on or after 29 June 2008.

9.2 Combined Code

Provisions of the Combined Code	
Directors' responsibilities	
The board	Should **meet regularly**, and have a **formal schedule of matters** reserved to it for its decision.
	There should be clear division of responsibilities between chairman and chief executive.
	Non-executive directors should comprise 50% of the board with the Chairman having a casting vote. Directors should submit themselves for re-election every three years and NEDs should not normally exceed two three-year terms of office.
The AGM	Companies should propose **separate resolutions** at the AGM on each substantially different issue. The chairman should ensure that members of the audit, remuneration and nomination committees are available at the AGM to **answer questions**. Notice of AGMs should be sent out at least 20 days before the meeting.
Remuneration	There should be remuneration committees composed of non-executive directors to set directors' pay, which should provide pay which attracts, retains and motivates quality directors but avoids paying more than is necessary for the purpose. The company's annual report should contain a statement of remuneration policy and details of the remuneration of each director.
Accountability and audit	The directors should **explain** their **responsibility for preparing accounts**. They should **report that the business is a going concern**, with supporting assumptions and qualifications as necessary.
Internal control	The directors should review the **effectiveness of internal control** systems, at least annually, and also **review the need for an internal audit function**.
Audit committee	The board **should establish an audit committee**.
External auditors' responsibilities	
Statement of responsibilities	The external auditors **should include** in their report a statement of their reporting responsibilities.
Directors' remuneration	Under the Directors' Remuneration Regulations of 2002, external auditors are also required to check the accuracy of disclosure in the financial statements of some elements of directors' remuneration.

NOTES

9.3 Turnbull recommendations

The Turnbull Report adds some additional guidelines in relation to internal control systems.

Definition

> An **internal control system** comprises the control environment and control procedures. It includes all the policies and procedures (internal controls) adopted by the directors and management of an entity to ensure, as far as practicable, the orderly and efficient conduct of its business, including adherence to internal policies, the safeguarding of assets, the prevention and detection of fraud and error, the accuracy and completeness of the accounting records, and the timely preparation of reliable financial information. Internal controls may be incorporated within computerised accounting systems. However the internal control system extends beyond those matters which relate directly to the accounting system.

TURNBULL GUIDELINES

- Have a defined process for the review of effectiveness of internal control.
- Review regular reports on internal control.
- Consider key risks and how they have been managed.
- Check the adequacy of action taken to remedy weaknesses and incidents.
- Consider the adequacy of monitoring.
- Conduct an annual assessment of risks and the effectiveness of internal control.
- Make a statement on this process in the annual report.

9.4 Assurance provision

As you can see from the above tables, many of the requirements in relation to corporate governance necessitate **communication** between the directors and the shareholders.

By law, **directors** of all companies are **required to produce financial statements** annually which give a **true and fair view** of the affairs of the company and its profit or loss for the period. They are also **encouraged** to **communicate with shareholders** on matters relating to **directors' pay** and benefits (this is required by law in the case of public limited companies), **going concern** and **management of risks.**

But how are the shareholders to know whether the directors' communications are **accurate**, or present a **fair picture?** Part of the external auditor's duty is to provide a report on the financial statements prepared by the directors. As the external auditor is independent of the directors, the shareholders can then rely on this report to confirm that the directors have prepared the companies financial statements so as to present a 'true and fair view'. In other words, an audit is an 'assurance' engagement.

Definition

> An **assurance engagement** is one where a professional accountant evaluates or measures a subject matter that is the responsibility of another party against suitable criteria, and expresses an opinion which provides the intended user with a level of assurance about that subject matter.

A statutory external audit is just one example of an assurance engagement. In this case the assurance is provided to the users of the financial statements – the company's shareholders.

FOR DISCUSSION

Discuss with your tutor and fellow learners what other types of assurance and assurance provider might be asked to offer and who would require such assurance.

Chapter roundup

- Business risk comprises operational, financial and compliance risk.

- It is the responsibility of the directors to install and maintain a satisfactory accounting system to minimise business risk.

- An internal control system comprises the control environment and control procedures. It extends beyond those matters which relate directly to the accounting system.

- **ISA 315** covers accounting and internal control systems and audit risk assessments.

- Segregation of duties is a vital aspect of the control system.

- Fraud is the use of deception to obtain advantage, while an error is an unintentional mistake.

- There are many control procedures for reducing the risk of fraud.

- Corporate governance is a contributory factor in the elimination of fraud.

Quick quiz

1   What should a company's accounting records be able to do, according to the Companies Act 2006?

2   What is the control environment?

3   What is meant by segregation of duties?

4   Give two examples of controls over documents.

5   What is 'teeming and lading'?

6   What are the main safeguards to prevent fraud?

7   What is the responsibility of the external auditor with regard to fraud?

Answers to Quick quiz

1   Every company must keep adequate accounting records that are sufficient to:

(a)   Show and explain the company's transactions and to disclose with reasonable accuracy, at any time, the financial position of the company at that time and to enable the directors to ensure that any accounts required to be prepared comply with the requirements of the Act.

(b)   The records must contain entries from day to day of all sums of money received and expended by the company and the matters in respect of which the receipt and expenditure takes place.

(c)   A record of the assets and liabilities of the company.

(d)   Where the company's business involves dealing in goods, the accounting records must enable the company to establish the statement of inventory at the end of each financial year end including the stock taking records.

2   The framework within which controls operate.

3   It is segregation of function and the segregation of staff carrying out various accounting operations.

4   Multi-part documents
Pre-numbering of documents
Standardisation of documents

5   It is a fraud whereby a cashier steals money from the company and then applies money received later on from someone else to cover up the original theft. It is a 'rolling fraud'.

6   A good system of internal control
Continuous supervision of all employees
Surprise audit visits
Thorough personnel procedures

7   To report all instances of fraud that they find to management, unless they suspect management of being involved in the fraud.

Answers to Activities

1   *Purchasing department*

A key risk is the risk that suppliers will not deliver goods when the company needs them in order to be able to produce goods on time for its customers.

The company can reduce this risk by setting up a system of internal control in respect of contracting with suppliers and ensuring that it does not contract with suppliers unless they have certain quality standards in place.

Human resources department

A key risk is the risk that the HR will recruit staff who are not capable of carrying out their roles in the organisation.

The company can reduce this risk by setting up a system of internal control so that no one is employed until they have provided evidence of their qualifications and references from previous employers.

2   This will depend very much on the type of organisation involved. You would certainly expect to see a good handful of those controls in operation, although bear in mind that it is often more difficult for a small company with few employees to operate a cohesive system of internal controls.

3   Reasons for weaknesses in small company PC-based systems include the following.

(a) Small companies generally have few accounting staff, so that it will often be difficult to create good conditions for segregation of duties. The accountant, for instance, may be the only person in the company fully conversant with the accounting system. This weakens security and problems may arise if the computer 'expert' is ill or away on holiday. If one person has specialised programming knowledge not shared by others, s/he may easily be able to put through unauthorised program changes undetected.

(b) Controls over access to the system may be poor or non-existent. In a small office, it will probably be difficult to create physical security by putting the computer in a secure area. Controls over programs and disks may also be poor.

(c) Clerical staff in a small company may be required to use the computer for routine processing without an understanding of the system or of its possible risks and pitfalls. If a malfunction occurs or if an error is made, untrained staff may not be able to take proper corrective action, and there is a risk that files may be corrupted or data lost as a result.

(d) Poor access controls, combined with real-time processing, may result in poor control over input; there is a risk that data may be input twice or not at all.

(e) Small companies with few resources may not have adequate provision for maintenance or stand-by equipment in case of breakdown or damage.

4   Clearly, it is in the interest of all shareholders that all companies are well-managed so as to maximise returns from their investment. However, in the UK, only public limited companies are entitled to sell shares to the general public. This means that in **many** cases (although not all), shareholders in private (Ltd) companies will be more closely connected to the directors than in public limited

company (plcs). In fact, many Ltd companies in the UK are 'owner-managed', in other words, their shareholders and directors are one and the same. This is not always the case, and some Ltd companies are large affairs where owners and managers are very clearly distinct from one another.

While all public limited companies are entitled to sell shares to the public, in practice, the public are most likely to invest in shares that are **listed** on an exchange, for example, the Stock Exchange. This makes them key candidates for the need of good corporate governance.

Chapter 3
THE ROLE OF THE AUDITOR AND THE AUDITING ENVIRONMENT

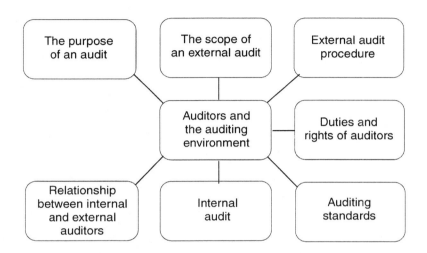

Introduction

The Edexcel guidelines require you to appreciate the distinction between and the importance of both internal and external audit. Although this chapter refers to internal audit, it is mainly concerned with the law and professional standards relating to external audit, in order for you to fulfil the learning outcome 'explain the environment in which the audit of a business organisation takes place'.

You should appreciate that although it is only large limited companies which are required by law to undergo an audit, many other business organisations do so on a voluntary basis. These include partnerships, sole traders, clubs and societies. The main reason for this is the fact that a set of audited accounts is of great value in supporting applications for finance and in providing credibility to the organisation as a whole.

Your objectives

In this chapter you will learn about the following.

(a)   The purpose of an audit and the responsibilities of the various parties involved

(b)   The scope of external audit

(c)   The procedure for the conduct of an external audit

(d)   The duties and rights of the external auditor

(e)   The role of International Standards on Auditing (ISAs)

(f)   The role and scope of internal audit and the relationship between external and internal audit

1 THE PURPOSE OF AN AUDIT

1.1 The role of the auditors

In the modern commercial environment, businesses which are operated as companies with limited liability need to produce accounts in order to show their owners (shareholders) how their investment has been used, and how successfully the businesses are performing. However the owners of a business require something more than accounts because the managers responsible for preparing them may, either unintentionally or by deliberate manipulation, produce accounts which are misleading (put another way, there is **information risk** about the accounts). An independent examination of the accounts is needed so that the owners of the business can rely on the financial statements when assessing how well management have discharged their stewardship and whether shares in the business remain a worthwhile investment.

1.2 Definition of an audit

The Auditing Practices Board (APB) is the main standard setting body in the United Kingdom. The APB gives general guidance on what constitutes an audit.

Definition

According to ISA 200: The objective of an **audit** of financial statements is to enable the auditor to express an opinion whether the financial statements are prepared, in all material respects, in accordance with an applicable financial reporting framework. The phrases used to express the auditor's opinion are 'give a true and fair view' or 'present fairly, in all material respects' which are equivalent terms.

This wording follows very closely that of the auditors' report on financial statements, which we will look at later.

First of all, though, we need to look at what an audit is really about. This is the subject matter of the APB's ISA 200 *Objective and General Principles Governing an Audit of Financial Statements*.

1.3 ISA 200

In undertaking an audit of financial statements auditors should:

(a) comply with the Ethical Standards issued by the Auditing Practices Board (APB)

(b) conduct an audit in accordance with the ISAs

(c) plan and perform an audit with an attitude of professional scepticism – in other words the auditor should realise that circumstances may exist which cause the financial statements to be materially misstated.

(d) plan and perform the audit to reduce audit risk to an acceptably low level that is consistent with the objective of an audit.

The ISAs explanatory material highlights an audit peformed in accordance with ISA's is designed to provide **reasonable assurance** that the financial statements are free from material misstatement.

Materiality is discussed in detail in chapter 4.

An auditor cannot obtain absolute (i.e. 100%) assurance because there are inherent limitations in an audit that affect the auditor's ability to detect material misstatements, such as:

(a) Use of testing

(b) Inherent limitations in internal control systems (e.g. possibility of human error)

(c) Most audit evidence is persuasive rather than conclusive

(d) Impracticality of examining all items

(e) The possibility of collusion or misrepresentation for fraudulent purposes.

1.4 Responsibility of directors

Most importantly, the standard makes clear that the auditors do not bear any responsibility for the preparation and presentation of the financial statements.

The responsibility for the preparation and presentation of the financial statements is that of the management of the entity, with oversight from those charged with governance. Auditors are responsible for forming and expressing an opinion on the financial statements. The audit of the financial statements does not relieve the directors of any of their responsibilities.

1.5 The expectations gap

Definition

> The **expectations gap** is the 'gap' between the role of the auditor as laid down by statute and the Auditing Standards, and the public's perception of the role of the auditor, which usually encompasses being responsible for finding frauds.

There are some common misconceptions in relation to the role of the auditors, even among 'financially aware' people, including the following examples.

(a) Many people think that the auditors report to the directors of a company, rather than the members.

(b) Some think that a qualified audit report is more favourable than an unqualified audit report, whereas the converse is true.

(c) There is a perception that it is the auditors' duty to detect fraud, when in fact the detection of fraud is the responsibility of the directors.

These findings highlight the 'expectations gap' between what auditors do and what people in general think that they do. Add the fact that many 'financially aware' people do not look at the report and accounts of a company they are considering investing in, and you have some sobering facts for the auditors to contemplate!

Some of the recent large company collapses have emphasised the need to reduce the expectation gap. For this reason, reports such as those of the Cadbury and Hampel Committee reports on corporate governance have been published. They aim to reduce the expectations gap by laying out a code of conduct for directors, as well as making suggestions for the content of company reports.

2 THE SCOPE OF EXTERNAL AUDIT

2.1 Statutory and non-statutory audits

Audits are required under statute in the case of a large number of undertakings, including the following.

Undertaking	Principal Act
Limited companies	Companies Act 2006
Building societies	Building Societies Act 1986
Trade unions and employer associations	Trade Union and Labour Relations Act 1974
Housing Associations	Various Acts depending on the legal constitution of the housing association, including: Industrial and Provident Societies Act 1965; Friendly and Industrial and Provident Societies Act 1968; Housing Act 1980; Companies Act 1985; Housing Association Act 1985.
Certain charities	Various Acts depending on the status of the charity, including special Acts of Parliament.
Unincorporated investment businesses	Regulations made under the Financial Services and Markets Act 2000

Non-statutory audits and **other assurance engagements** are performed by independent auditors because the owners, proprietors, members, trustees, professional and governing bodies or other interested parties want them, rather than because the law requires them.

2.2 External and internal audit

We have discussed auditing in particular in the context of the APB definition in section 1.2. The definition relates to the work of **external** auditors, independent persons brought in from outside an organisation to review the accounts prepared by management. **Internal auditors** perform a different role.

The management of an organisation will wish to establish systems to ensure that business activities are carried out efficiently. They will institute clerical, administrative and financial controls.

Larger organisations may appoint full-time staff whose function is to monitor and report on the running of the company's operations. **Internal** audit staff members are one type of control. Although some of the work carried out by internal auditors is similar to that performed by external auditors, there are important distinctions between the nature of the two functions.

We shall look at internal audit in more detail later in this chapter.

3 DUTIES AND RIGHTS OF EXTERNAL AUDITORS

The duties and rights of auditors are enshrined in law, indicating their importance.

3.1 Duties

The principal statutory duties of auditors in respect of the audit of a limited company are set out in ss. 475–6 and 495–502 CA 2006. Auditors are required to:

(a) Form an independent opinion on the truth and fairness of the accounts

(b) Confirm that the accounts have been properly prepared in accordance with the Companies Act 2006

(c) State in their audit report whether in their opinion the information given in the directors' report is consistent with the financial statements.

The Companies Act lists other factors which auditors must consider whether:

(a) adequate accounting records have not been kept;

(b) returns adequate for audit have been received from branches not visited;

(c) the financial statements are in agreement with the accounting records and returns;

(d) disclosures of directors' remuneration specified by law are made;

(e) all the information and explanations required for the audit have been received

Auditors must report if any of (a) to (e) is not true.

3.2 Rights

The principal statutory rights auditors have, excepting those dealing with resignation or removal, are set out in the table below. All references are to the Companies Act 1985. Some of these rights will change under the Companies Act 2006 as limited companies (as compared to public companies) will no longer be required to hold general meetings).

s 499(1)(a)	*Access to records*	A right of access at all times to the books, accounts and vouchers of the company
s 499(1)(b)	*Information and explanations*	A right to require from the company's officers such information and explanations as they think necessary for the performance of their duties as auditors
s 502 (2)	*Attendance at/notices of general meetings*	A right to attend any general meetings of the company and to receive all notices of and communications relating to such meetings which any member of the company is entitled to receive
s 502 (2)	*Right to speak at general meetings*	A right to be heard at general meetings which they attend on any part of the business that concerns them as auditors
s 502 (2)	*Rights in relation to written resolutions*	A right to receive a copy of any written resolution proposed

4   AUDITING STANDARDS

4.1   The APB and International Standards on Auditing (ISAs)

Auditing standards are initially set by the International Auditing and Assurance Standards Board in New York. These standards are then tailored for use in the UK and Ireland by the Auditing Practices Board (APB).

(a)   The APB can issue auditing standards in its own right without having to obtain the approval of all the professional accounting bodies.

(b)   It has strong representation from outside the accounting profession.

(c)   It has a commitment to openness, with agenda papers being circulated to interested parties, and an annual report being published.

4.2   Scope of ISAs

The APB sets out the the scope of ISA's and it's other pronouncements in *The Auditing Practices Board – Scope and Authority of Pronouncements (Revised). The APB makes several categories of pronouncements:*

- The auditors' code
- Quality control standards
- International Standards on Auditing (ISAs)
- Ethical Standards for Auditors
- Practice Notes
- Bulletins

The auditors' code contains the fundamental principles that apply to all auditors and the work they carry out.

Quality control standards and ISAs contain basic principles and essential procedures ('Auditing Standards') which are indicated by bold type and with which auditors are required to comply, except where otherwise stated in the ISA concerned, in the conduct of any audit of financial statements.

The ethical standards explain the ethical principles that apply to all work undertaken by accountants with specific standards relating to different areas of service provided including non-audit services.

Apart from statements in bold type, ISAs also contain other material which is not prescriptive but which is designed to help auditors interpret and apply auditing standards. The APB document also states that auditing standards need not be applied to immaterial items (items which are not significant to the accounts).

The authority of ISAs is defined as follows.

> 'Auditors and reporting accountants should not claim compliance with APB standards unless they have complied fully with all of those standards relevant to an engagement.'

4.3   Other pronouncements

Practice Notes are issued 'to assist auditors in applying Auditing Standards of general application to particular circumstances and industries'.

Bulletins are issued 'to provide auditors with timely guidance on new or emerging issues'.

Practice Notes and Bulletins are persuasive rather than prescriptive, but they indicate good practice and have a similar status to the explanatory material in ISAs. Both Practice Notes and Bulletins may be included in later ISAs.

5   INTERNAL AUDIT

The management of an organisation will wish to establish systems to ensure that business activities are carried out efficiently. They will institute clerical, administrative and financial controls. Even in very small businesses with simple accounting systems it will be found that some limited checks and controls are present.

5.1   Differences between internal and external audit

Larger organisations may appoint full-time **internal audit** staff whose function is to monitor and report on the running of the company's operations. Internal audit staff are one kind of control. Although some of the work carried out by internal auditors is similar to that performed by external auditors, there are important distinctions between the nature of the two functions.

(a)   External auditors are independent of the organisation, whereas internal auditors (as employees) are responsible to the management.

(b)   The responsibility of external auditors is fixed by statute, but internal auditors' responsibilities are decided by management.

(c)   External auditors report to the members, not to the management (directors), as in the case of internal auditors.

(d)   External auditors perform work to enable them to express an opinion on the truth and fairness of the accounts. Internal auditors' work may range over many areas and activities, both operational and financial, as determined by management.

Definition

> **Internal audit** is an appraisal or monitoring activity established by management and directors for the review of the accounting and internal control systems as a service to the entity. It functions by, amongst other things, examining, evaluating and reporting to management and the directors on the adequacy and effectiveness of components of the accounting and internal control systems.

Internal audit was originally concerned entirely with the financial records, checking for weaknesses in the accounting systems and errors in the accounts. The function of internal audit has now been extended to the monitoring of all aspects of an organisation's activities.

NOTES

> ### Activity 1 (10 minutes)
>
> What consequences do you think the above differences have for the scope of internal and external auditors' work? Which difference do you think is most important?

5.2 Objectives of internal audit

The Institute of Internal Auditors states:

> 'The objective of internal auditing is to assist members of the organisation in the effective discharge of their responsibilities. To this end internal auditing furnishes them with analyses, appraisals, recommendations, counsel and information concerning the activities reviewed.'

The role of the internal auditor has expanded in recent years as internal auditors seek to add value to their organisation. The work of the internal auditor is still prescribed by management, but it may cover the following broad areas.

(a) **Monitoring of internal control.** The establishment of adequate accounting and internal control systems is a responsibility of management and the directors which demands proper attention on a continuous basis. Often, internal audit is assigned specific responsibility for:

    (i)   Reviewing the design of the systems
    (ii)   Monitoring operation of the systems
    (iii) Recommending improvements

(b) **Examination of financial and operating information**. This may include review of the means used to identify, measure, classify and report such information and specific enquiry into individual items including detailed testing of transactions, balances and procedures.

(c) **Review of the economy, efficiency and effectiveness of operations** (often called a 'value for money' audit) including non-financial controls of an organisation.

(d) **Review of compliance** with laws, regulations and other external requirements and with internal policies and directives and other requirements including appropriate authorisation of transactions.

(e) **Special investigations** into particular areas, for example suspected fraud.

5.3 Essential criteria for internal auditors

(a) The internal auditors should have the **independence** in terms of organisational status and personal objectivity which permits the proper performance of their duties.

(b) Like external audit teams, the internal audit unit should be **appropriately staffed** in terms of numbers, grades, qualifications and experience, having regard to its responsibilities and objectives. Training should be a planned and continuing process at all levels.

(c)   The internal auditors should seek to foster constructive **working relationships** and mutual understanding with management, with external auditors, with any other review agencies and, where one exists, with the audit committee.

(d)   The internal auditors cannot be expected to give total assurance that control weaknesses or irregularities do not exist, but they should exercise **due care** in fulfilling their responsibilities.

(e)   Like the external auditors, the internal auditors should adequately **plan, control and record** their work. As part of the planning process the internal auditors should identify the whole range of systems within the organisation.

(f)   The internal auditors should identify and **evaluate the organisation's internal control system** as a basis for reporting upon its adequacy and effectiveness.

(g)   The internal auditors should obtain **sufficient, relevant and reliable evidence** on which to base reasonable conclusions and recommendations.

(h)   For **reporting and follow-up,** the internal auditors should ensure that findings, conclusions and recommendations arising from each internal audit assignment are communicated promptly to the appropriate level of management and they should actively seek a response.

6   RELATIONSHIP BETWEEN INTERNAL AND EXTERNAL AUDIT

Co-ordination between the external and internal auditors of an organisation will minimise duplication of work and encourage a wide coverage of audit issues and areas. This co-ordination will involve:

(a)   Periodic meetings to plan the overall audit to ensure adequate coverage
(b)   Periodic meetings to discuss matters of mutual interest
(c)   Mutual access to audit programmes and working papers
(d)   Exchange of audit reports and management letters
(e)   Common development of audit techniques, methods and terminology

Where the external auditors wish to rely on the work of the internal auditors, then the external auditors must assess the internal audit function, as with any part of the system of internal control.

Although the reliability of records and adequacy of the reporting and accounting systems are interests shared by both types of auditor:

(a)   Internal audit must not be seen merely as a service to the external audit and internal audit work should not be so distorted in order to fit with external audit needs that its own function is lost, and

(b)   Internal audit is not always a cheaper way of carrying out an external audit function because:

(i)   The internal role extends into many other areas, and

(ii)   The special position of the external auditors makes them more effective and appropriate sometimes.

NOTES

Activity 2 (15 minutes)

Explain why the internal and external auditors' review of internal control procedures differ in purpose.

Chapter roundup

- The purpose of a statutory audit is to enable external auditors to give an opinion as to whether the financial statements give a true and fair view.

- There are common misconceptions as to the role of the external auditor, known as the expectation gap.

- Internal audit is designed to assure management that the controls of the business are operating effectively.

- The external audit has a precise procedure involving testing both of controls and transactions.

- External auditors have specific duties and rights which are laid down by statute.

- Auditing standards (ISAs) are issued by the Auditing Practices Board, and external auditors are expected to follow them unless there are extremely valid reasons for not doing so.

Quick quiz

1   What is an audit?

2   What is the expectation gap?

3   List three statutory rights of the auditor.

4   To whom does the internal auditor report?

BPP
LEARNING MEDIA

Answers to Quick quiz

1   An exercise whose objective is to enable the auditor to express an opinion as to whether the financial statements give a true and fair view.

2   The difference between the role of the auditor as laid down by statute and auditing standards, and the public perception of that role.

3   Access to records
Receive information and explanations
Receive notice of and attend general meetings
Speak at general meetings
Require laying of accounts before members

4   Management of the organisation.

Answers to Activities

1   The difference in objectives is particularly important, although internal and external auditors use many similar methods to achieve their respective objectives. Every definition of internal audit suggests that it has a much wider scope than external audit, which has the objective of considering whether the accounts give a true and fair view of the organisation's financial position.

2   The internal auditors review and test the system of internal control and report to management in order to improve the information received by managers and to help in their task of running the company. The internal auditors will recommend changes to the system to make sure that the management receives objective information which is efficiently produced. The internal auditors will also have a duty to search for and discover fraud.

The external auditors review the system of internal control in order to determine the extent of the substantive work required on the year end accounts. The external auditors report to the shareholders rather than the managers or directors.

External auditors usually however issue a letter of weakness to the managers, laying out any areas of weakness and recommendations for improvement in the system of internal control. The external auditors report on the truth and fairness of the financial statements, not directly on the system of internal control. The auditors do not have a specific duty to detect fraud, although they should plan their audit procedures so as to detect any material misstatement in the accounts on which they give an opinion.

NOTES

Chapter 4

PLANNING THE AUDIT

Introduction

Audit planning is a critical part of the audit process as it is at this stage that the key decisions are made including the assessment of risk and materiality. Information obtained will determine the overall approach or audit strategy as well as the detailed audit procedures which will be performed.

Your objectives

In this chapter you will learn about the following.

(a) How to determine the audit approach

(b) The implications of the assessment of controls

(c) The components of audit risk

(d) The importance of materiality

1 OVERALL AUDIT APPROACH

1.1 Scope

The first stage in any audit should be to determine its scope and the auditors' general approach. For statutory audits the scope is clearly laid down in the Companies Act 2006 as expanded by auditing standards.

1.2 Audit strategy

Auditors should prepare an **audit strategy** to be placed on the audit file. The purpose of this document is to provide a record of the major areas to which the auditors attach special significance and to highlight any particular difficulties or points of concern peculiar to the audit client.

Adequate planning ensures that audit risk is kept to an acceptably low level and that appropriate attention is devoted to important areas of the audit, that potential problems are identified and resolved on a timely basis and that the audit is properly organised and managed in order to be carried out in an efficient and effective manner.

Audit risk will be covered in more detail in the next section of this chapter.

ISA 300 *Planning an Audit of Financial Statements* sets out the key planning activities that should be undertaken by the external auditor:

- **Overall audit strategy**

  The overall audit strategy sets the scope, timing and direction of the audit and guides the development of a more detailed plan. It will assist the auditor in determining the nature, timing and extent of resources needed.

- **Audit plan**

  The audit plan is more detailed that the audit strategy and includes the nature, timing and extent of audit procedures to be performed by the audit team.

  Both the audit strategy and audit plan should be updated during the course of the audit for changes in circumstances where they arise.

- **Direction, supervision and review**

  The auditor will need to plan how the work of the audit team is to be directed, supervised and reviewed.

- **Documentation**

  All of the above activities should be documented.

- **Communications of those charged with governance**

  The auditor will need to discuss with management elements of planning such as the timing of the audit and the approach being taken. This should improve the effectiveness and efficiency of the audit.

1.3 Documenting accounting systems

As part of the process of determining the overall audit strategy the auditor should obtain an understanding of the entity and its environment, including its internal control, sufficient to identify and assess the risks of material misstatement of the financial statements whether due to fraud or error, and sufficient to design and perform further audit procedures. (ISA 315.2)

This **understanding** of the accounting system must enable auditors to identify and understand:

- Major classes of transactions in the entity's operations
- How such transactions are initiated
- Significant accounting records, supporting documents and accounts
- The accounting and financial reporting process

The factors affecting the **nature, timing and extent** of the **procedures** performed in order to understand the systems include:

- The auditor's judgement regarding **materiality**

- The **size** of the entity

- The **nature of the entity's business**, including its organisation and ownership characteristics

- The **diversity and complexity** of the entity's operations

- Applicable **legal and regulatory requirements**

- The nature and complexity of the systems that are a part of the entity's **internal control**, including the use of service organisations

1.4 Ascertain the system and internal controls

The objective at this stage is to determine the **flow of documents** and **extent of controls** in existence. This is very much a fact-finding exercise, achieved by discussing the accounting system and document flow with all the relevant departments, including typically, sales, purchases, cash, stock and accounts personnel. It is good practice to make a rough record of the system during this fact-finding stage, which will be converted to a formal record.

The objective here is to prepare a **comprehensive record** to facilitate evaluation of the systems. Records may be in various formats.

- Charts, for example organisation charts and records of the books of account
- Narrative notes
- Internal control questionnaires
- Flowcharts

The auditors' objective here is to confirm that the **system recorded** is the same as that in **operation**.

After completion of the preparation (or update) of the systems records the auditors will confirm their understanding of the system by performing **walk-through** tests. These involve tracing literally a handful of transactions of each type through the system and observing the operation of controls over them. This procedure will establish whether the accounting system operates in the manner ascertained and recorded.

The need for this check arises as the client's staff will occasionally tell the auditors what they should be doing (the established procedures) rather than what is actually being done in practice.

1.5 Assess the system and internal controls

The purpose of **evaluating the systems** is to gauge their reliability and formulate a basis for testing their effectiveness in practice. Following the evaluation, the auditors will be able to recommend improvements to the system and determine the extent of the further tests to be carried out as described.

1.6 Test the system and internal controls

Given effective controls, the objective is to select and perform tests designed to establish compliance with the system. One of the most important points underlying modern auditing is that, if the controls are strong, the records should be reliable and consequently the amount of detailed testing can be reduced.

Auditors should however check that the controls are as effective in practice as they are on paper. They will therefore carry out **tests of controls**. These are like walk-through checks in so far as they are concerned with the workings of the system. There are a number of differences between the two.

- Tests of control are concerned only with those areas subject to effective control.

- Tests of control cover a representative sample of transactions throughout the period.

- Tests of control are likely to cover a larger number of items than walk-through tests.

The conclusion drawn from the results of a test of controls may be either that:

(a) The **controls are effective**, in which case the auditors will only need to carry out restricted substantive procedures.

(b) The **controls are ineffective** in practice, although they had appeared strong on paper, in which case the auditors will need to carry out more extensive substantive procedures.

These procedures should only be carried out if the controls are evaluated at Stage 5 as being effective. If the auditors know that the controls are ineffective then there is no point in carrying out tests of controls which will merely confirm what is already known. Instead the auditors should go straight on to carry out full substantive procedures.

Having assessed the accounting system and control environment, the auditors can make a **preliminary assessment** of whether the system is capable of producing reliable financial statements and of the likely mix of tests of control and substantive procedures (see Chapter 6).

The following diagram sets out the audit process. Steps 1–5 essentially cover those steps discussed above that are undertaken during the planning process. Steps 7–9 represent the fulfilment of those activities planned and steps 10–12 cover the process by which the auditor reaches the audit opinion.

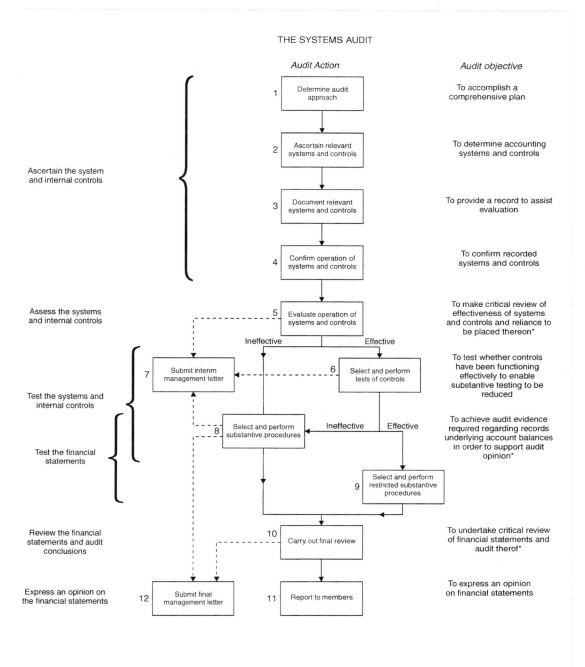

Figure 4.1 The external audit procedure

2   AUDIT RISK

Definition

> **Audit risk** is the risk that auditors may give an inappropriate opinion on the financial statements.

2.1   Components of audit risk

Audit risk has three components: inherent risk, control risk and detection risk.

Audit risk is the risk that the auditors give an unqualified opinion on the accounts when they should have given a qualified opinion (or *vice versa*) **or** they give an opinion qualified for a particular reason where that reason was not justified.

In recent years there has been a shift towards risk-based auditing. This refers to the development of auditing techniques which are responsive to **risk factors** in an audit. Auditors apply judgement to determine what level of risk pertains to different areas of a client's system and devise appropriate audit tests. This approach should ensure that the greatest audit effort is directed at the riskiest areas, so that the chance of detecting errors is improved and excessive time is not spent on 'safe' areas.

The increased use of risk-based auditing reflects two factors.

(a)   The growing **complexity** of the business environment increases the danger of fraud or misstatement. Factors such as the developing use of computerised systems and the growing internationalisation of business are relevant here.

(b)   Pressures are increasingly exerted by audit clients for the auditors to keep **fee levels down** while providing an improved level of service.

Risk-based auditing is responsive to both factors.

ISA 200 *Objective and general principles governing an audit of financial statements* introduces audit risk. ISA 315 provides more detail on how to plan to miminise that risk to an acceptable level.

Auditors should:

(a)   obtain an understanding of the entity and its environment including its internal control, sufficient to identify and assess the risks of material misstatement of the financial statements whether due to fraud or error, and sufficient to design and perform further audit tests (ISA 315.2); and

(b)   plan and perform the audit to reduce audit risk to an acceptably low level that is consistent with the objective of the audit (ISA 200.15).

Audit risk can never be completely eliminated. The auditors are called upon to make subjective judgements in the course of forming an opinion and so fraud or error may possibly go undetected.

A **risk-based approach** gives the auditors an overall measure of risk, but at the same time it provides a quantification of each stage of the audit. The extent of detailed testing required is determined by a purely risk-based perspective. A diagrammatic view of the risk-based approach is given here.

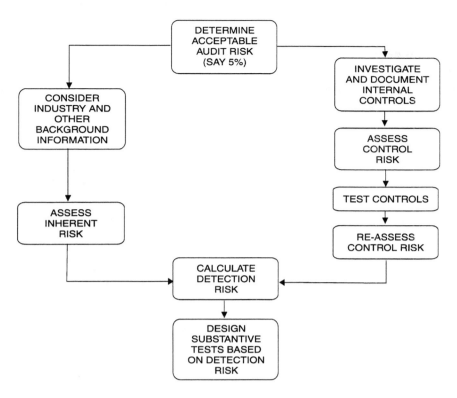

Figure 4.2: Risk-based approach

2.2 Inherent risk

Definition

> **Inherent risk** is the susceptibility of an assertion to a misstatement that could be material, either individually or when aggregated with other misstatements, assuming that there are no related controls (ISA 200.20).

Inherent risk is the risk that items will be misstated due to characteristics of those items, such as the fact they are **estimates** or that they are **important** items in the accounts. The auditors must use their professional judgement and all available knowledge to assess inherent risk. If no such information or knowledge is available then the inherent risk is **high**.

The results of the assessment must be properly documented and, where inherent risk is assessed as not high, then audit work may be reduced.

In developing their audit approach and detailed procedures, auditors should assess inherent risk in relation to financial statement assertions about material account balances and classes of transactions, taking account of factors relevant both to the entity as a whole and to the specific assertions. For more detail on audit assertions, see chapter 6. Factors that indicate higher risk are set out in the tables below. ISA 315 Appendix 3 contains a similar list although this is not split by client and individual account balances.

FACTORS AFFECTING CLIENT AS A WHOLE	
Integrity and **attitude to risk** of directors and management	Domination by a single individual can cause problems
Management experience and **knowledge**	Changes in management and quality of financial management
Unusual pressures on management	Examples include tight reporting deadlines, or market or financing expectations
Nature of business	Potential problems include technological obsolescence or over-dependence on a single product
Industry factors	Competitive conditions, regulatory requirements, technology developments, changes in customer demand
Information technology	Problems include lack of supporting documentation, concentration of expertise in a few people, potential for unauthorised access

FACTORS AFFECTING INDIVIDUAL ACCOUNT BALANCES OR TRANSACTIONS	
Financial statement **accounts prone to misstatement**	Accounts which require adjustment in previous period, require high degree of estimation or judgement, or which may significantly affect profitability or liquidity
Complex accounts	Accounts which require expert valuations or are subjects of current professional discussion
Assets at risk of being **lost or stolen**	Cash (consider opportunities for unauthorised payments), stock, portable fixed assets (computers)
High volume of **transactions**	Accounting system may have problems coping
Quality of **accounting systems**	Strength of individual departments (sales, purchases, cash etc)
Unusual transactions	Transactions for large amounts, with unusual names, not settled promptly (particularly important if they occur at period-end)
	Transactions that do not go through the system, that relate to specific clients or processed by certain individuals
Staff	Staff changes or areas of low morale

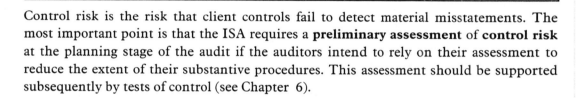

Activity 1   **(15 minutes)**

You are the newly appointed auditor of CME Ltd. CME sells fashion clothing to high street retailers. Clothing is purchased from overseas suppliers who invoice CME in their own local currency. CME invoices retailers in UK Sterling and grants each retailer a period of credit up to 60 days. Recently economic conditions have seen a decline in orders and one retailer has gone into liquidation with monies still owed to CME.

Identify the inherent risks associated with CME and explain what risks they pose for the financial statements.

2.3 Control risk

Definition

Control risk is the risk that a misstatement that could occur in an assertion and that could be material, either individually or when aggregated with other misstatements, will not be prevented, or detected and corrected, on a timely basis by the entity's internal control (ISA 200.20).

Control risk is the risk that client controls fail to detect material misstatements. The most important point is that the ISA requires a **preliminary assessment** of **control risk** at the planning stage of the audit if the auditors intend to rely on their assessment to reduce the extent of their substantive procedures. This assessment should be supported subsequently by tests of control (see Chapter 6).

2.4 Detection risk

Definition

Detection risk is the risk that the auditor will not detect a misstatement that exists in an assertion that could be material, either individually, or when aggregated with other misstatements (ISA 200.22).

Detection risk is the risk that audit procedures will fail to detect material errors. Detection risk relates to the inability of the auditors to examine all evidence. Audit evidence is usually persuasive rather than conclusive so some detection risk is usually present, allowing the auditors to seek 'reasonable confidence'.

Auditors should consider the assessed levels of inherent and control risk in determining the nature, timing and extent of substantive procedures required to reduce audit risk to an acceptable level.

Effectively this is the management of detection risk based on the auditor's assessment of inherent and control risks. Where inherent and/or control risk is assessed as being 'high' the audit will want to reduced detection risk by carry out more audit procedures. Equally, where inherent and control risk are assessed as low there is no need to carry out extensive testing and so the auditor will carry out more limited audit procedures (resulting in a higher detection risk).

The auditors' **inherent and control risk assessments** influence the **nature, timing and extent of substantive procedures** required to reduce detection risk and thereby audit risk.

(a) Auditors need to be careful when relying on their **assessment** of **control risk**, as good controls may impact upon some but not other aspects of audit areas. For example, good controls over the recording of sales and debtors would not reduce audit testing on bad debts, as the amounts recorded may represent amounts that will not be collected.

(b) To design an efficient audit strategy, auditors should not just consider reducing the number of items they test substantively, the **extent** of testing, if inherent and control risks are low. They may also alter the tests they do, the **design** of testing, by placing for instance more reliance on analytical procedures. They may also change the **timing** of tests, for example carrying out certain procedures such as circularisation at a date that is not the year-end, and placing reliance upon internal controls functioning at the year-end.

Misstatements discovered in substantive procedures may cause the auditors to modify their previous assessment of control risk.

Regardless of the assessed levels of inherent and control risks, auditors should perform some substantive procedures for financial statement assertions of material account balances and transaction classes.

Substantive procedures can never be abandoned entirely because control and inherent risk can never be assessed at a low enough level, although substantive procedures may be restricted to analytical procedures if appropriate.

Where the auditors' assessment of the components of audit risk changes during the audit, they should modify the planned substantive procedures based on the revised risk levels.

When both inherent and control risks are assessed as high, the auditors should consider whether substantive procedures can provide sufficient appropriate audit evidence to reduce detection risk, and therefore audit risk, to an acceptably low level. For example, they may not be able to obtain sufficient evidence about the completeness of income in the absence of some internal controls. If sufficient evidence cannot be obtained, auditors may have to qualify their audit report.

Activity 2   **(20 minutes)**

Hippo Ltd is a long established client of your firm. It manufactures bathroom fittings and fixtures, which it sells to a range of wholesalers in the UK, on credit.

You are the audit senior and have recently been sent the following extract from the draft balance sheet by the finance director.

	Budget		Actual	
	£'000s	£'000s	£'000s	£'000s
Tangible non-current assets		453		367
Current assets				
Account receivables	1,134		976	
Cash	-		54	
Current liabilities				
Account payables	967		944	
Bank overdraft	9		-	
Net current assets		158		86
Total assets		611		453

During the course of conversation with the finance director, you establish that a major new customer the company had included in its budget went bankrupt during the year.

Identify any potential risks for the audit of Hippo and explain why you believe they are risks.

---

3 MATERIALITY

3.1 What is materiality?

Definition

Materiality A matter is material if its omission or misstatement could influence the economic decisions of users taken on the basis of the financial statements. Materiality depends on the size of the item or error judged in the particular circumstances of its omission or misstatement. Thus, materiality provides a threshold or cut-off point rather than being a primary qualitative characteristic which information must have if is to be useful. (ISA 320.3)

Although the definition refers to the decision of the user of the financial statements (that is, the members of the company), their decisions may well be influenced by how the accounts are used. For example if the accounts are to be used to secure a bank loan, what is significant to the bank will influence the way members act. The views of other users of the accounts must be taken into account.

Materiality is often a question of the relative size of an item in the financial statements. However, items may also be material due to their very nature – for example remuneration paid directors would always be considered to be a material amount and disclosures in this respect should be completely accurate.

3.2 ISA 320 Audit materiality

ISA 320 states that auditors should consider materiality and its relationship with audit risk when conducting an audit. (ISA 320.2)

Auditors plan and perform the audit to be able to provide reasonable assurance that the financial statements are free of material misstatement and give a true and fair view. The assessment of what is material is a matter of professional judgement.

Small amounts should be considered if there is a risk that they could occur more than once and together add up to an amount which is material in total. As well as quantitative aspects, qualitative aspects must also be considered, for example the inaccurate and therefore misleading description of an accounting policy.

Materiality considerations will differ depending on the aspect of the financial statements being considered.

Materiality is considered at both the overall financial statement level and in relation to individual account balances, classes of transactions and disclosures.

A good example is directors' pay which make normal materiality considerations irrelevant, because it **must** be disclosed by the auditors if they are not disclosed correctly by the directors in the financial statements.

Materiality considerations during **audit planning** are extremely important. The assessment of materiality when determining the nature, timing and extent of audit procedures should be based on the most recent and reliable financial information and will help to determine an effective and efficient audit approach. Materiality assessment in conjunction with risk assessment will help the auditors to make a number of decisions.

- What items to examine

- Whether to use sampling techniques (see Chapter 6)

- What level of error is likely to lead to an opinion that the accounts do not give a true and fair view

The resulting combination of audit procedures should help to reduce detection risk to an appropriately low level.

3.3 Practical implications

Because many users of accounts are primarily interested in the **profitability** of the company, the materiality level is often expressed as a proportion of its profits before tax. Some argue, however, that materiality should be thought of in terms of the **size** of the business. Hence, if the company remains a fairly constant size, the materiality level should not change; similarly if the business is growing, the level of materiality will increase from year to year.

The **size** of a company can be measured in terms of turnover and total assets before deducting any liabilities (sometimes referred to in legislation as 'the balance sheet total') both of which tend not to be subject to the fluctuations which may affect profit. The auditors will often calculate a range of values, such as those shown below, and then take an average or weighted average of all the figures produced as the materiality level.

Value	%
Profit before tax	5
Gross profit	½ – 1
Turnover	½ – 1
Total assets	1 – 2
Net assets	2 – 5
Profit after tax	5 – 10

The effect of planning materiality on the audit process is shown in the diagram below.

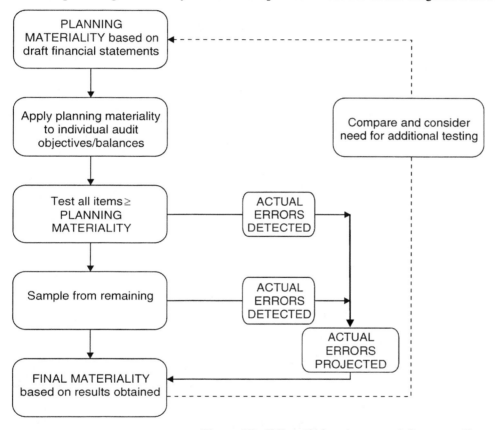

Figure 4.3: Effect of planning materiality on audit process

3.4 Changes to the level of materiality

The level of materiality must be reviewed constantly as the audit progresses. Changes to audit procedures may be required for various reasons.

- Draft accounts are altered (due to material error and so on) and therefore overall materiality changes.

- External factors cause changes in the control or inherent risk estimates.

- Changes are caused by errors found during testing.

Activity 3   **(10 minutes)**

Which measures of the business would an audit firm use when setting a level of materiality:

(a)   If the client had a stable asset base, steady turnover over the last few years, but had only made a small pre-tax profit this year owing to a large one-off expense?

(b)   If the directors had expressed concern over declining profits over the last few years?

Chapter roundup

- The auditor will formulate an overall audit plan which will be translated into a detailed audit programme for audit staff to follow.

- The audit programme documents the nature, timing and extent of planned audit procedures.

- There is no single accepted approach to audit. The more commonly used approach is the systems based audit, which has evolved into a risk-based approach.

Quick quiz

1   What is a systems audit?

2   What is risk based auditing?

3   What are the components of audit risk?

4   Which factors affecting the client as a whole increase inherent risk?

5   What impact does the auditor's assessment of inherent risk and control risk have on audit planning?

6   Why cannot substantive procedures be abandoned entirely?

7   What decisions are made on the basis of the materiality assessment?

8   At which levels should materiality be considered?

Answers to Quick quiz

1   The audit of internal controls within a system

2   The use of auditing techniques which are responsive to risk factors in an audit, so that the greatest audit effort is directed at the riskiest areas.

3   Inherent risk
Control risk
Detection risk

4   Integrity and attitude of management
Unusual pressures
Nature of business
Industry factors
Information technology problems

5   It influences the nature, timing and extent of substantive procedures

6   Control risk and inherent risk cannot be eliminated entirely

7   • How many and what items to examine
    • Whether to use sampling techniques
    • What level of error is likely to lead to a qualified audit report.

8   • Overall financial statement level
    • Individual accounts balance level

Answers to Activities

1   **Inherent risks for CME Ltd**

(1)   Nature of business: being in the fashion industry CME will face risk of their clothing becoming unfashionable and therefore not being able to continue to trade.

(2)   Complex transactions: errors could be made when translating payments to suppliers

(3)   Bad debts: the fact CME extend credit to retailers, particularly in a weak economic climate, increases the risk that the account receivables balance will be overstated

(4)   Fashion items: the value of items in inventory may be incorrectly valued if there is no longer any demand for them – inventory is likely to become obsolete relatively quickly.

2   **Potential risks relevant to the audit of Hippo**

(1)   **Credit sales**. Hippo makes sales on credit. This increases the risk that Hippo's sales will not be converted into cash. Debtors is likely to be a risky area and the auditors will have to consider what the best evidence that debtors are going to pay their debts is likely to be.

(2)   **Related industry**. Hippo manufactures bathroom fixtures and fittings. These are sold to wholesalers, but it is possible that Hippo's ultimate market is the building industry. This is a notoriously volatile industry, and Hippo may find that their results fluctuate too, as demand rises and falls. This suspicion is added to by the bankruptcy of the wholesaler in the

year. The auditors must be sure that accounts which present Hippo as a viable company are in fact correct.

(3) **Controls**. The fact that a major new customer went bust suggests that Hippo did not undertake a very thorough credit check on that customer before agreeing to supply them. This implies that the controls at Hippo may not be very strong.

(4) **Variance**. The actual results are different from budget. This may be explained by the fact that the major customer went bankrupt, or it may reveal that there are other errors and problems in the reported results, or in the original budget.

(5) **Debtors**. There is a risk that the result reported contains debt from the bankrupt wholesaler, which is likely to be irrecoverable.

3 (a) Because the business is stable, auditors are likely to base overall materiality on a % of turnover or gross assets, or possibly an average of both. Profit before tax is unlikely to be used overall as its fluctuation does not appear to be significant. However a different materiality level may be set when considering the one-off expense, since it may be particularly significant to readers of the accounts.

(b) Auditors are likely here to pay some attention to the level of profit when setting materiality, because the outside members regard profit as significant. However the auditors are also likely to take into account gross and net assets. Low profits will be of less significance if the business has a strong asset base, but of more significance if the business is in long-term financial difficulty.

Chapter 5

RECORDING AUDIT WORK

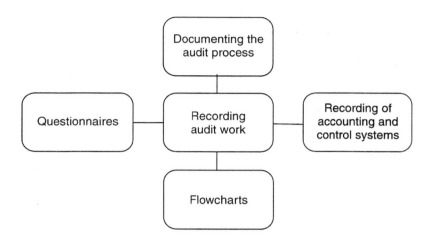

Introduction

Recording audit work is a vital part of the audit procedure, as it provides documentary evidence of how the audit has been carried out, what work has been done and what conclusions have been reached. This is essential in order that the work of the audit team can be reviewed and should the auditor subsequently have to justify his audit opinion on the financial statements.

Adequate recording of audit work can also be helpful in subsequent years, as it is common practice for the auditor to look back at last year's files to see what work was done and problems found, in case they should impact on the current year's work.

Your objectives

In this chapter you will learn about the following.

    (a)   Working papers and their different forms

    (b)   The different ways of recording accounting and control systems

    (c)   Flowcharting techniques

    (d)   Questionnaires

NOTES

1   DOCUMENTING THE AUDIT PROCESS

All audit work must be documented: the working papers are the tangible evidence of the work done in support of the audit opinion. ISA 230 *Audit Documentation* covers this area.

Definition

> **Audit documentation** means the record of audit procedures performed, relevant audit evidence obtained and conclusions the auditor reached (terms such as 'working papers' or 'workpapers' are also sometimes used). (ISA 230.6)
>
> Audit documentation may be in the form of data stored on paper, film, electronic media or other media.
>
> Audit documentation supports, amongst other things, the statement in the auditors' report as to the auditors' compliance or otherwise with Auditing Standards to the extent that this is important in supporting their report.

1.1   Form and content of working papers

ISA 230.2 indicates that working papers should provide (a) a sufficient and appropriate record of the basis for the auditor's report and (b) evidence that the audit was performed in accordance with ISAs and applicable legal and regulatory requirements .

Auditors should record in their working papers their reasoning on all significant matters which require the exercise of judgement, and their conclusions thereon.

Auditors cannot record everything they consider. Therefore judgement must be used as to the extent of working papers, based on the following test.

> What would be necessary to provide an experienced auditor, with no previous connection with the audit, with an understanding of the audit procedures performed, the results of those procedures and the audit evidence obtained and the conclusions reached on each significant matter?

The form and content of working papers are affected by various matters.

(a)   The nature of the audit procedures performed

(b)   The identified risks of material misstatement

(c)   The extent of judgement required in performing the work and evaluating the results

(d)   The significance of the audit evidence obtained

(e)   The nature and extent of exceptions identified

(f)   The need to document a conclusion or the basis for a conclusion not readily determinable from the documentation of the work performed or audit evidence obtained, and

(g)   The audit methodology tools used.

Standardised working papers, eg checklists, standard audit programmes, specimen letters can be used as they may improve the efficiency with which such working papers are prepared and reviewed. But while they facilitate the delegation of work and provide a means to control its quality, it is never appropriate to follow mechanically a standard

BPP
LEARNING MEDIA

approach to the conduct and documentation of the audit without regard to the need to exercise professional judgement.

While auditors may utilise schedules, analyses etc prepared by the entity, they require evidence that such information is properly prepared.

1.2   Typical contents of working papers

These include the following.

- Information concerning the legal and organisational structure of the client

- Information concerning the client's industry, economic and legal environment

- Evidence of the planning process

- Evidence of the auditors' understanding of the accounting and internal control systems

- Evidence of inherent and control risk assessments and any revisions

- Analyses of transactions and balances

- Analyses of significant ratios and trends

- A record of the nature, timing, extent and results of auditing procedures

- Copies of communications with other auditors, experts and other third parties

- Copies of correspondence with the client

- Reports to directors or management

- Notes of discussions with the entity's directors or management

- A summary of the significant aspects of the audit

- Copies of the approved financial statements and auditors' reports

1.3 Format of working papers

Client: *Example Ltd* ①

Subject: *Creditors* ⑥

Year end: *31 December 20X3* ②

	Prepared by	Reviewed by
④	*PC*	⑦ *AD*
	Date: *16.2.X4* ⑤	⑧ Date: *3.3.X4*

③ $E^3/_1$

⑨ **Objective**	To ensure purchase ledger balance fairly stated.							
⑪ **Work done**								⑩
	Selected a sample of trade creditors as at 31 December and reconciled the supplier's statement to the							
	year end purchase ledger balance. Vouched any reconciling items to source documentation.							
	⑩							
⑬ **Results**	See $E^3/_2$							
	One credit note, relating to Woodcutter Ltd, has not been accounted for. An adjustment is required. ⑭							
	DEBIT	Trade creditors	£4,975					
	CREDIT	Purchases		£4,975 *H1/2*				
	One other error was found, which was immaterial, and which was the fault of the supplier.							
	⑭							
	In view of the error found, however, we should recommend that the client management checks							
	supplier statement reconciliations at least on the larger accounts. Management letter point.							
⑮ **Conclusion**								
	After making the adjustment noted above, purchase ledger balances are fairly stated							
	as at 31 December 20X3.							

Client: _Example Ltd_

Subject: _Creditors_

Year end: _31 December 20X3_

Prepared by	Reviewed by
PC	*AD*
Date: *16.2.X4*	Date: *3.3.X4*

ε ³/₂

Client	Purchase ledger £		Supplier statement £		Difference		Agreed		Reconciling item			
A Ltd	↘ 300	00	300	00	-		✓		-			
B Ltd	↘ 747	00	732	00	15	00	✕		15	00	Credit note	
											not yet	
											received	
				⑫	Key							
					✓ Agreed							
					✕ Not agreed							
					⌃ Adds checked							
					↘ Agreed to purchase ledger							
	1,047	00										
	⌃											

KEY

①	The **name** of the **client**	⑨	The **objective** of the work done
②	The balance sheet **date**	⑩	The **sources of information**
③	The **file reference** of the working paper	⑪	The **work done**
④	The **name** of the **person** preparing the working paper	⑫	A **key** to any audit ticks or symbols
⑤	The **date** the working paper was **prepared**	⑬	The **results obtained**
⑥	The **subject** of the working paper	⑭	**Analysis** of **errors** or other significant observations
⑦	The **name** of the person **reviewing** the working paper	⑮	The **conclusions drawn**
⑧	The **date** of the **review**		*Figure 5.1: Format of working papers*

1.4 Computerised working papers

Automated working paper packages have been developed which can make the documenting of audit work much easier. These are automatically cross referenced and balanced by the computer. Whenever an adjustment is made, the computer will automatically update all the necessary schedules.

The **advantages** of automated working papers are as follows.

(a) The **risk** of **errors** is **reduced**.

(b) The **working papers** will be **neater** and **easier to review**.

(c) The **time saved** will be **substantial** as adjustments can be made easily to all working papers, including working papers summarising the key analytical information.

(d) **Standard** forms **do not have** to be **carried** to audit locations. Forms can be designed to be called up and completed on the computer screen.

(e) **Audit working papers** can be **transmitted** for review via a computer network, or fax facilities (if both the sending and receiving computers have fax boards and fax software).

1.5 Confidentiality, safe custody and ownership

Auditors should adopt appropriate procedures for maintaining the confidentiality and safe custody of their working papers.

Working papers are the property of the auditors. They are not a substitute for, nor part of, the client's accounting records.

Auditors must follow ethical guidance on the confidentiality of audit working papers. They may find themselves in a position where they have access to privileged information that would not ordinarily be available. In some circumstance this information could influence the decision making of others – for example if it would affect the share price.

They may, at their discretion, release parts of or whole working papers to the client, as long as disclosure does not undermine 'the independence or validity of the audit process'. Information should not be made available to third parties without the permission of the entity.

1.6 Audit files

For recurring audits, working papers may be split between permanent and current audit files.

(a) **Permanent audit files** are updated with new information of continuing importance such as legal documents, background information and correspondence with the client of relevance for a number of years. The file should also contain a copy of each year's final accounts.

(b) **Current audit files** contain information relating primarily to the audit of a single period.

Activity 1 **(15 minutes)**

Describe the benefits that auditors will obtain from documenting their work in accordance with ISA 230.

Activity 2 **(10 minutes)**

(a) With what details should working papers of audit tests performed be headed?

(b) What other details should working papers covering audit tests contain?

2 RECORDING OF ACCOUNTING AND CONTROL SYSTEMS

In Chapter 4 you saw the importance of recording the accounting and control systems present at a company subject to statutory audit. There are several techniques for recording accounting and internal control systems.

- Narrative notes
- Flowcharts
- Questionnaires (eg ICQ)
- Checklists

Often a combination may be used, with narrative notes and/or flowcharts recording the accounting system, and questionnaires recording controls.

Whatever method of recording the system is used, the record will usually be retained on the permanent file and updated each year.

2.1 Narrative notes

Narrative notes have the advantage of being simple to record. However they are awkward to change if written manually. Editing in future years will be easier if they are computerised. The purpose of the notes is to **describe** and **explain** the **system,** at the same time making any comments or criticisms which will help to demonstrate an intelligent understanding of the system.

For each system notes need to deal with the following questions.

- What functions are performed and by whom?
- What documents are used?
- Where do the documents originate and what is their destination?
- What sequence are retained documents filed in?
- What books are kept and where?

Narrative notes can be used to support flowcharts.

3 FLOWCHARTS

There are two methods of flowcharting in regular use.

- Document flowcharts
- Information flowcharts

3.1 Document flowcharts

Document flowcharts are more commonly used because they are relatively easy to prepare.

- *All* documents are followed through from 'cradle to grave'.
- *All* operations and controls are shown.

We shall concentrate on document flowcharts.

3.2 Information flowcharts

Information flowcharts are prepared in the reverse direction from the flow: they start with the entry in the accounting records and work back to the actual transaction. They concentrate on significant information flows and key controls and ignore any unimportant documents or copies of documents.

3.3 Advantages and disadvantages of flowcharts

Advantages include the following.

(a) After a little experience they can be **prepared quickly**.

(b) As the information is presented in a standard form, they are fairly **easy to follow** and to review.

(c) They generally ensure that the system is **recorded in its entirety**, as all document flows have to be traced from beginning to end. Any 'loose ends' will be apparent from a quick examination.

(d) They **eliminate** the need for **extensive narrative** and can be of considerable help in highlighting the salient points of control and any weaknesses in the system.

On the other hand, flowcharts do have some disadvantages.

(a) They are **only really suitable for describing standard systems**. Procedures for dealing with unusual transactions will normally have to be recorded using narrative notes.

(b) They are useful for recording the flow of documents, but once the **records** or the assets to which they relate have **become static** they **can no longer be used for describing the controls** (for example over fixed assets).

(c) Major **amendment is difficult** without redrawing.

(d) **Time** can be **wasted** by **charting areas** that are of no **audit significance** (a criticism of *document* not information flowcharts).

3.4 Design of flowcharts

Flowcharts should be kept simple, so that the overall structure or flow is clear at first sight.

(a) There must be **conformity of symbols**, with each symbol representing one and only one thing.

(b) The direction of the flowchart should be from **top to bottom** and from **left to right**.

(c) There must be no **loose ends.**

(d) The main flow should finish at the **bottom right hand corner,** not in the middle of the page.

(e) Connecting lines should cross *only* where absolutely necessary to preserve the chart's simplicity.

3.5 Flowcharting symbols

Basic symbols will be used for the charting of all systems, but where the client's system involves mechanised or computerised processing, then further symbols may be required to supplement the basic ones. The basic symbols used are shown below.

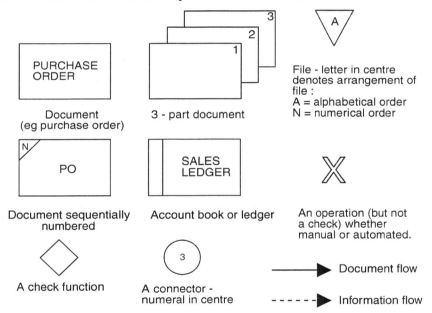

Figure 5.2: Flow chart symbols

Preparation of a basic flowchart will involve the procedures laid out in the next few paragraphs.

3.6 Document flows

The symbols showing the sequence of operations taking place within the one department are joined by a vertical line as illustrated in the figure below.

NOTES

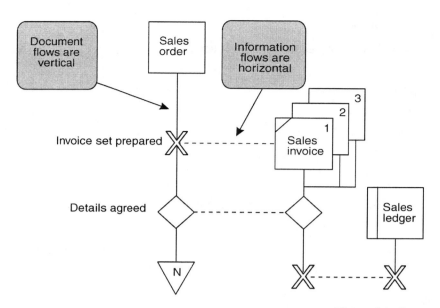

Figure 5.3: Document flows

3.7 Division of duties

One of the key features of any good system of internal control is that there should be a system of 'internal check'. Internal check is the requirement for a segregation of duties amongst the available staff so that one person's work is independently reviewed by another, no one person having complete responsibility for all aspects of a transaction.

This method of flowcharting shows the division of duties. This is achieved by dividing the chart into **vertical columns**. In a **smaller** enterprise there would be one column to show the duties of each **individual**, whereas in a **large** company the vertical columns would show the division of duties amongst the various **departments**.

The following figure shows, in a small company, the division of duties between Mr Major and Mr Minor.

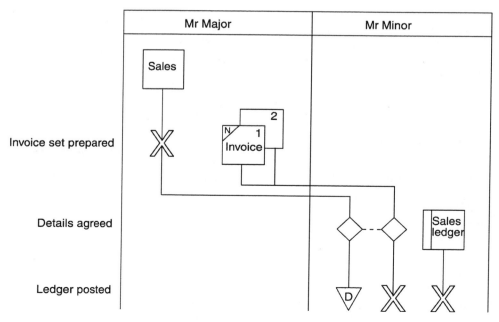

Figure 5.4: Division of duties

3.8 Sequence and description of operations

To facilitate ease of reference each operation shown on the chart is numbered in sequence on the chart, a separate column being used for this purpose.

Finally, the chart will be completed by the inclusion of a narrative column which will describe significant operations. Narrative should be kept to a minimum and only included where in fact it is required.

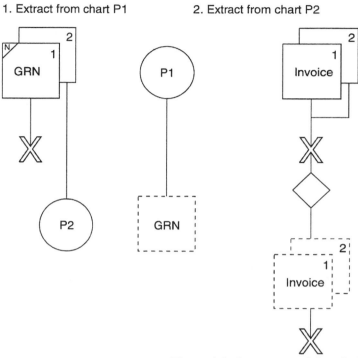

Figure 5.5: Sequence and description of operations

On the following pages you will find two charts which illustrate typical procedures in a company's purchasing system.

- Ordering and receiving of goods
- Approval of invoices

NOTES

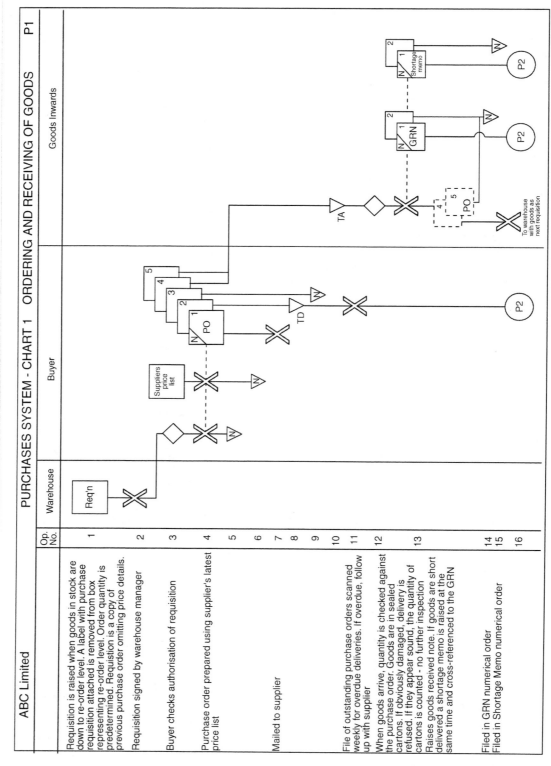

Figure 5.6: Ordering and receiving of goods

BPP LEARNING MEDIA

Each situation must therefore be judged on its own merits and hence, although the ICQs often take the form of a standard pre-printed pack, they should be used with imagination. As using ICQs is a skilled and responsible task, the evaluation should be performed by a senior member of the audit team.

4.2 Advantages and disadvantages of ICQs

ICQs have various advantages.

(a) **If drafted** thoroughly, they can ensure **all controls** are **considered.**

(b) They are **quick** to **prepare.**

(c) They are **easy** to **use** and **control.** A manager or partner reviewing the work can easily see what has been done.

However they also have disadvantages:

(a) The client may be able to **overstate controls.**

(b) They may contain a large number of **irrelevant controls.**

(c) They can give the impression that all controls are of **equal weight.** In many systems one 'no' answer (for example lack of segregation of duties) may cancel the apparent value of a string of 'yes' answers).

(d) They may not include unusual controls, which are nevertheless effective in particular circumstances.

4.3 Internal Control Evaluation Questionnaires (ICEQs)

In recent years many auditing firms have developed and implemented an evaluation technique more concerned with assessing whether specific errors (or frauds) are possible rather than establishing whether certain desirable controls are present.

This is achieved by reducing the control criteria for each transaction stream down to a handful of key questions (or control questions). The characteristic of these questions is that they concentrate on criteria that the controls present should fulfil.

The nature of an ICEQ can be illustrated by the following example.

Internal control evaluation questionnaire: control questions

The sales cycle

Is there reasonable assurance that:

(a) Sales are properly authorised?

(b) Sales are made to reliable payers?

(c) All goods despatched are invoiced?

(d) All invoices are properly prepared?

(e) All invoices are recorded?

(f) Invoices are properly supported?

(g) All credits to customers' accounts are valid?

(h) Cash and cheques received are properly recorded and deposited?

(i) Slow payers will be chased and that bad and doubtful debts will be provided against?

NOTES

(j) All transactions are properly accounted for?

(k) Cash sales are properly dealt with?

(l) Sundry sales are controlled?

(m) At the period end the system will neither overstate nor understate debtors?

The purchases cycle

Is there reasonable assurance that:

(a) Goods or services could not be received without a liability being recorded?

(b) Receipt of goods or services is required in order to establish a liability?

(c) A liability will be recorded:

- Only for authorised items; and
- At the proper amount?

(d) All payments are properly authorised?

(e) All credits due from suppliers are received?

(f) All transactions are properly accounted for?

(g) At the period end liabilities are neither overstated nor understated by the system?

(h) The balance at the bank is properly recorded at all times?

(i) Unauthorised cash payments could not be made and that the balance of petty cash is correctly stated at all times?

Each key control question is supported by detailed control points to be considered. For example, the detailed control points to be considered in relation to key control question (b) for the expenditure cycle (Is there reasonable assurance that receipt of goods or services is required to establish a liability?) are as follows.

(1) Is segregation of duties satisfactory?

(2) Are controls over relevant master files satisfactory?

(3) Is there a record that all goods received have been checked for:

- Weight or number?
- Quality and damage?

(4) Are all goods received entered in the detailed stock ledgers:

- By means of the goods received note?

- Or by means of purchase invoices?

- Are there, in a computerised system, sensible control totals (hash totals, money values and so on) to reconcile the stock system input with the creditors system?

(5) Are all invoices initialled to show that:

- Receipt of goods has been checked against the goods received records?
- Receipt of services has been verified by the person using it?
- Quality of goods has been checked against the inspection?

(6) In a computerised invoice approval system are there print-outs (examined by a responsible person) of:

- Cases where order, GRN and invoice are present but they are not equal ('equal' within predetermined tolerances of minor discrepancies)?

- Cases where invoices have been input but there is no corresponding GRN?

(7) Is there adequate control over direct purchases?

(8) Are receiving documents effectively cancelled (for example cross-referenced) to prevent their supporting two invoices?

Alternatively, ICEQ questions can be phrased so that the weakness which should be prevented by a key control is highlighted, such as the following.

Question	Answer	Comments or explanation of 'yes' answer
Can goods be sent to unauthorised suppliers?		

In these cases a 'yes' answer would require an explanation, rather than a 'no' answer.

4.4 Advantages and disadvantages of ICEQs

ICEQs have various advantages:

(a) Because they are drafted in terms of **objectives** rather than specific controls, they are easier to apply to a variety of systems than **ICQs**.

(b) Answering ICEQs should enable auditors to **identify the most important controls** which they are most likely to test during control testing.

(c) ICEQs can **highlight areas of weakness** where extensive substantive testing will be required.

However, the principal disadvantage is that they can be **drafted vaguely**, hence **misunderstood** and important controls not identified.

When the auditor discovers weaknesses or failings in the system, he will produce a report to management (sometimes called a management letter), which will point out the problems, the risks arising from it and the auditor's recommendations to eliminate the weakness. We cover these in detail in Chapter 7.

Chapter roundup

- The proper completion of working papers is fundamental to the recording of audits. They should show:
    - When and by whom the audit work was performed and reviewed
    - Details of the client
    - The year-end
    - The subject of the paper

- Working papers should also show:
    - The objectives of the work done
    - The sources of information
    - How any sample was selected and the sample size determined
    - The work done
    - A key to any audit ticks or symbols
    - Results obtained
    - Errors or other significant observations
    - Conclusions drawn
    - Key points highlighted

- Computerised working papers are being used more by auditors. Their main advantages are that they are neat and easy to update and the risk of errors is reduced.

- Auditors can use a number of methods to record accounting and control systems.
    - Narrative notes
    - Flowcharts
    - ICQs (which ask if various controls exist)
    - ICEQs (which ask if controls fulfil key objectives)
    - Checklists

Quick quiz

1   What is the main danger of using standardised working papers?

2   Explain the importance of maintaining the confidentiality of working papers?

3   What is the main disadvantage of recording systems by means of manual narrative notes?

4   In what directions should a flowchart be prepared?

5   What is the main difference between ICQs and ICEQs?

Answers to Quick quiz

1   The main danger of using standardised working papers is that they can mean auditors mechanically follow a standard approach to the audit without using professional judgement.

2   Auditors are often subject to privileged information that is not generally available. In some cases this information might affect the decisions others make with respect to their interest in the company and ultimately the company's share price.

3   The main disadvantage of manual narrative notes is that they can be difficult to change.

4   Flowcharts should be prepared going from top to bottom and left to right on a page.

5   ICQs concentrate on whether specific controls exist, whereas ICEQs concentrate on whether the control system has specific strengths or can prevent specific weaknesses.

Answers to Activities

1   Key benefits that auditors will obtain from preparing working papers that meet the requirement stated in the ISA are as follows.

(a)   They provide a sufficient and appropriate record of the basis for the auditor's report.

(b)   Evidence that the work was carried out in accordance with ISAs and applicable legal and regulatory requirements.

(d)   Assisting the audit team to plan and perform the audit

(e)   Assisting members of the audit team responsible for supervision to direct and supervise the audit work, and to discharge their review responsibilities

(f)   Enabling the audit team to be accountable for its work

(g)   Retaining a record of matters of continuing significance to future audits

(h)   Enabling an experienced auditor to conduct quality control reviews and inspections

(i)   Enabling an experienced auditor to conduct external inspections in accordance with applicable legal, regulatory or other requirements.

2   (a)   Working papers should be headed with:

(i)   The name of the client
(ii)   The balance sheet date
(iii)   The file reference of the working paper
(iv)   The name of the person preparing the working paper
(v)   The date the working paper was prepared
(vi)   The subject of the working paper
(vii)   The name of the person reviewing the working paper
(viii)   The date of the review

BPP LEARNING MEDIA

(b) Working papers should also show:

    (i)   The objective of the work done

    (ii)   The source of information

    (iii)   How any sample was selected and the sample size determined

    (iv)   The work done

    (v)   A key to any audit ticks or symbols

    (vi)   The results obtained

    (vii)   Analysis of errors or other significant observations

    (viii) The conclusions drawn

    (ix)   The key points highlighted

Chapter 6
AUDIT EVIDENCE AND AUDIT PROCEDURES

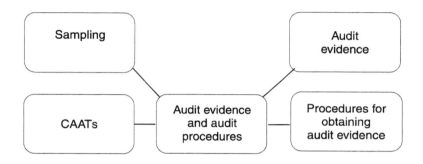

Introduction

It is the procedures carried out during the audit, and the obtaining of audit evidence, which ultimately enable the auditor to form an opinion and produce an audit report. The degree of evidence required and the procedures to be carried out will have been determined at the planning stage, as discussed in the previous chapter.

It is important to realise that the procedures and amount of evidence needed to come to a conclusion will differ from audit to audit (depending on the auditor's assessment of risk and materiality) and the auditor needs to be flexible and adaptable in his approach.

Learning objectives

In this chapter you will learn about the following.

(a) The different kinds of audit evidence

(b) The distinction between tests of control (compliance tests) and substantive procedures

(c) Tests of control and substantive procedures for a variety of accounting areas

(d) How computer assisted audit techniques can be used in the audit

(e) The factors considered when choosing a sample size and how to select an appropriate sample

1 AUDIT EVIDENCE

Definition

> **Audit evidence** is all the information used by the auditor in arriving at the conclusions on which the audit opinion is based, and included the information contained in the accounting records underlying the financial statements and other information. (ISA 500.3)

In order to reach a position in which they can express a professional opinion, the auditors need to gather evidence from various sources. ISA 500 *Audit Evidence* covers this area.

1.1 Sufficient appropriate audit evidence

ISA 500.2 says that auditors should obtain sufficient appropriate audit evidence to be able to draw reasonable conclusions on which to base the audit opinion.

'Sufficiency' and 'appropriateness' are interrelated and apply to both tests of controls and substantive procedures.

- **Sufficiency** is the measure of the **quantity** of audit evidence.

- **Appropriateness** is the measure of the **quality** of the audit evidence: that is its **relevance** and **reliability**

Audit evidence will be **relevant** where it provides support, or detects misstatements in, the classes of transactions, account balances, and disclosures and related assertions.

Assertions will be covered later in this chapter.

The reliability of audit evidence is determined by its source. We will see that certain sources of audit evidence are likely to be more persuasive than others.

Sufficient appropriate audit evidence can be obtained by the auditor through different types of audit tests - tests of control and substantive tests.

Definitions

> **Tests of control** are tests performed to obtain audit evidence about the operationing effectiveness of controls in preventing, or detecting and correcting, material misstatements at the assertion level. **Substantive procedures** are audit procedures performed to detect material misstatements at the assertion level; they include:
>
> (a) Substantive analytical procedures
>
> (b) Tests of details of classes of transactions, account balances, and disclosures.

Activity 1   **(10 minutes)**

Can you state which of the following tests are tests of control and which are substantive procedures?

(a) Checking that invoices have been approved by the managing director

(b) Attending the year-end stocktake

(c) Reviewing accounting records after the year-end for events that affect this year's accounts

(d) Obtaining confirmation from the bank of balances held at the year-end

(e) Checking how unauthorised personnel are prevented from entering stock-rooms

(f) Checking if references are sought for all new major customers

Audit evidence is usually persuasive rather then conclusive (usually indicates what is probable rather than what is definite) so different sources are examined by the auditors. Auditors can only give reasonable assurance that the financial statements are free from misstatement, as not *all* sources of evidence will be examined.

The auditors' judgement as to what is sufficient appropriate audit evidence is influenced by various factors.

- Assessment of risk
- The nature of the accounting and internal control systems
- The materiality of the item being examined
- The experience gained during previous audits.
- The auditors' knowledge of the business and industry
- The results of audit procedures
- The source and reliability of information available

If they are unable to obtain sufficient appropriate audit evidence, the auditors may have to consider the effect on their audit report.

1.2 Tests of control

In seeking to obtain audit evidence from tests of control, auditors should consider the sufficiency and appropriateness of the audit evidence to support the assessed level of control risk.

There are two aspects of the relevant parts of the accounting and internal control systems about which auditors should seek to obtain audit evidence.

(a) **Design**: the accounting and internal control systems are designed so as to be capable of preventing or detecting material misstatements.

(b) **Operation**: the systems exist and have operated effectively throughout the relevant period.

For example, the auditor might carry out the following tests on ordering and granting of credit in the sales system.

- Check that references are being obtained for all new customers.

- Check that all new accounts on the sales ledger have been authorised by senior staff.

- Check that orders are only accepted from customers who are within their credit terms and credit limits.

- Check that customer orders are being matched with production orders and despatch notes.

1.3 Substantive procedures

In seeking to obtain audit evidence from substantive procedures, auditors should consider the extent to which that evidence, together with any evidence from tests of controls, supports the relevant financial statement assertions.

Substantive procedures are designed to obtain evidence about the financial statement assertions which are basically what the accounts say about the assets, liabilities and transactions of the client, and the events that affect the client's accounts.

Financial statement assertions are the representations of the directors that are embodied in the financial statements. By approving the financial statements, the directors are making representations about the information therein. These representations or assertions may be described in general terms in a number of ways.

ISA 500 states that 'the auditor should use assertions for **classes of transactions, account balances,** and **presentation and disclosures** in sufficient detail to form a basis for the assessment of risks of material misstatement and the design and performance of further audit procedures'. It gives examples of assertions in these areas.

Assertions used by the auditor	
Assertions about **classes of transactions** and events for the period under audit	**Occurrence**: transactions and events that have been recorded have occurred and pertain to the entity.
	Completeness: all transactions and events that should have been recorded have been recorded.
	Accuracy: amounts and other data relating to recorded transactions and events have been recorded appropriately.
	Cut-off: transactions and events have been recorded in the correct accounting period.
	Classification: transactions and events have been recorded in the proper accounts.
Assertions about **account balances** at the period-end	**Existence**: assets, liabilities and equity interests exist.
	Rights and obligations: the entity holds or controls the rights to assets, and liabilities are the obligations of the entity.
	Completeness: all assets, liabilities and equity interests that should have been recorded have been recorded.
	Valuation and allocation: assets, liabilities, and equity interests are included in the financial statements at appropriate amounts and any resulting valuation or allocation adjustments are appropriately recorded.

Assertions used by the auditor	
Assertions about **presentation and disclosure**	**Occurrence and rights and obligations**: disclosed events, transactions and other matters have occurred and pertain to the entity.
	Completeness: all disclosures that should have been included in the financial statements have been included.
	Classification and understandability: financial information is appropriately presented and described, and disclosures are clearly expressed.
	Accuracy and valuation: financial and other information are disclosed fairly and at appropriate amounts.

Activity 2   **(20 minutes)**

Different financial statement assertions will be relevant to different classes of transactions and account balances, for each of the following identify the most relevant financial statement assertions:

(a) Account receivables
(b) Admininstrative expenses
(c) Cash
(d) Share capital
(e) Inventory
(f) Revenue

1.4   Reliability of evidence

(i) *Evidence originated by the auditors*

Evidence originated by the auditors is in general the most reliable type of audit evidence because there is little risk that it can be manipulated by management.

Examples

(1) Analytical procedures, such as the calculation of ratios and trends in order to examine unusual variations

(2) Physical inspection or observation, such as attendance at physical stock counts

(3) Re-performance of calculations making up figures in the accounts, such as the computation of total stock values

(ii) *Evidence created by third parties*

Third party evidence is more reliable than client-produced evidence to the extent that it is obtained from independent sources. Its reliability will be reduced if it is obtained from sources which are not independent, or if there is a risk that client personnel may be able to and have reason to suppress or manipulate it. This, for instance, is an argument against having replies to circularisations sent to the client instead of the auditors.

Examples

(1)   Circularisation of trade debtors or creditors, confirmation of bank balances.

(2)   Reports produced by experts, such as property valuations, actuarial valuations, legal opinions. In evaluating such evidence, the auditors need to take into account the expert's qualifications, independence and the terms of reference for the work.

(3)   Documents held by the client which were issued by third parties, such as invoices, price lists and statements. These may sometimes be manipulated by the client and so are less reliable than confirmations received directly.

(iii) *Evidence created by management*

The auditors cannot place the same degree of reliance on evidence produced by client management as on that produced outside the company. However, it will often be necessary to place some reliance on such evidence. The auditors will need to obtain audit evidence that the information supplied is complete and accurate, and apply judgement in doing so, taking into account previous experience of the client's reliability and the extent to which the client's representations appear compatible with other audit findings, as well as the materiality of the item under discussion.

Examples

(1)   The company's accounting records and supporting schedules. Although these are prepared by management, the auditors have a statutory right to examine such records in full: this right enhances the quality of this information.

(2)   The client's explanations of, for instance, apparently unusual fluctuations in results. Such evidence requires interpretation by the auditors and, being oral evidence, only limited reliance can be placed upon it.

(3)   Information provided to the auditors about the internal control system. The auditors need to check that this information is accurate and up-to-date, and that it does not simply describe an idealised system which is not adhered to in practice.

(b)   **General considerations in evaluating audit evidence**

Audit evidence will often not be wholly conclusive. The auditors must obtain evidence which is **sufficient and appropriate** to form the basis for their audit conclusions. The evidence gathered should also be **relevant** to those conclusions, and sufficiently **reliable** to form the basis for the audit opinion. The auditors must exercise skill and judgement to ensure that evidence is correctly interpreted and that only valid inferences are drawn from it.

Certain general principles can be stated. **Written evidence** is preferable to oral evidence; **independent evidence** obtained from outside the organisation is more reliable than that obtained internally; and **evidence generated by the auditors** is more reliable than that obtained from others.

> **Activity 3** (5 minutes)
>
> You are auditing the year-end cash at bank balance at JER Ltd and have obtained the following evidence. Rank the items for reliability starting with the most reliable:
>
> (a) A bank reconciliation prepared by a member the cashier and reviewed by the financial controller.
>
> (b) A bank confirmation letter obtained directly from JER's bank
>
> (c) An oral confirmation from the cashier that the bank balance per the nominal ledger is correct
>
> (d) A photocopy of the bank statement at year-end provided by the cashier

2 PROCEDURES FOR OBTAINING AUDIT EVIDENCE

2.1 How evidence is obtained

Audit evidence is usually obtained for assets, liabilities and transactions to support each financial statement assertion and evidence from one does not compensate for failure to obtain evidence for another. However, audit procedures may provide audit evidence of more than one assertion.

Auditors obtain evidence by one or more of the following procedures.

PROCEDURES

Inspection of records or documents	Confirmation to documentation of items recorded in accounting records confirms that an asset exists or a transaction occurred. Confirmation that items recorded in supporting documentation are recorded in accounting records tests completeness.
	Cut-off can be verified by inspecting the reverse population ie checking transactions recorded after the balance sheet date to supporting documentation to confirm that they occurred after the balance sheet date.
	Inspection also provides evidence of valuation/measurement, rights and obligations and the nature of items (presentation and disclosure). It can also be used to compare documents (and hence test consistency of audit evidence) and confirm authorisation.
Inspection of tangible assets	Inspection of assets that are recorded in the accounting records confirms existence, gives evidence of valuation, but does not confirm rights and obligations.
	Confirmation that assets seen are recorded in accounting records gives evidence of completeness.

NOTES

PROCEDURES	
Observation	This involves watching a procedure being performed (for example, post opening). It is of limited use, as it only confirms the procedure took place when the auditor was watching.
Inquiry	This involves seeking information from client staff or external sources. Strength of evidence depends on the knowledge and integrity of the source of the information.
Confirmation	This involves seeking confirmation from another source of details in client's accounting records eg, confirmation from bank of bank balances.
Recalculation	Checking arithmetic of client's records for example, adding up ledger account.
Reperformance	Independently executing procedures or controls, either manually or through the use of computer assisted audit techniques (CAATs, see next section).
Analytical procedures	Evaluating and comparing financial and/or non-financial data for plausible relationships.

Activity 4   **(30 minutes)**

The examination of evidence is fundamental to the audit process. ISA 500 *Audit Evidence* states that: 'the auditors should obtain sufficient appropriate audit evidence to be able to draw reasonable conclusions on which to base the audit opinion'.

Evidence is available to the auditors from sources under their own control, from the management of the company and from third parties. Each of these sources presents the auditors with differing considerations as to the quality of the evidence so produced.

Tasks

(a) Discuss the quality of the following types of audit evidence, giving two examples of each form of evidence.

    (i) Evidence originated by the auditors

    (ii) Evidence created by third parties

    (iii) Evidence created by the management of the client

(b) Describe the general considerations which the auditors must bear in mind when evaluating audit evidence.

3   COMPUTER ASSISTED AUDIT TECHNIQUES (CAATs)

Computer-based accounting systems allow auditors to use either the client's computer or another computer during their audit work. Techniques performed with computers in this way are known as Computer Assisted Audit Techniques (CAATs).

There is no mystique about using CAATs to help with auditing.

(a)   Most modern accounting systems allow data to be manipulated in various ways and extracted into a **report**.

(b)   Even if reporting capabilities are limited, the data can often be exported directly into a **spreadsheet** package (sometimes using simple Windows-type cut and paste facilities in modern systems) and then analysed.

(c)   Most systems have **searching** facilities that are much quicker to use than searching through print-outs by hand.

There are a variety of packages specially designed either to ease the auditing task itself, or to carry out audit interrogations of computerised data automatically. There are also a variety of ways of testing the processing that is carried out.

Auditors can use PCs such as laptops that are independent of the organisation's systems when performing CAATs.

3.1   Types of CAAT

There are various types of CAAT.

(a)   **Audit interrogation software** is a computer program used for audit purposes to examine the content of the client's computer files.

(b)   **Test data** is data used by the auditors for computer processing to test the operation of the client's computer programs.

(c)   **Embedded audit facilities** are elements set up by the auditor which are included within the client's computer system. They allow the possibility of continuous checking.

3.2   Audit interrogation software

Interrogation software performs the sort of checks on data that auditors might otherwise have to perform by hand. Its use is particularly appropriate during substantive testing of transactions and especially balances. By using audit software, the auditors may scrutinise large volumes of data and concentrate skilled manual resources on the investigation of results, rather than on the extraction of information.

For example, the auditor could use such software to ensure that the balances in the accounts receivable ledger add up correctly or to extract a random sample of balances for subsequent circularisation.

3.3   Test data

An obvious way of seeing whether a system is **processing** data in the way that it should be is to input some test data and see what happens. The expected results can be calculated in advance and then compared with the results that actually arise.

For example, the auditor might process a sale to ensure that the correct VAT is calculated and posted to the VAT account and that the balance due is posted to the correct account receivable.

The problem with test data is that any resulting corruption of the data files has to be corrected. This is difficult with modern real-time systems, which often have built in (and highly desirable) controls to ensure that data entered *cannot* easily be removed without leaving a mark. Consequently test data is used less and less as a CAAT.

3.4 Embedded audit facilities

The results of using test data would, in any case, be completely distorted if the programs used to process it were not the ones *normally* used for processing. For example a fraudulent member of the IT department might substitute a version of the program that gave the correct results, purely for the duration of the test, and then replace it with a version that siphoned off the company's funds into his own bank account.

To allow a **continuous** review of the data recorded and the manner in which it is treated by the system, it may be possible to use CAATs referred to as 'embedded audit facilities'.

An embedded facility consists of audit modules that are incorporated into the computer element of the enterprise's accounting system.

EXAMPLES OF EMBEDDED AUDIT FACILITIES	
Integrated test facility (ITF)	Creates a **fictitious entity** within the company application, where transactions are posted to it alongside regular transactions, and actual results of fictitious entity compared with what it should have produced
Systems control and review file (SCARF)	Allows auditors to have transactions above a **certain amount** from **specific ledger account** posted to a file for later auditor review

3.5 Simulation

Simulation (or 'parallel simulation') entails the preparation of a separate program that simulates the processing of the organisation's real system. Real data can then be passed not only through the system proper but also through the simulated program. For example the simulation program may be used to re-perform controls such as those used to identify any missing items from a sequence.

3.6 Knowledge-based systems

Decision support systems and expert systems can be used to assist with the auditors' own judgement and decisions.

3.7 Planning CAATs

In certain circumstances the auditors will need to use CAATs in order to obtain the evidence they require, whereas in other circumstances they may use CAATs to improve the efficiency or effectiveness of the audit.

In choosing the appropriate combination of CAATs and manual procedures, the auditors will need to take the following points into account.

(a)   Computer programs often perform functions of which **no visible evidence** is available. In these circumstances it will frequently not be practicable for the auditors to perform tests manually.

(b)   In many audit situations the auditors will have the choice of performing a test either **manually** or with the **assistance of a CAAT**. In making this choice, they will be influenced by the respective efficiency of the alternatives, which is influenced by a number of factors.

  (i)   The extent of tests of controls or substantive procedures achieved by both alternatives

  (ii)   The pattern of cost associated with the CAAT

  (iii)   The ability to incorporate within the use of the CAAT a number of different audit tests

(c)   Sometimes auditors will need to report within a comparatively **short time-scale**. In such cases it may be more efficient to use CAATs because they are quicker to apply.

(d)   If using a CAAT, auditors should ensure that the **required computer facilities, computer files** and **programs are available**.

(e)   The operation of some CAATs requires **frequent attendance** or access by the auditors.

3.8   Controlling CAATs

Where CAATs are used, however, particular attention should be paid to the need to **co-ordinate the work of staff** with specialist computer skills with the work of others engaged on the audit. The **technical work** should be **approved** and **reviewed** by someone with the necessary computer expertise.

3.9   Audit trails

The original purpose of an **audit trail** was to preserve details of all stages of processing on *paper*. This meant that transactions could be followed stage-by-stage through a system to ensure that they had been processed correctly.

3.10   Around the computer?

Traditionally, therefore, it was widely considered that auditors could fulfil their function without having any detailed knowledge of what was going on inside the computer.

The auditors would commonly audit '**round the computer**', ignoring the procedures which take place within the computer programs and concentrating solely on the input and corresponding output. Audit procedures would include checking authorisation, coding and control totals of input and checking the output with source documents and clerical control totals.

3.11   Through the computer

The 'round the computer approach' is now frowned upon. Typical audit problems that arise as audit trails move further away from the hard copy trail include testing computer generated totals when no detailed analysis is available and testing the completeness of output in the absence of control totals. One of the principal problems facing the auditors is that of acquiring an understanding of the workings of electronic data processing and of the computer itself.

Auditors now customarily audit '**through the computer**'. This involves an examination of the detailed processing routines of the computer to determine whether the controls in the system are adequate to ensure complete and correct processing of all data. In these situations it will often be necessary to employ computer assisted audit techniques.

Activity 5   **(15 minutes)**

(a)   What is meant by the term 'loss of audit trail' in the context of computerised accounting procedures?

(b)   How can auditors gain assurance about the operation of computerised accounting procedures given the 'loss of audit trail'?

4   AUDIT SAMPLING

ISA 530 *Audit Sampling and Other Means of Testing* covers this topic in depth.

This ISA is based on the premise that auditors do not normally examine all the information available to them; it would be impractical to do so and using audit sampling will produce valid conclusions. We also saw in chapter 3 that the auditor is required to give reasonable (and not absolute) assurance and therefore testing all items that make up a class or transactions or account balance is not necessary.

Definitions

Audit sampling involves the application of audit procedures to less than 100% of items within a class of transactions or an account balance such that all the sampling units have an equal chance of selection. This will enable the auditor to obtain and evaluate audit evidence about some characteristic of the items selected in order to form or assist in forming a conclusion concerning the population from which the sample is drawn. Audit sampling can use either a statistical or non-statistical approach.

Sampling units are the individual items constituting the population.

Error is an unintentional misstatement in the financial statements, including the omission of an amount or a disclosure

Tolerable error is the maximum error in the population that the auditors are willing to accept.

Sampling risk is the possibility that the auditors' conclusion, based on a sample, may be different from the conclusion that would be reached if the entire population was subject to the same audit procedure.

Non-sampling risk arises from factors that cause the auditor to reach an erroneous conclusion for any reason not related to the size of the sample.

> **Statistical sampling** is any approach to sampling that has the following characteristics: (a) random selection of a sample; (b) use of probability theory to evaluate sample results, including measurement of sampling risk.
>
> **Non-statistical sampling** is any sampling approach that does not have the characteristics of statistical sampling.

The ISA points out that some testing procedures do *not* involve sampling.

(a)   Testing 100% of items in a population (this should be obvious)

(b)   Testing all items with a certain characteristic (eg over a certain value) as selection is not representative

The ISA distinguishes between **statistically based sampling**, which involves the use of techniques from which mathematically constructed conclusions about the population can be drawn, and **non-statistical or judgmental methods**, from which auditors draw a judgmental opinion about the population. However, the principles of the ISA apply to both methods.

4.1   Design of the sample

Audit objectives

Auditors must consider the **specific audit objectives** to be achieved and the audit procedures which are most likely to achieve them.

The auditors also need to consider the **nature and characteristics** of the **audit evidence** sought and **possible error conditions**. This will help them to define what constitutes an error and what population to use for sampling.

Furthermore auditors must consider the **level of error** they are prepared to accept and **how confident** they wish to be that the population does not contain an error rate greater than what is acceptable.

Thus for a test of controls auditors may wish to be 95% confident that controls have failed to work on no more than 3 occasions. For a substantive test of fixed assets, they may wish to be 90% confident that fixed assets are not mis-stated by more than £10,000.

The % confidence auditors wish to have is the 'confidence level' and it is related to the degree of audit risk auditors are prepared to accept.

Population

The population from which the sample is drawn must be **appropriate** and **complete** for the specific audit objectives.

In the case of assets in the Statement of Financial Position (Balance Sheet) this is relatively straight forward – the auditor will take the list of items making up the account balance and seek to obtain audit evidence from a sample of items on that list. For example, when testing accounts receivable the auditor might select a sample from the accounts receivable ledger and circularise those accounts for confirmation of the balance owing.

In the case of liabilities however, we need to be more careful. The risk associated with liabilities is one of completeness. The auditor will be concerned that the list of balances, making up the total balance in the Statement of Financial Position, has items missing. Therefore selecting a sample of items from this list will not be relevant to testing the financial statement assertion of completeness. In this instance the auditor needs to look for a different population from which to draw his sample. An example of this might be the outstanding invoices file held by the accounts payables clerk when auditing accounts payable.

4.2 Sample size

When determining sample sizes, auditors should consider sampling risk, the amount of error that would be acceptable and the extent to which they expect to find errors.

4.3 Sampling risk

Sampling risk is encountered by the auditors in both tests of control and substantive procedures. It is the risk of drawing a **wrong conclusion** from audit sampling. It is part of detection risk.

For tests of control, drawing a wrong conclusion means making an **incorrect assessment** (too high or too low) of **control risk**. For substantive procedures it means either stating a population is **materially mis-stated when it is not**, or stating a population is **not materially mis-stated when it is**.

The **greater** their reliance on the results of the procedure in question, the **lower** the sampling risk auditors will be willing to accept and the **larger** the sample size needs to be.

Thus if inherent risk is high, control risk is high and sampling is the only substantive procedure auditors are carrying out, then auditors are placing maximum reliance on sampling. Hence the level of sampling risk auditors will be prepared to accept will be at minimum, and sample sizes will be high.

4.4 Tolerable error

For **tests** of **control,** the tolerable error is the **maximum rate** of **deviation** from a control that auditors are willing to accept in the population and still conclude that the preliminary assessment of control risk is valid. Often this rate will be very low, since the auditor is likely to be concentrating on testing important controls.

Sometimes even a single failure of an important control will cause auditors to reject their assessment of control risk. If for example, an important control is that all major capital expenditure is approved by the board, failure to approve expenditure on one item may be an unacceptable deviation as far as the auditors are concerned.

For substantive procedures, the **tolerable error** is the **maximum monetary error** in an account balance or class of transactions, that auditors are willing to accept so that when the results of all audit procedures are considered, they are able to conclude with reasonable assurance, that the financial statements are not materially mis-stated.

Sometimes the tolerable error rate will be the materiality rate. Some accounting firms set tolerable error as being a fixed percentage of materiality, say 50% or 70% for reasons of prudence.

4.5 Expected error

Larger samples will be required when errors are expected than would be required if none were expected, in order to conclude that the *actual* error is *less* than the *tolerable* error. If the expected error rate is high then sampling may not be appropriate and auditors may have to examine 100% of a population.

4.6 Selection of the sample

Auditors should select sample items in such a way that the sample can be expected to be representative of the population in respect of the characteristics being tested.

For a sample to be representative of the population, all items in the population are required to have an equal or known probability of being selected.

There are a number of selection methods available, but the ISA identifies four that are commonly used.

(a) Use of a computerised **random number generator** ensures that all items in the population have an equal chance of selection, alternatively random number tables can be used.

(b) **Systematic selection** (or interval sampling) involves selecting items using a constant interval between selections, the first interval having a random start.

Suppose the auditors decide to pick every 50th item and start at random at item number 11. They will then pick item number 61 (11 + 50), item number 111 (11 + (50 × 2)), item number 161 (11 + (50 × 3)) and so on. Auditors must when using this method, guard against the risk of errors occurring systematically in such a way as not to be detected by sampling. In our example this could be errors occurring at item number 41, 91, 141, 191 etc.

(c) **Haphazard selection** involves auditors choosing items subjectively without using formal random methods but also avoiding bias. The biggest danger of haphazard selection is that bias does in fact occur. Auditors may for example end up choosing items that are easily located, and these may not be representative. Haphazard selection is more likely to be used when auditors are using judgmental rather than statistical sampling.

(d) **Block selection** involves selecting a block of contiguous items from within the population. However, this method is not recommended as it is not statistically based which means that results from testing cannot be used to determine any population error.

In addition the auditors may also consider for certain tests:

(a) **Stratification.** This involves division of the population into a number of parts. Each sampling unit can only belong to one, specifically designed, stratum. The idea is that each stratum will contain items which have significant characteristics in common. This enables the auditors to direct audit effort towards items which, for example, contain the greatest potential monetary error.

(b) **Selection by value** is selecting the largest items within a population. This will only be appropriate if auditors believe that the size of the item is related to the risk of the item being seriously misstated.

(c) **Sequence sampling** may be used to check whether certain items have particular characteristics. For example an auditor may use a sample of 50 consecutive cheques to check whether cheques are signed by authorised signatories rather than picking 50 single cheques throughout the year. Sequence sampling may however produce samples that are not representative of the population as a whole particularly if errors occurred only during a certain part of the year.

Certain items may be tested because they are considered unusual, for example debit balances on a purchase ledger or a nil balance with a major supplier.

4.7 Statistical and judgmental sampling

As mentioned above, auditors need to decide when sampling whether to use statistical or non-statistical methods. Statistical sampling means using statistical theory to measure the impact of sampling risk and evaluate the sample results. Non-statistical sampling relies on judgement to evaluate results.

Whether statistical or non-statistical methods are used, auditors will still have to take account of risk, tolerable and expected error, and population value for substantive tests when deciding on sample sizes.

If these conditions are present, **statistical sampling** normally has the following **advantages**.

(a) At the conclusion of a test the auditors are able to state with a **definite level of confidence** that the whole population conforms to the sample result, within a stated precision limit.

(b) **Sample size** is **objectively determined**, having regard to the degree of risk the auditors are prepared to accept for each application.

(c) The process of fixing required precision and confidence levels compels the auditors to consider and **clarify their audit objectives**.

(d) The **results of tests** can be **expressed** in precise **mathematical terms**.

(e) **Bias is eliminated**.

4.8 Evaluation of sample results

Having carried out, on each sample item, those audit procedures which are appropriate to the particular audit objective, auditors should:

(a) analyse any errors detected in the sample; and
(b) draw inferences for the population as a whole.

4.9 Analysis of errors in the sample

To begin with, the auditors must consider whether the items in question are **true errors**, as they defined them before the test, eg a misposting between customer accounts will not count as an error as far as total debtors are concerned.

Assuming the problems are errors, auditors should consider the **nature and cause** of the error and any possible **effects** the error might have on other parts of the audit.

4.10 Inferences to be drawn from the population as a whole

The auditors should project the error results from the sample on to the relevant population. The projection method should be consistent with the method used to select the sampling unit. The auditors will estimate the **probable error** in the population by extrapolating the errors found in the sample. They will then estimate any **further error** that might not have been detected because of the imprecision of the sampling technique (in addition to consideration of the nature and effects of the errors).

The auditors should then compare the **projected population error** (net of adjustments made by the entity in the case of substantive procedures) to the **tolerable error**, taking account of other audit procedures relevant to the specific control or financial statement assertion.

If the projected population error *exceeds* tolerable error, then the auditors should **re-assess sampling risk**. If it is unacceptable, they should consider **extending auditing procedures** or **performing alternative procedures**, either of which may result in a proposed adjustment to the financial statements.

4.11 Summary

Key stages in the sampling process are as follows.

- Determining objectives and population
- Determining sample size
- Choosing method of sample selection
- Analysing the results and projecting errors

Activity 6 **(15 minutes)**

Describe three commonly-used methods of sample selection and describe the main risks involved in using each method.

Activity 7 **(10 minutes)**

For each of the following audit areas suggest what population the auditor would use in order to extract a sample for testing:

(a) Tangible fixed assets

(b) Inventory

(c) Trade Payables

(d) Accruals

NOTES

Chapter roundup

- The auditors must be able to evaluate all types of audit evidence in terms of its sufficiency and appropriateness.

- Evidence can be in the form of tests of controls or substantive procedures.

- Tests of control concentrate on the design and operation of controls.

- Substantive testing aims to test all the financial statement assertions, including:

  ° Existence
  ° Rights and obligations (ownership)
  ° Occurrence
  ° Completeness
  ° Valuation
  ° Measurement
  ° Presentation and disclosure

  These can be applied to specific account balances eg fixed assets.

- The reliability of audit evidence is influenced by its source and by its nature eg circularisation of debtors provides third party evidence.

- Audit evidence can be obtained by the following techniques.

  ° Inspection
  ° Observation eg attendance at a stocktake
  ° Enquiry and confirmation
  ° Computation
  ° Analytical procedures

- Auditors may use a number of computer assisted audit techniques including audit interrogation software, test data and embedded audit facilities.

- The main stages of audit sampling are:

  ° Design of the sample
  ° Selection of the sample
  ° Evaluation of sample results

- Sample sizes for tests of control are influenced by sampling risk, tolerable error rate and expected error rate.

- Sample sizes for substantive tests are influenced by inherent, control and detection risk, tolerable error rate, expected error rate, population value and stratification.

- Sample items can be picked by a variety of means including random selection, systematic selection and haphazard selection.

- When evaluating results, auditors should:

  ° Analyse any errors considering their amount and the reasons why they have occurred

  ° Draw conclusions for the population as a whole

Quick quiz

1   What does ISA 500 say about the evidence that auditors should obtain?

2   When auditors are testing controls, about which two aspects are they seeking evidence?

3   Of which type of audit procedure are the following examples?

   (a) Physical check of fixed assets

   (b) Watching the payment of wages

   (c) Receiving a letter from the client's bank concerning balances held at the bank by the client

   (d) Adding up the client's trial balance

4   What tasks are most important in controlling the use of CAATs?

5   What is the difference between auditing round the computer and auditing through the computer?

6   Define:

   (a) Error
   (b) Tolerable error
   (c) Sampling risk

7   Summarise the factors that affect sample sizes for substantive tests.

Answers to Quick quiz

1   ISA 500 states that auditors should obtain sufficient appropriate audit evidence to be able to draw reasonable conclusions on which to base their opinion.

2   When testing controls, auditors are concentrating on their design and operation.

3   (a) Inspection
     (b) Observation
     (c) Confirmation
     (d) Computation

4   The most important tasks in controlling the use of CAATs are:

     (a) Co-ordination of the work of specialist computer staff with the rest of the audit team

     (b) Approval and review of the work by someone with the necessary computer experience

5   Auditing 'round the computer' involves comparisons of input and output, neglecting procedures that take place within the computer.

     Auditing 'through the computer' involves examination of the detailed routines that take place within the computer.

6   (a) An error is an unintentional mistake in the financial statements.

     (b) Tolerable error is the maximum error in the population that auditors are willing to accept and still conclude the audit objectives have been achieved.

     (c) Sampling risk is the risk that the auditors' conclusion, based on a sample, may be different from the conclusion that would be reached if the entire population was subject to the audit procedure.

7   Factors that affect the sample sizes of substantive tests are:

     (a) Inherent risk
     (b) Control risk
     (c) Detection risk
     (d) Tolerable error rate
     (e) Expected error rate
     (f) Population value
     (g) Number of items (in small population)

     Stratification may also lead to smaller sample sizes.

Answers to Activities

1   (a)   Control
    (b)   Substantive
    (c)   Substantive
    (d)   Substantive
    (e)   Control
    (f)   Control

2   (a)   Accounts receivables: Existence, valuation, cut off

    (b)   Administrative expenses: Occurrence, completeness, accuracy, cut off, classification

    (c)   Cash: Existence

    (d)   Share capital: Completeness, classification

    (e)   Inventory: Existence, valuation, cut off

    (f)   Revenue: Occurence, accuracy, cut of

3   (b)
    (a)
    (d)
    (c)

4   (a)   (i)   There is little risk that evidence originated by the auditors can be manipulated by management. It is therefore, in general, the most reliable type of audit evidence. Examples include the following.

                (1)   Analytical procedures, such as the calculation of ratios and trends in order to examine unusual variations

                (2)   Physical inspection or observation, such as attendance at physical stocktakes or inspection of a fixed asset

                (3)   Re-performance of calculations making up figures in the accounts, such as the computation of total stock values

          (ii)   Third party evidence is more reliable than client-produced evidence to the extent that it is obtained from sources independent of the client. Its reliability will be reduced if it is obtained from sources which are not independent, or if there is a risk that client personnel may be able to and have reason to suppress or manipulate it. This, for instance, is an argument against having replies to circularisations sent to the client instead of the auditors.

                 Examples of third party evidence include the following.

                (1)   Circularisation of debtors or creditors and other requests from the auditors for confirming evidence, such as requests for confirmation of bank balances.

                (2)   Reports produced by experts, such as property valuations, actuarial valuations, legal opinions. In evaluating such evidence, the auditors need to take into account the qualifications of the expert, his or her independence of the client and the terms of reference under which the work was carried out.

(3) Documents held by the client which were issued by third parties, such as invoices, price lists and statements. These may sometimes be manipulated by the client, to the extent that items may be suppressed or altered, and to this extent they are less reliable than confirmations received direct.

(iii) The auditors cannot place the same degree of reliance on evidence produced by client management as on that produced outside the client organisation. It will, however, often be necessary to place some reliance on the client's evidence. The auditors will need to apply judgement in doing so, taking into account previous experience of the client's reliability and the extent to which the client's representations appear compatible with other audit findings, as well as the materiality of the item under discussion. Examples of evidence originating from client management include the following.

(1) The company's accounting records and supporting schedules. Although these are prepared by management, the auditors have a statutory right to examine such records in full: this right enhances the quality of this information.

(2) The client's explanations of, for instance, apparently unusual fluctuations in results. Such evidence requires interpretation by the auditors and, being oral evidence, only limited reliance can be placed upon it.

(3) Information provided to the auditors about the internal control system. The auditors need to check that this information is accurate and up-to-date, and that it does not simply describe an idealised system which is not adhered to in practice.

(b) Audit evidence will often not be wholly conclusive. The auditors must obtain evidence which is sufficient and appropriate to form the basis for their audit conclusions. The evidence gathered should also be relevant to those conclusions, and sufficiently reliable ultimately to form the basis for the audit opinion. The auditors must exercise skill and judgement to ensure that evidence is correctly interpreted and that only valid inferences are drawn from it.

Certain general principles can be stated. Written evidence is preferable to oral evidence; independent evidence obtained from outside the organisation is more reliable than that obtained internally; and that evidence generated by the auditors is more reliable than that obtained from others.

5 (a) Loss of audit trail means that auditors do not have full details of the accounting process that goes on within the computer, and cannot therefore check that process for accuracy. In addition auditors cannot be sure that the output of the computer is complete. Certain procedures may also take place entirely within the computer without any visible evidence.

(b) Auditors can overcome the loss of audit trail in the following ways.

(i) Placing reliance on application and general controls. Application controls such as check digit verification or record counts can give assurance on the completeness and accuracy of processing. General controls can give assurance that the programs run have been developed properly and access to those programs is limited.

(ii) Audit interrogation software can be used to reperform reconciliations, analyse accounts and identify items which do not fulfil criteria set down by the auditors and may therefore be subject to fraud.

(iii) Test data can be used to see whether the system produces the results expected.

(iv) Likewise an integrated test facility, involving the creation of a fictitious department, can be used to test the operation of processes.

(v) The results of processing can be subject to analytical review, comparisons with previous years, budgets etc.

(vi) Similarly the results of processing can be compared with other audit evidence, for example computer stock balances being compared with actual stock counts.

(vii) Procedures can be reperformed manually but this is very time-consuming.

6   (a)   **Random selection** involves using random number tables or other methods to select items. Random selection means that bias cannot affect the sample chosen; it means that all items in the population have an equal chance of being chosen.

However, if the auditors are more concerned about some items than others, they can modify their approach, either by selecting certain items automatically because they are above a certain value, and selecting the rest of the sample by random numbers, or by stratifying the sample.

(b)   **Systematic selection** involves selecting items using a constant interval between selections, the first interval having a random start.

The main danger is that errors occur systematically in a pattern that means that none of the items in error will be selected.

(c)   **Haphazard selection** involves auditors choosing items subjectively without using formal random methods but avoiding bias.

The main danger is that bias (conscious or unconscious) does affect the auditor's judgement, and that certain items are selected because for example they are easy to obtain.

7   (a)   Tangible fixed asset register

(b)   Inventory listing produced at the stock count or perpetual inventory system

(c)   Unpaid invoices file, post year end payments on bank statement

(d)   Post year end payments on bank statement, prior year accruals listing

Chapter 7
AUDIT REPORTS AND AUDITORS' LIABILITY

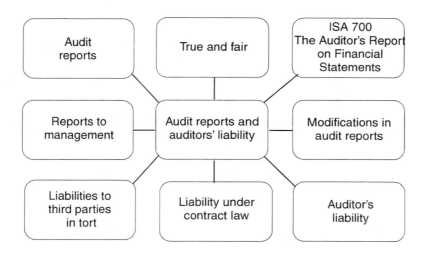

Introduction

The **audit report** is the means by which the external auditors express their opinion on the **truth and fairness** of a company's financial statements. This is for the benefit principally of the shareholders, but also for other users as the audit report is usually kept on public record, with the filed financial statements.

As we have seen, many of the contents of the auditor's report are prescribed by statute. They are also subject to professional requirements in the form of ISA 700 *The Auditor's Report on Financial Statements*. This makes it extremely different from the private 'reports to management' auditors produce which we will look at in more detail at the end of this chapter.

There are two key differences between the report to the shareholders and the report to management:

- Purpose
- Understandability

The **purpose** of the publicised audit report is to report to the **shareholders** on whether the accounts show a **true and fair view.** The private reports are for the purposes of directors and management.

The second issue is that of **understandability,** how the purpose and conclusion of the public report is **communicated** to shareholders. Directors and management work in the business, the report submitted to them may well be more meaningful to them than the audit report is to more isolated shareholders.

Learning objectives

In this chapter you will learn about the following.

(a) Unqualified audit reports

(b) The meaning of the phrase 'true and fair'

(c) ISA 700 on the Auditor's Report on Financial Statements

(d) Qualifications in audit reports

(e) The liability of the auditor to those relying on the financial statements

(f) The auditors' report to management

1 AUDIT REPORTS

The audit report is the end product of the auditor's work, whether the audit took a week, in the case of a small company, or a number of months, in the case of a large conglomerate. The content and format of the audit report are set out in law, reflecting its importance.

1.1 Unqualified reports

An **unqualified** audit report communicates an assurance to the user, that an independent examination of the accounts has discovered no material problems and that the accounts show a '**true and fair view**'. We will discuss truth and fairness in the next section of this chapter.

An unqualified report also conveys certain implications. These are unstated because the auditors only report **by exception**. In other words, these assumptions will only be mentioned (by a **qualified** audit report) if they do not hold true. An unqualified report implies that (under Companies Act 2006):

(a) adequate accounting records have not been kept;

(b) returns adequate for audit have been received from branches not visited;

(c) the financial statements are in agreement with the accounting records and returns;

(d) disclosures of directors' remuneration specified by law are made;

(e) all the information and explanations required for the audit have been received

2 TRUE AND FAIR

The accounts of a limited company are required by Companies Act 2006 to show a **true and fair view** of the company's financial position as at the balance sheet date and of its profit or loss for the year ending on that date. The auditors are required to state in their report whether, in their opinion, the accounts satisfy that requirement.

Most commentators give definitions of truth and fairness along the following lines.

Definitions

True: Information is factual and conforms with reality, not false. In addition the information conforms with required standards and law. The accounts have been correctly extracted from the books and records.

Fair: Information is free from discrimination and bias and in compliance with expected standards and rules. The accounts should reflect the commercial substance of the company's underlying transactions.

3 ISA 700 THE AUDITOR'S REPORT ON FINANCIAL STATEMENTS

3.1 Main provisions of ISA 700

Auditors' reports on financial statements should contain a clear expression of opinion, based on review and assessment of the conclusions drawn from evidence obtained in the course of the audit.

The auditors' report should be placed before the financial statements. The directors' responsibilities statement (explained later) should be placed before the auditors' report.

3.2 Basic elements of the auditors' report

ISA 700 explains the contents of a basic auditors report as follows:

Basic elements of audit report	Explanation
Title	The title should indicate that the report is by an **independent** auditor to confirm all the relevant ethical standards have been met, to distinguish it from reports issued by the board of directors and to add credibility to the financial statements
Addressee	The addressee will be determined by national law, but is likely to be the **shareholders** or **board of directors**.
Introductory paragraph	This should identify the entity being audited, state that the financial statements have been audited, identify the financial statements being audited (for example, profit and loss account, balance sheet, cash flow statement and the period they cover), specify the date and period covered by the financial statements. The auditor may be able to refer to specific page numbers if the financial statements are contained in a larger report.

Basic elements of audit report	Explanation
Statement of management's responsibility	The report must contain a statement that management is responsible for the presentation of the financial statements. This responsibility includes designing, implementing and maintaining internal controls, selecting appropriate accounting policies and making reasonable accounting estimates.
Statement of auditor's responsibility	The report must state that the auditor is responsible for expressing an opinion on the financial statements. The auditor should distinguish his duties from the relevant responsibilities of those charged with governance by referring to the summary of the responsibilities of those charged with governance contained elsewhere in the published information. If this information has not been published elsewhere, the auditor should include it in the report.
Basis of audit opinion	The basis of audit opinion paragraph should explain that the auditor adhered to international standards on auditing and ethical requirements and that he planned and performed the audit so as to obtain reasonable assurance that the financial statements are free from material misstatements.

The report should describe the audit as including:

(a) Examining, on a test basis, evidence to support the financial statement amounts and disclosures

(b) Assessing the accounting policies used in the preparation of the financial statements

(c) Assessing the significant estimates made by management in the preparation of the financial statements

(d) Evaluating the overall financial statement presentation

The paragraph should also include a statement by the auditor that the audit provides a reasonable basis for the opinion. |

Basic elements of audit report	Explanation
Opinion paragraph	If the auditor concludes that the financial statements give a true and fair view, he should express an **unqualified** opinion. An unqualified opinion states that the financial statements give a true and fair view or present fairly, in all material respects, in accordance with the applicable financial reporting framework. It should clearly indicate the financial reporting framework used, and, if IFRSs are not used, the country of origin of the framework, such as UK accounting standards.
	In addition the auditor must state his opinion whether the directors' report is consistent with the financial statements.
Date of the report	The report must be dated. This date shows the completion date of the audit and should not be before management has approved the financial statements.
Auditor's address	The location where the auditor practises must be included. This is usually the city where the auditor has his office.
Auditor's signature	The report must contain the auditor's signature, whether this is the auditor's own name or the audit firm's name.

EXAMPLE

The following is an example of an unqualified audit report in the UK.

Example 1. Unqualified opinion: company incorporated in Great Britain

INDEPENDENT AUDITOR'S REPORT TO THE SHAREHOLDERS OF XYZ LIMITED

We have audited the financial statements of XYZ Limited for the year ended ... which comprise [state the primary financial statements such as the profit and loss account, the balance sheet, the cash flow statement, the statement of total recognised gains and losses] and the related notes. These financial statements have been prepared under the accounting policies set out therein.

Respective responsibilities of directors and auditors

The directors' responsibilities for preparing the annual report and the financial statements in accordance with applicable law and United Kingdom Accounting Standards (UK Generally Accepted Accounting Practice) are set out in the Statement of Directors' Responsibilities.

Our responsibility is to audit the financial statements in accordance with relevant legal and regulatory requirements and International Standards on Auditing (UK and Ireland).

We report to you our opinion as to whether the financial statements give a true and fair view and are properly prepared in accordance with the Companies Act 2006. We report to you whether in our opinion the information given in the directors' report is consistent with the financial statements. [The information given in the directors' report includes that specific information presented in the Operating and Financial Review that is cross referred from the Business Section of the directors' report.]

In addition we report to you if, in our opinion, the company has not kept adequeate accounting records, if we have not received all the information and explanations we require for our audit, or if information specified by law regarding directors' remuneration and other transactions is not disclosed.

We read the Directors' Report and consider the implications for our report if we become aware of any apparent misstatements within it.

Basis of audit opinion

We conducted our audit in accordance with International Standards on Auditing (UK and Ireland) issued by the Auditing Practices Board. An audit includes examination, on a test basis, of evidence relevant to the amounts and disclosures in the financial statements. It also includes an assessment of the significant estimates and judgments made by the directors in the preparation of the financial statements, and of whether the accounting policies are appropriate to the company's circumstances, consistently applied and adequately disclosed.

We planned and performed our audit so as to obtain all the information and explanations which we considered necessary in order to provide us with sufficient evidence to give reasonable assurance that the financial statements are free from material misstatement, whether caused by fraud or other irregularity or error. In forming our opinion we also evaluated the overall adequacy of the presentation of information in the financial statements.

Opinion

In our opinion the financial statements:

- give a true and fair view, in accordance with United Kingdom Generally Accepted Accounting Practice, of the state of the company's affairs as at ... and of its profit [loss] for the year then ended;

- have been properly prepared in accordance with the Companies Act 2006; and

- the information given in the directors' report is consistent with the financial statements.

Registered auditors   *Address*
Date

The report should use a standard format as an aid to the reader, including headings for each section, for example 'Opinion'. The title and addressee and the introductory paragraph are fairly self explanatory. You may have noticed that the audit report does not refer to the company's cash flow statement in the opinion paragraph. This is discussed in the next section.

3.3 Statements of responsibility and basic opinion

(a) Auditors should distinguish between their responsibilities and those of the directors by including in their report:

    (i) a statement that the financial statements are the responsibility of the reporting entity's directors;

    (ii) a reference to a description of those responsibilities when set out elsewhere in the financial statements or accompanying information; and

    (iii) a statement that the auditors' responsibility is to express an opinion on the financial statements.

(b) Where the financial statements or accompanying information (for example the directors' report) do not include an adequate description of directors' relevant responsibilities the auditors' report should include a description of those responsibilities.

3.4 Explanation of auditors' opinion

Auditors should explain the basis of their opinion by including in their report:

(a) a statement as to their compliance or otherwise with Auditing Standards, together with the reasons for any departure therefrom;

(b) a statement that the audit process includes:

    (i) examining, on a test basis, evidence relevant to the amounts and disclosures in the financial statements;

    (ii) assessing the significant estimates and judgements made by the reporting entity's directors in preparing the financial statements;

    (iii) considering whether the accounting policies are appropriate to the reporting entity's circumstances, consistently applied and adequately disclosed;

(c) a statement that they planned and performed the audit so as to obtain reasonable assurance that the financial statements are free from material misstatement, whether caused by fraud or other irregularity or error, and that they have evaluated the overall presentation of the financial statements.

Other than in exceptional circumstances, a departure from an auditing standard is a limitation on the scope of work undertaken by the auditors (see section 4).

3.5 Expression of opinion

An auditors' report should contain a clear expression of opinion on the financial statements and on any further matters required by statute or other requirements applicable to the particular engagement.

An unqualified opinion on financial statements is expressed when in the auditors' judgement they give a true and fair view and have been prepared in accordance with relevant accounting or other requirements. This judgement entails concluding whether *inter alia*:

(a) The financial statements have been prepared using **appropriate, consistently applied accounting policies**.

(b) The financial statements have been **prepared** in accordance with **relevant legislation, regulations** or **applicable accounting standards** (and that any departures are justified and adequately explained in the financial statements).

(c) There is **adequate disclosure** of all information relevant to the proper understanding of the financial statements.

3.6 Date and signature of the auditors' report

(a) Auditors should not express an opinion on financial statements until those statements and all other financial information contained in a report of which the audited financial statements form a part have been approved by the directors, and the auditors have considered all necessary available evidence.

(b) The date of an auditors' report on a reporting entity's financial statements is the date on which the auditors sign their report expressing an opinion on those statements.

If the date on which the auditors sign the report is later than that on which the directors approve the financial statements, then the auditors must check that the post balance sheet event review has been carried out up to the date they sign their report and that the directors would also have approved the financial statements on that date.

3.7 Forming an opinion on financial statements

The principal matters which auditors consider in forming an opinion may be expressed in three questions.

(a) Have they **completed all procedures necessary** to meet auditing standards and to obtain all the information and explanations necessary for their audit?

(b) Have the financial statements been **prepared in accordance** with the **applicable accounting requirements**?

(c) Do the financial statements, as prepared by the directors, give **a true and fair view**?

This measure of uniformity in the auditor's report is desirable because it helps to promote the reader's understanding and to identify unusual circumstances when they do occur.

NOTES

Activity 1   **(15 minutes)**

The following is a series of extracts from an unqualified audit report which has been signed by the auditors of Little Panda Limited.

AUDITORS' REPORT TO THE SHAREHOLDERS OF LITTLE PANDA LIMITED

We have audited *the financial statements on pages .... to ....* which have been prepared under the historical cost convention.

We have conducted our audit *in accordance with Auditing Standards* issued by the Auditing Practices Board. An audit includes examination on a test basis of evidence relevant to the amounts and disclosures in the financial statements.

In our opinion the financial statements give a true and fair view of the state of the company's affairs as at 31 December 20X7 and of its profit for the year then ended and have been properly prepared in accordance with the Companies Act 2006.

Tasks

Explain the purpose and meaning of the following phrases taken from the above extracts of an unqualified audit report.

(a)   '... the financial statements on pages .... to ....'
(b)   '... in accordance with Auditing Standards.'
(c)   'In our opinion ...'

---

4   MODIFICATIONS IN AUDIT REPORTS

4.1   Modifications to the auditor's report

ISA 700 goes on to deal with situations where the auditor cannot issue an unmodified report.

The options available to the auditor with respect to the audit option are summarised in the diagram below:

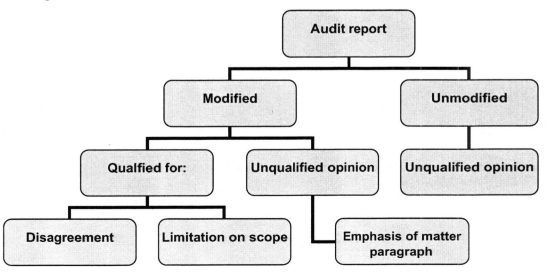

4.2   Unqualified audit opinions

In certain circumstances, an auditor's report may be modified by adding an **emphasis of matter** to highlight a matter affecting the financial statements which is included in a note to the financial statements that more extensively discusses the matter. The addition of such an emphasis of matter paragraph **does not affect** the auditor's opinion. The auditor may also modify the auditor's report by using an emphasis of matter paragraph(s) to report matters other than those affecting the financial statements.

The paragraph would preferably be included after the opinion paragraph and would ordinarily refer to the fact that the auditor's opinion is not qualified in this respect.

The ISA distinguishes between **going concern matters** and other matters, saying 'the auditor should modify the auditor's report by adding a paragraph to highlight a material matter regarding a going concern problem. The auditor should consider modifying the auditor's report by adding a paragraph if there is a **significant uncertainty** (other than a going concern problem), the resolution of which is dependent upon future events and which may affect the financial statements.'

Definition

> An **uncertainty** is a matter whose outcome depends on future actions or events not under the direct control of the entity but that may affect the financial statements.

The following is an example of an emphasis of matter paragraph.

Unqualified opinion with emphasis of matter describing a fundamental uncertainty

Significant uncertainty (insert just after opinion paragraph)

In forming our opinion, we have considered the adequacy of the disclosures made in the financial statements concerning the possible outcome to litigation against B Limited, a subsidiary undertaking of the company, for an alleged breach of environmental regulations. The future settlement of this litigation could result in additional liabilities and the closure of B Limited's business, whose net assets included in the consolidated balance sheet total £... and whose profit before tax for the year is £... . Details of the circumstances relating to this uncertainty are described in note .... . Our opinion is not qualified in this respect.

This type of paragraph will usually be sufficient to meet the auditor's reporting responsibilities. In extreme cases, however, which involve multiple uncertainties that are significant to the financial statements, a **disclaimer of opinion** may be required instead (see below).

The auditor may also modify the report by using an emphasis of matter paragraph for matters which do **not** affect the financial statements. This might be the case if amendment is necessary to other information in documents containing audited financial statements and the entity refuses to make the amendment. An emphasis of matter paragraph could also be used for **additional statutory reporting responsibilities**.

4.3 Qualified audit opinions

An auditor may not be able to express an unqualified opinion when either of the following circumstances exist and, in the auditor's judgement, the effect of the matter is or may be **material** to the financial statements:

(a) There is a **limitation on the scope** of the auditor's work.

(b) There is a **disagreement** with management regarding the acceptability of the accounting policies selected, the method of their application or the adequacy of financial statement disclosures.

There are different types and degrees of modified opinion.

- A limitation on scope may lead to a **qualified opinion ('except for....')** or a **disclaimer of opinion**.

- A disagreement may lead to a **qualified opinion ('except for....')** or an **adverse opinion**.

The following table summarises the different types of qualified opinion, and we will look at the detail of each of these in turn:

Nature of circumstances	*Material but not pervasive*	*Pervasive*
Disagreement	Except for .. (auditors disclaim an opinion on a particular aspect of the accounts which is not considered pervasive)	Disclaimer of opinion (auditors state they are unable to form an opinion on truth and fairness)
Limitation in scope	Except for ... (auditors express an adverse opinion on a particular aspect of the accounts which is not considered pervasive)	Adverse opinion (auditors state that the accounts do not give a true and fair view)

The ISA describes these different modified opinions and the circumstances leading to them as follows. 'A **qualified opinion ('except for...')** should be expressed when the auditor concludes that an unqualified opinion cannot be expressed but that the effect of any disagreement with management, or limitation on scope is not so material and pervasive as to require an adverse opinion or a disclaimer of opinion. A qualified opinion should be expressed as being 'except for the effects of the matter to which the qualification relates.'

A **disclaimer of opinion** should be expressed when the possible effect of a limitation on scope is so material and pervasive that the auditor has not been able to obtain sufficient, appropriate audit evidence and accordingly is unable to express an opinion on the financial statements.

An **adverse opinion** should be expressed when the effect of a disagreement is so material and pervasive to the financial statements that the auditor concludes that a qualification of the report is not adequate to disclose the misleading or incomplete nature of the financial statements'.

The concept of materiality was discussed earlier and you can now see its fundamental importance in auditing. ISA 700 says 'whenever the auditor expresses an opinion that is other than unqualified, a clear description of all the substantive reasons should be included in the report and, unless impracticable, a quantification of the possible effect(s) on the financial statements'.

This would usually be set out in a **separate paragraph** preceding the opinion or disclaimer of opinion and may include a reference to a more extensive discussion (if any) in a note to the financial statements.

Limitation on scope

There are two circumstances identified by the standard where there might be a limitation on scope.

Firstly, a limitation on the scope of the auditor's work may sometimes be **imposed by the entity** (for example, when the terms of the engagement specify that the auditor will not carry out an audit procedure that the auditor believes is necessary).

However, when the limitation in the terms of a proposed engagement is such that the auditor believes the need to express a disclaimer of opinion exists, the auditor would usually not accept such a limited audit engagement, unless required by statute. Also, a statutory auditor would not accept such an audit engagement when the limitation infringes on the auditor's statutory duties.

Secondly, a scope limitation may be **imposed by circumstances** (for example, when the timing of the auditor's appointment is such that the auditor is unable to observe the counting of physical stock). It may also arise when, in the opinion of the auditor, the entity's accounting records are inadequate or when the auditor is unable to carry out an audit procedure believed to be desirable. In these circumstances, the auditor would attempt to carry out reasonable alternative procedures to obtain sufficient, appropriate audit evidence to support an unqualified opinion.

Where there is a limitation on the scope of the auditor's work that requires expression of a qualified opinion or a disclaimer of opinion, the auditor's report should describe the limitation and indicate the possible adjustments to the financial statements that might have been determined to be necessary had the limitation not existed.

The following examples are reports given under a limitation of scope.

Qualified opinion: limitation on the auditors' work

(Basis of opinion: extract)

Except for the financial effects of such adjustments, if any, as might have been determined to be necessary had we been able to satisfy ourselves as to physical stock quantities, in our opinion the financial statements:

- Give a true and fair view, in accordance with United Kingdom Generally Accepted Accounting Practice, of the state of the company's affairs as at 31 December 20X1 and of its profit [loss] for the year then ended; and

- Have been properly prepared in accordance with the Companies Act 2006.In respect solely of the limitation on our work relating to stocks:

- We have not obtained all the information and explanations that we considered necessary for the purpose of our audit; and

- We were unable to determine whether proper accounting records had been maintained

---

In our opinion the information given in the Directors' Report is consistent with the financial statements.

Disclaimer of opinion

(Basis of opinion: extract)

.... or error. However, the evidence available to us was limited because we were unable to observe the counting of physical stock having a carrying amount of £X and send confirmation letters to trade debtors having a carrying amount of £Y due to limitations placed on the scope of our work by the directors of the company. As a result of this we have been unable to obtain sufficient appropriate audit evidence concerning both stock and trade debtors. Because of the significance of these items, we have been unable to form a view on the financial statements.

In forming our opinion we also evaluated the overall adequacy of the presentation of information in the financial statements.

Activity 2 **(20 minutes)**

For each of the following scenarios reach a conclusion, with reasons, as to the audit opinion that you would give:

(a) The directors of A Ltd have refused to make the necessary disclosures in the financial statements regarding some related party transactions that occurred in the year. Under accounting standards the auditor has concluded that the disclosures should be made.

(b) The auditor of B Ltd has been unable to verify the year-end inventory balance as the records taken at the year-end inventory count were lost in a fire.

(c) The directors of C Ltd have included a disclosure in the financial statements regarding a legal claim against the company for unfair dismissal by an ex-employee. The amount is potentially material although the matter will not be resolved until after the audit report is signed. The auditors are happy that the necessary information has been appropriately disclosed.

5 AUDITORS' LIABILITY

The main part of this section deals with **auditor liability** for professional negligence. This is a subject of great concern to auditors. Press reports of actions against auditors for large financial damages have become more common over the last few years. Audit firms can take out professional indemnity insurance to protect their assets, but this has its drawbacks, since arguably it provides a ready source of compensation which therefore makes auditors easy targets.

You have covered the basics of contract and tort, including professional negligence, back in Mandatory Unit 5, Aspects of Contract and Negligence for Business.

5.1 Contract

Auditors face potential liability to clients under the **law of contract**. A client who brings an action under contract law does so to enforce upon auditors responsibility for loss which has occurred through the failure of auditors to carry out their duties imposed by the contract with the client. In this chapter we shall discuss what these duties are, what a client has to prove in order to bring a successful action under the law of contract and whether auditors have any defences.

5.2 Tort

Auditors may also be liable under the **law of tort**. We cannot discuss the law of tort in detail but its effect may be to impose upon auditors a duty of care over and above what is imposed by statute or contract. In theory clients may sue in tort, but in practice the law of contract will most likely offer them better remedies. The law of tort is more likely to be a remedy for third parties. In this chapter we shall see how far auditor liability stretches, emphasising in particular the importance of the **Caparo case** which restricted the scope of auditor liability in this area.

One reason why auditors may face court actions is because of misunderstandings over the role of auditors – known as the expectation gap, which was defined back in Chapter 3.

5.3 Statute

The Companies Act 2006 introduces two new additional concepts to auditor liability.

Reckless auditing

The Act includes a new criminal offence, punishable by an unlimited fine, for 'knowingly or recklessly' to cause an audit report to include 'any matter that is misleading, false, deceptive in a material particular, or cause a report to omit a statement that is required under certain sections of the Act' – s. 507 CA2006. The offence can be committed by a partner, director, employee or agent of the audit firm if that person would be eligible for appointment as auditor of the company. In other words, the offence is not just related to the partners of the firm, but to any member of staff who has a practicing certificate.

The Government's view is that 'recklessness' has a very high hurdle and would only catch an auditor who is 'aware that an action or failure to act carried risks, that they personally knew that the risks were not reasonable ones to take, and that, despite knowing that, they went ahead. The real point is that this is a long way above negligence; one cannot be reckless inadvertently'. In other words, 'recklessly' is a subjective test because a risk taken must be unreasonable in the mind of the person taking it.

The offence has yet to be tested in court. However, professional bodies continue to argue that 'honest mistakes' should not be punishable.

Audit liability

Sections 534–538 of the Act allow members to pass an ordinary resolution to limit the liability of their auditors for negligence, default, breach of duty or breach of trust occurring during the course of an audit, by means of a limitation of liability agreement. Key points of this agreement are:

- Liability can only be limited where to do so would be 'fair and reasonable' in regard to all circumstances. In other words, the agreement could be set aside by the court where the auditor appeared to be contracting out of liability too much, or where a high standard of work was expected and the auditor failed to provide this

- Shareholder approval can be obtained either before or after the company enters into the agreement with the auditor

- The agreement must be disclosed in the directors' report

- The agreement must be renewed annually

- The members can terminate the agreement by ordinary resolution at any time

The actual terms of the agreement therefore have to be decided between the auditor and the client. However, the Act does not contain automatic proportional liability, which appeared to be the objective of the audit profession.

6 LIABILITY UNDER CONTRACT LAW

When auditors accept appointment, they enter into a contract which imposes certain obligations upon them. These obligations arise from the terms of the contract.

Both **express** and **implied** terms of contracts impact upon auditors. Express terms are those stated explicitly in the contract.

6.1 Express terms

The express terms of the audit contract cannot over-ride the Companies Act by restricting company auditors' statutory duties or imposing restrictions upon auditors' statutory rights which are designed to assist them in discharging those duties.

Express terms will however be significant if auditors and client agree that auditor responsibilities should be extended beyond those envisaged by the Companies Act. Additionally if auditors are involved in a non-statutory audit, the express terms will only be those contained in any specific contract that may exist with the client.

In these circumstances auditors are always likely to be judged on the content of any report which they have issued, and so they should always ensure that their report clearly states the effect of any limitations that there have been upon the extent and scope of their work. The auditors must take special care to ensure that their report does not in any way imply that they have in fact done more work than that required by the terms of the contract.

6.2 Implied terms

'Implied terms' are those which the parties to a contract may have left unstated because they consider them too obvious to express, but which, nevertheless, the law will impart into a contract.

The 'implied terms' which the law will impart into a contract of the type with which we are currently concerned are as follows:

- The auditors have a duty to exercise **reasonable care**.

- The auditors have a duty to carry out the work required with **reasonable expediency**.

- The auditors have a right to **reasonable remuneration**.

6.3   The auditors' duty of care

The auditors' duty of care arose under the Supply of Goods Act 1982; a higher degree of care arises in work of a specialised nature or where negligence is likely to cause substantial loss.

Auditors should use generally accepted auditing techniques. In addition, if auditors' suspicions are aroused (they are put upon enquiry) they must conduct further investigations until the suspicions are confirmed or put to rest.

When the auditors are exercising judgement they must act both honestly and carefully. Obviously, if auditors are to be 'careful' in forming an opinion, they must give due consideration to all relevant matters. Provided they do this and can be seen to have done so, then their opinion should be above criticism.

However if the opinion reached by the auditors is one that no reasonably competent auditor would have been likely to reach then they would still possibly be held negligent. This is because however carefully the auditors may appear to have approached their work, it clearly could not have been careful enough, if it enabled them to reach a conclusion which would be generally regarded as unacceptable.

6.4   Actions for negligence against auditors

Definition

Negligence is some act or omission which occurs because the person concerned has failed to exercise the degree of professional care and skill, appropriate to the case, which is expected of accountants or auditors.

If a client is to bring a successful action against an auditor then the client, as the claimant, must satisfy the court in relation to three matters, all of which must be established.

(a)   **Duty of care**

There existed a duty of care enforceable at law.

(b)   **Negligence**

In a situation where a duty of care existed, the auditors were negligent in the performance of that duty, judged by the accepted professional standards of the day.

(c)   **Damages**

The client has suffered some monetary loss as a direct consequence of the negligence on the part of the auditors.

6.5   Excluding or restricting liability to a client

The Companies Act 2006 introduced a new provision for auditors to agree limits on their liability to companies in respect of statutory audits. This had not previously been allowed. In order for such an agreement to be valid it must:

- cover only one financial year

- be approved by a resolution of the company's shareholders

- be considered to be 'fair and reasonable' in the particular circumstances of that company

Liability could be limited in a number of ways:

- a monetary cap on liability

- based on a proportionate share of the responsibility for any loss

- based on what is 'fair and reasonable'

7   LIABILITY TO THIRD PARTIES IN TORT

An accountant may be liable for negligence not only in contract, but also in tort if a person to whom he owed a **duty of care** has suffered **loss** as a result of the accountant's negligence. The key question in the law of tort is to whom does an auditor owe a duty of care.

7.1   To whom does the auditor owe a duty of care?

An accountant will almost always owe a duty of care to his own client. However that duty is likely to be co-existent with his contractual duty. In practice, the possibility of liability in tort will be important mainly in the context of claims by third parties.

In Royal Bank of Scotland v Bannerman Johnstone Maclay (the auditors) the courts concluded that the Royal Bank of Scotland were entitled to rely on the financial statements of a company for the purposes of lending the company money. This called into question previous cases where the courts had concluded that the auditors legal duty of care was restricted to their client.

Many UK auditors now insert an additional paragraph in their audit report in order to attempt to limit reliance by third parties on their audit reports. The APB has not included this in their standard audit report in ISA 700 however.

The wording of the so-called 'Bannerman paragraph' is:

'This report is made solely to the company's members, as a body, in accordance with Companies Act 2006. Our audit work has been undertaken so that we might state to the company's members those matters we are required to state to them in an auditor's report and for no other purpose. To the fullest extent permitted by law, we do not accept or assume responsibility to anyone other than the company and the company's members as a body for our audit work , for this report, or for the opinion we have formed.'

8 REPORTS TO MANAGEMENT

Auditors should report any weaknesses discovered in the system of internal control to the management of the company. This report usually takes the form of a **management letter** (or report to management), but other types of report are acceptable. ISA 260 *Communication of Audit Matters with Those Charged with Governance* covers this topic.

8.1 Reasons for a report to management

The main purposes of reports to directors or management are for auditors to communicate various points that have come to their attention during the audit. ISA 260 provides a list of matters that the auditor can report on including:

(a) Material weaknesses in internal control identified during the audit

(b) The auditors' views about the qualitative aspects of the entity's accounting practices and financial reporting

Note that such a report to management is *not* a substitute for a qualified audit report, when such a qualification is required. Inconsistencies between reports to management and the auditors' report should be avoided.

8.2 Material weaknesses in the accounting and internal control systems

When material weaknesses in the accounting and internal control systems are identified during the audit, auditors should report them in writing to the directors, the audit committee or an appropriate level of management on a timely basis.

A **material weakness** is one which may result in a **material misstatement** in the financial statements. If it is corrected by management, it need not be reported, but the discovery and correction should be documented.

To be effective, the report should be made **as soon as possible** after **completion** of the **audit procedures**. A written report is usual, but some matters may be raised orally with a file note to record the auditors' observation and the directors' response.

Where no report is felt to be necessary, the auditors should inform the directors that no material weaknesses have been found.

8.3 Interim letters

Where the audit work is performed on more than one visit, the auditors will normally report to management after the interim audit work has been completed as well as after the final visit.

8.4 Final letters

The final management letter can cover the following issues.

(a) Additional matters under the same headings as the interim letter, if sent

(b) Details of inefficiencies or delays in the agreed timetable for preparation of the accounts or of working schedules which delayed the completion of the audit and may have resulted in increased costs

(c)   Any significant differences between the accounts and any management accounts or budgets which not only caused audit problems but also detract from the value of management information

(d)   Any results of the auditors' analytical procedures of which management may not be aware and may be of benefit to them.

8.5   Other matters regarding reports to directors or management

If the auditors choose not to send a formal letter or report but consider it preferable to discuss any weaknesses with management, the discussion should be **minuted** or otherwise recorded in writing. Management should be provided with a copy of the note.

The auditors should explain in their report to management that it **only** includes those matters which came to their attention as a result of the audit procedures, and that it should not be regarded as a comprehensive statement of all weaknesses that exist or all improvements that might be made.

The auditors should request a **reply** to all the points raised, indicating what action management intends to take as a result of the comments made in the report.

If **previous points** have **not** been **dealt with effectively** and they are still considered significant, the auditors should enquire why action has not been taken.

The report may contain matters of varying levels of significance and thus make it difficult for senior management to identify points of significance. The auditors can deal with this by giving the report a '**tiered**' **structure** so that major points are dealt with by the directors or the audit committee and minor points are considered by less senior personnel.

Other points to note about the management letter are as follows.

(a)   The recommendations should take the form of **suggestions** backed up by **reason and logic**.

(b)   The letter should be in **formal terms** unless the client requests otherwise.

(c)   **Weaknesses** that **management** are aware of but **choose not to do anything about** should be **mentioned** to protect the auditors.

(d)   If management or staff have **agreed to changes**, this should be mentioned in a letter.

8.6   Third parties interested in reports to directors or management

Any report made to directors or management should be regarded as a confidential communication. The auditors should therefore not normally reveal the contents of the report to any third party without the prior written consent of the directors or management of the company.

In practice, the auditors have little control over what happens to the report once it has been despatched. Occasionally management may provide third parties with copies of the report, for example their bankers or certain regulatory authorities.

Thus care should be taken to protect the auditors' position from exposure to liability in negligence to any third parties who may seek to rely on the report. Accordingly, the auditors should state clearly in their report that it has been prepared for the private use of the client.

8.7 Specimen management letter

A specimen letter is provided below which demonstrates how the principles described in the previous paragraphs are put into practice.

EXAMPLE

SPECIMEN MANAGEMENT LETTER

ABC & Co
Certified Accountants
29 High Street
London, N10 4KB

The Board of Directors,
Manufacturing Co Limited,
15 South Street
London, S20 1CX

1 April 200X

Members of the board,

Financial statements for the year ended 31 May 200X

In accordance with our normal practice we set out in this letter certain matters which arose as a result of our review of the accounting systems and procedures operated by your company during our recent interim audit.

We would point out that the matters dealt with in this letter came to our notice during the conduct of our normal audit procedures which are designed primarily for the purpose of expressing our opinion on the financial statements of your company. In consequence our work did not encompass a detailed review of all aspects of the system and cannot be relied on necessarily to disclose defalcations or other irregularities or to include all possible improvements in internal control.

1   *Purchases: ordering procedures*

  Present system

  During the course of our work we discovered that it was the practice of the stores to order certain goods from X Ltd orally without preparing either a purchase requisition or purchase order.

  Implications

  There is therefore the possibility of liabilities being set up for unauthorised items and at a non-competitive price.

  Recommendations

  We recommend that the buying department should be responsible for such orders and, if they are placed orally, an official order should be raised as confirmation.

2   *Purchase ledger reconciliation*

  Present system

  Although your procedures require that the purchase ledger is reconciled against the control account on the nominal ledger at the end of every month, this was not done in December or January.

  Implications

  The balance on the purchase ledger was short by some £2,120 of the nominal ledger control account at 31 January 200X for which no explanation could be offered. This implies a serious breakdown in the purchase invoice and/or cash payment batching and posting procedures.

  Recommendations

  It is important in future that this reconciliation is performed regularly by a responsible official independent of the day to day purchase ledger, cashier and nominal ledger functions.

---

3   *Sales ledger: credit control*

Present system

As at 28 February 200X debtors account for approximately 12 weeks' sales, although your standard credit terms are cash within 30 days of statement, equivalent to an average of about 40 days (6 weeks) of sales.

Implications

This has resulted in increased overdraft usage and difficulty in settling some key suppliers accounts on time.

Recommendations

We recommend that a more structured system of debt collection be considered using standard letters and that statements should be sent out a week earlier if possible.

4   *Preparation of payroll and maintenance of personnel records*

Present system

Under your present system, just two members of staff are entirely and equally responsible for the maintenance of personnel records and preparation of the payroll. Furthermore, the only independent check of any nature on the payroll is that the chief accountant confirms that the amount of the wages cheque presented to him for signature agrees with the total of the net wages column in the payroll. This latter check does not involve any consideration of the reasonableness of the amount of the total net wages cheque or the monies being shown as due to individual employees.

Implications

It is a serious weakness of your present system, that so much responsibility is vested in the hands of just two people. This situation is made worse by the fact that there is no clearly defined division of duties as between the two of them. In our opinion, it would be far too easy for fraud to take place in this area (eg by inserting the names of 'dummy workmen' into the personnel records and hence on to the payroll) and/or for clerical errors to go undetected.

Recommendations

(i)   Some person other than the two wages clerks be made responsible for maintaining the personnel records and for periodically (but on a surprise basis) checking them against the details on the payroll;

(ii)   The two wages clerks be allocated specific duties in relation to the preparation of the payroll, with each clerk independently reviewing the work of the other;

(iii) When the payroll is presented in support of the cheque for signature to the chief accountant, that he should be responsible for assessing the reasonableness of the overall charge for wages that week.

Our comments have been discussed with your finance director and the chief accountant and these matters will be considered by us again during future audits. We look forward to receiving your comments on the points made. Should you require any further information or explanations do not hesitate to contact us.

This letter has been produced for the sole use of your company. It must not be disclosed to a third party, or quoted or referred to, without our written consent. No responsibility is assumed by us to any other person.

We should like to take this opportunity of thanking your staff for their co-operation and assistance during the course of our audit.

Yours faithfully

ABC & Co

BPP
LEARNING MEDIA

NOTES

Activity 3 (15 minutes)

During the audit of AJ (Paper) Ltd you have ascertained the following weaknesses within the systems of internal control.

(a) The ordering, recording and payment for purchases of materials are made by the administration department manager.

(b) All production department workers are paid on an hourly basis as per the hours on their time records. These records are completed by each worker on a weekly basis and are not checked by the supervisor prior to being submitted to the payroll department.

Tasks

Based on the above information

(i) Describe the weakness
(ii) Explain the implications of the weakness
(iii) Give recommendations to address the weakness

Chapter roundup

- An unqualified audit report demonstrates to the user that an independent examination of the accounts has discovered no material problems and that the accounts show a true and fair view.

- True and fair means that the accounts are factually materially correct, comply with relevant standards and the law and are free from bias.

- The standard unqualified audit report is set out in ISA 700.

- Wherever possible a qualified audit report should provide a full explanation of the reasons for the qualification and a quantification of its effect on the financial statements.

- Qualifications can arise due to limitations on scope or disagreements.

- Companies Act 2006 contains new provisions for auditors to agree to limit their liability to the company and its members.

- Auditors may chose to attempt to limit their liability to third parties through the insertion of a 'Bannerman' paragraph in their audit reports.

- Auditors should report any weaknesses that they discover in the system of internal control to the management of the company.

Quick quiz

1 What is implied by an unqualified audit report?

2 What are the two categories of circumstance giving rise to a qualification?

3 What is an auditor saying in a disclaimer of opinion?

4 Explain the purpose of a Bannerman paragraph

LEARNING MEDIA

Answers to Quick quiz

1   Adequate accounting records have been kept
The accounts agree with the underlying records and returns
All information and explanations have been received
Directors' emoluments, benefits and loans have been correctly disclosed

2   Limitation in scope of work, leading to uncertainty, and disagreement.

3   That he is unable to form an opinion on the truth and fairness of the financial statements.

4   To limit the possibility of auditors becoming liable to 3rd parties who choose to rely on the financial statements and auditor's report for a company.

Answers to Activities

1   (a)   '...the financial statements on pages ... to ...'

Purpose

The purpose of this phrase is to make it clear to the reader of an audit report the part of a company's annual report upon which the auditors are reporting their opinion.

Meaning

An annual report may include documents such as a chairman's report, employee report, five year summary and other voluntary information. However, under the Companies Act, only the profit and loss account, balance sheet and associated notes are required to be audited in true and fair terms. Thus the page references (for instance, 8 to 20) cover only the profit and loss account, balance sheet, notes to the accounts, cash flow statement and statement of total recognised gains and losses. The directors' report, although examined and reported on as to whether it contains inconsistencies, is not included in these page references.

(b)   '...in accordance with Auditing Standards...'

Purpose

This phrase is included in order to confirm to the reader that best practice, as laid down in Auditing Standards, has been adopted by the auditors in both carrying out their audit and in drafting their audit opinion. This means that the reader can be assured that the audit has been properly conducted, and that should he or she wish to discover what such standards are, or what certain key phrases mean, he or she can have recourse to Auditing Standards to explain such matters.

Meaning

Auditing Standards are those auditing standards prepared by the Auditing Practices Board.

These prescribe the principles and practices to be followed by auditors in the planning, designing and carrying out various aspects of their audit work, the content of audit reports, both qualified and unqualified and so on. Members are expected to follow all of these standards.

BPP
LEARNING MEDIA

(c) 'In our opinion ...'

Purpose

Under the Companies Act, auditors are required to report on every balance sheet, profit and loss account or group accounts laid before members. In reporting, they are required to state their opinion on those accounts. Thus, the purpose of this phrase is to comply with the statutory requirement to report an opinion.

Meaning

An audit report is an expression of opinion by suitably qualified auditors as to whether the financial statements give a true and fair view, and have been properly prepared in accordance with the Companies Act. It is not a certificate; rather it is a statement of whether or not, in the professional judgement of the auditors, the financial statements give a true and fair view.

2 (a) In this scenario the auditors **disagree** with the absence of the necessary disclosures in the financial statements. As the failure to disclose appears to be material (but not pervasive) the auditors should issue a qualified opinion for disagreement ("except for.....").

(b) The lack of availability of the inventory records means that the auditors have not been able to confirm the year end inventory balance. This represents a limitation on scope of the audit. The auditors would therefore issue a qualified opinion for limitation on scope. As the inventory balance does not pervade the financial statements an "except for" opinion would be appropriate.

(c) The outcome of the legal case against the company represents a significant uncertainty. As the directors have made the appropriate disclosures there is no disagreement. The auditors should therefore issue an unqualified audit opinion but include an emphasis of matter paragraph in order to highlight the uncertainty to the reader of the financial statements.

3 (a) **Segregation of duties in administration department**

Weakness

Segregation of duties in the administration department is **inadequate**, as the administration manager is responsible for all the tasks involved in purchasing goods.

Implication

Unauthorised purchases may be made and posted to the purchase ledger.

Recommendation

Different members of staff should perform the tasks of ordering, recording and payment.

(b) **Wages of production staff**

Weakness

Timesheets completed by production department workers are **submitted** to the payroll department **without being checked**.

Implication

Staff in the production department could **complete** their **timesheets incorrectly** and hence be **paid** the **wrong amounts**.

Recommendation

The **production department supervisor** should **check** all **timesheets** before they are submitted to the payroll department. The company should also consider introducing a **computerised clock in system**.

Part B

Taxation
(Finance Act 2009)

Chapter 8

THE TAX PRACTITIONER AND THE UK TAX ENVIRONMENT

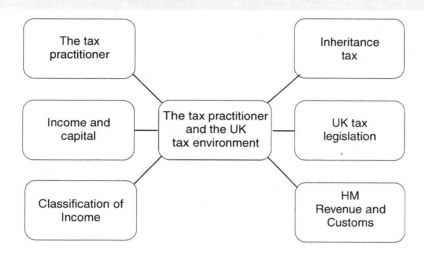

Introduction

Taxation is a fact of life, which will affect everyone in many different ways. The purpose of taxation is to enable central government to raise funds which then effectively pay for the running of the country, for example, education, roads and the health service.

Taxation is largely administered by the HM Revenue and Customs on behalf of the government.

Your objectives

In this chapter you will learn about the following.

(a) The main sources of UK tax legislation

(b) The key reference sources for UK tax legislation

(c) The organisation of HM Revenue and Customs and its terms of reference including the appeals system

(d) The appeals process

(e) The classification of income and the aggregation of income which is then subject to income tax.

(f) The difference between income and capital profits/losses

1   UK TAX LEGISLATION

1.1   The role of government and HM Revenue & Customs (HMRC)

Central government raises revenue through a wide range of taxes. Tax law is made by **statute** (ie by Acts of Parliament). This comprises not only **Acts of Parliament** but also regulations laid down by **Statutory Instruments**. Statute is interpreted and amplified by **case law**.

HM Revenue and Customs also issue:

(a) **Statements of practice,** setting out how they intend to apply the law

(b) **Extra-statutory concessions**, setting out circumstances in which they will not apply the strict letter of the law where it would be unfair

(c) A wide range of **explanatory leaflets**

(d) **Business economic notes.** These are notes on particular types of business, which are used as background information by HMRC and are also published

(e) The **Tax Bulletin**. This is a newsletter giving HMRC's view on specific points

(f) The **Internal Guidance,** a series of manuals used by HMRC staff

A great deal of information and HMRC publications can be found on the HM Revenue and Customs' Internet site (www.hmrc.gov.uk).

1.2   The main taxes

The main taxes, their incidence and their sources, are set out in the table below.

Tax	Suffered by	Source
Income tax	**Individuals Partnerships**	Capital Allowances Act 2001 (CAA 2001); Income Tax (Earnings and Pensions) Act 2003 (ITEPA 2003); Income Tax (Trading and Other Income) Act 2005 (ITTOIA 2005); Income Tax Act 2007 (ITA 2007)
Corporation tax	**Companies**	Income and Corporation Taxes Act 1988 (ICTA 1988), Corporation Tax Act 2009 (CTA 2009) and subsequent Finance Acts, CAA 2001 as above
Capital gains tax	**Individuals Partnerships Companies** (which pay tax on capital gains in the form of corporation tax)	Taxation of Chargeable Gains Act 1992 (TCGA 1992) and subsequent Finance Acts

The taxes set out in the table are the main ones with which the Edexcel guidelines expect you to be familiar.

However, the guidelines also mention one further tax of which you should be aware: inheritance tax (IHT). This will be discussed in brief at the end of this chapter.

1.3   Finance Acts

Finance Acts are passed each year, incorporating proposals set out in the **Budget**. They make changes which apply mainly to the tax year ahead. This book includes the provisions of the Finance Act 2009.

Definition

> The **tax year**, or fiscal year, or year of assessment, runs from 6 April to 5 April the following year. For example, the tax year 2009/10 runs from 6 April 2009 to 5 April 2010.

2   THE ORGANISATION OF HM REVENUE & CUSTOMS

2.1   The framework

The **Treasury** formally imposes and collects taxation. The management of the Treasury is the responsibility of the Chancellor of the Exchequer. **The administrative function for the collection of tax is undertaken by Her Majesty's Revenue and Customs (HMRC).** Previously there were two separate bodies called the Inland Revenue (responsible for direct taxes such as income tax and corporation tax) and HM Customs and Excise (responsible for indirect taxes such as VAT). Rules on these administrative matters are contained in the **Taxes Management Act 1970 (TMA 1970)**.

2.2   Administration and collection of income tax

HMRC consists of the commissioners for Her Majesty's Revenue and Customs and staff known **as Officers of Revenue and Customs.**

The UK has historically been divided into **tax districts**. These are being merged into larger **areas**, with the separate offices in each area being responsible for different aspects of HMRC's work. For example, one office may be designated to deal with taxpayer's queries, another to deal with the PAYE procedures for joiners and leavers, whilst end of year PAYE returns may be dealt with by a third office. Some offices also act as **enquiry offices**, where taxpayers can visit the office and see a member of HMRC staff in person without an appointment.

Each area is headed by an area director. HMRC staff were historically described as 'Inspectors' and 'Collectors'. The legislation now refers to an '**Officer of the Revenue and Customs**' when setting out HMRC's powers. They are responsible for supervising the self-assessment system and agreeing tax liabilities. Collectors (or **receivable management officers**) are local officers who are responsible for following up amounts of unpaid tax referred to them by the **HMRC Accounts Office.**

Taxpayer service offices do routine checking, computation *and* collection work, while **Taxpayer district offices** investigate selected accounts, deal with corporation tax and enforce the payment of tax when it is not paid willingly. **Taxpayer assistance offices** handle enquiries and arrange specialist help for taxpayers.

2.3 Appeals

Tax appeals are heard by the **Tax Tribunal** which is made up of **two tiers**:

(a) **First Tier Tribunal,** and
(b) **Upper Tribunal**

The **First Tier Tribunal deals with most cases** other than complex cases. The **Upper Tribunal deals** with complex cases which either involve an important issue of tax law or a large financial sum. The Upper Tribunal also hears appeals against decisions of the First Tier Tribunal.

3 THE CLASSIFICATION OF INCOME

Some income is received in full, with no tax deducted in advance. An example of such income is gilt interest (interest paid on government securities) which is normally paid gross.

Other income is received after deduction of tax. This is income taxed at source. The taxable income for a tax year (6 April in one year to 5 April in the next) is the **gross** amount (that is, adding back any tax deducted at source). We will look at taxed income in the context of the personal tax computation in the next chapter.

Dividends on UK shares are received net of a 10% tax credit. The taxable income for a tax year is the gross dividend (that is, the dividends received multiplied by 100/90). We will look at dividends in the next chapter.

3.1 Classification of Income

All income received must be classified according to the nature of the income. This is because different computational rules apply to different types of income. The main types of income are:

(a) **Income from employment and pensions**
(b) **Profits of trades, professions and vocations**
(c) **Income from property letting**
(d) **Savings and investment income, including interest and dividends.**
(e) **Miscellaneous income**

4 INCOME AND CAPITAL PROFITS/LOSSES

As a general rule, income tax is charged on income profit which might be expected to recur (such as weekly wages or profits from running a business) whereas capital gains tax is charged on one-off capital profits (for example from selling a painting owned for 20 years).

5 THE ROLE OF THE TAX PRACTITIONER

Many taxpayers arrange for their accountants to prepare and submit their tax returns. The taxpayer is still the person responsible for submitting the return and for paying whatever tax becomes due; the accountant is only acting as the taxpayer's agent.

The role of the tax practitioner in dealing with the HMRC on behalf of the client is dealt with fully in Chapter 12, *Tax documentation and payment of tax.*

6 INHERITANCE TAX

Inheritance tax (IHT) is primarily a tax on wealth left by an individual on death. It also applies to gifts made by individuals in the seven years prior to their death, and to some other large lifetime transfers of wealth.

IHT is different from the other taxes which you deal with in this Unit (such as income tax, corporation tax and capital gains tax) in that it is not concerned with the profit or income made by an individual, but with the amount of wealth **given away** by that person. The amount which is taxed is the amount transferred out of their estate, whether on death or in the period beforehand.

6.1 Rate of tax

The first £325,000 of transfers is tax free, although technically it is described as being the 'nil band'. However, it is not possible to evade IHT by making a number of separate transfers of just under £325,000 each, as transfers made are regarded on a cumulative basis over a seven year period.

Transfers above the £325,000 threshold are then taxed at 40%, known as the full rate.

These rates apply to lifetime transfers made in the seven years before death, that are taxed on death and on the value of an estate being taxed on death. This is death tax and calculated at the time of death. Lifetime tax can sometimes apply to large lifetime transfers of wealth and is calculated at the time of the gift, at half the death rate (currently 20%).

6.2 Exemptions

There are various exemptions available to eliminate or reduce the chargeable (taxable) amount of a lifetime transfer or property passing on a person's death.

These are:

(a) Outright gifts to individuals totalling £250 or less per donee in any one tax year (so that the donor can give £250 tax-free each year to each of as many donees as he wants)

(b) There is an overall annual exemption of £3,000 per tax year. This exemption, if unused, can only be carried forward for one year. This is to prevent someone making a lifetime transfer of £30,000 and then applying ten years' worth of unused annual exemption to the amount.

(c) Any transfers made between husband and wife, as long as the transferee (the recipient) is domiciled in the UK at the time of the transfer. This means that a spouse can leave their estate to their spouse free of IHT. However, the value of the estate would then be taxed on the death of the surviving spouse, when the estate passes to their children or others.

(d) Gifts to UK charities

(e) Gifts to UK political parties

(f) Gifts for national purposes (eg to museums, art galleries and the National Trust)

The first two of these exemptions apply only to lifetime transfers, not to property passing on death.

6.3 Valuation of assets

The value of any property for IHT is the value which it might reasonably be expected to fetch on the open market at the time of the transfer.

There are certain complex rules for the valuation of assets such as shares and securities, interests in family businesses and interests in agricultural property.

6.4 Administration of IHT

IHT is administered by HMRC Inheritance Tax. The personal representatives of the deceased (usually the executors) have to submit an account to HMRC showing the value of the estate on death and the amount of any chargeable lifetime transfers in the preceding seven years. This must be done within the 12 months following the month of death.

HMRC will then issue a notice of determination to the effect that IHT is payable.

The tax on the death estate is paid by the personal representatives, with the burden generally falling on the residuary legatee. This is the person named in the will as receiving the remainder of the estate after all specific gifts have been distributed.

Any tax due on lifetime transfers within the seven years before death, is suffered by the recipient.

Chapter roundup

- HM Revenue and Customs (HMRC) administers taxes.

- The First-tier Tribunal and Upper Tribunal hear appeals.

- Income is taxed classified according to the nature of the income.

- Income profits are receipts which recur regularly. Capital profits are one off receipts.

Quick quiz

1 What are the main UK taxes?

2 What tax do companies pay?

3 What are HMRC staff known as?

4 Under which type of income would you tax the profits from the trade of a self employed greengrocer?

5 How much is the IHT annual exemption?

Answers to Quick quiz

1   Income tax, capital gains tax and corporation tax.

2   Corporation Tax

3   'Officers of Revenue and Customs'

4   Profits of trades, professions and vocations

5   £3,000 per tax year, plus £3,000 carried forward from the previous year if unused

BPP
LEARNING MEDIA

NOTES

Chapter 9
THE PERSONAL TAX COMPUTATION

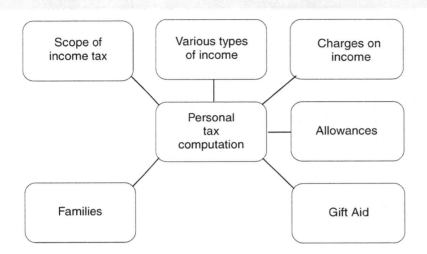

Introduction

Personal tax is a topic which will inevitably affect every reader of this book, and the subject matter of this chapter should be of practical as well as academic interest.

It is important that you understand the basic elements of the personal tax computation and when they are applicable.

The whole of this unit is based on the Finance Act 2009. You should be aware that although many of the figures used for allowances will change in each successive Finance Act, most of the principles will remain the same.

Your objectives

In this chapter you will learn about the following.

(a) The scope of income tax: chargeable persons, chargeable income

(b) The key elements of a personal income tax computation – total income (savings/non-savings/dividend), net income, taxable income, computation of income tax liability

(c) The key stages in the transition from computation of income tax liability to income tax payable

(d) The different categories of charges

(e) Personal allowances and the circumstances in which they can be claimed

(f) How to prepare income tax computations

1   THE SCOPE OF INCOME TAX

As a general rule, income tax is charged on receipts which might be expected to recur (such as weekly wages or profits from running a business). **An individual's income from all sources is brought together in a personal tax computation for the tax year.**

Definition

> The **tax year**, or **fiscal year**, or **year of assessment** runs from 6 April to 5 April. For example, the tax year 2009/10 runs from 6 April 2009 to 5 April 2010.

Three columns are needed in the computation. Here is an example. All items are explained later in this Course Book.

RICHARD: INCOME TAX COMPUTATION 2009/10

	Non-savings income £	Savings income £	Dividend income £	Total £
Income from employment	48,000			
Building society interest		1,000		
National savings & investments account interest		400		
UK dividends			1,000	
Total income	48,000	1,400	1,000	
Less interest paid	(2,000)			
Net income	46,000	1,400	1,000	48,400
Less personal allowance	(6,475)			
Taxable income	39,525	1,400	1,000	41,925

	£	£
Income tax on non savings income		
£37,400 × 20%		7,480
£2,125 × 40%		850
Tax on savings income		
£1,400 × 40%		560
Tax on dividend income		
£1,000 × 32.5%		325
		9,215
Less tax reducer		
Investment under the EIS £10,000 × 20%		(2,000)
Tax liability		7,215
Less tax suffered		
PAYE tax on salary (say)	6,100	
Tax on building society interest	200	
Tax credit on dividend income	100	
		(6,400)
Tax payable		815

Definitions

Total income is all income subject to income tax. Each of the amounts which make up total income is called a **component. Net income** is total income less deductible interest and trade losses. The **tax liability** is the amount charged on the individual's income. **Tax payable** is the balance of the liability still to be settled in cash.

Income tax is charged on 'taxable income'. Non-savings income is dealt with first, then savings income and then dividend income.

1.2 Tax rates

For non-savings income, the first £37,400 is taxed at the basic rate (20%) and the rest at the higher rate (40%).

There is a **tax rate of 10% for savings income between £0 and £2,440 (the starting rate band)**. This rate is called the **savings income starting rate**.

The savings income starting rate only applies where the savings income falls wholly or partly in the starting rate band. Remember that income tax is charged first on non-savings income. So, in most cases, an individual's non-savings income will exceed the starting rate limit and the savings income starting rate will not be available on savings income. In this case, the individual's savings income will be charged to tax at the 20% basic rate up to the basic rate limit of £37,400 and 40% thereafter.

However, **if an individual's non-savings income is less than the starting rate limit,** then **savings income will be taxable at the 10% savings income starting rate up to the starting rate limit, at 20% up to the basic rate limit of £37,400 and 40% thereafter.**

EXAMPLE

Joe is aged 55. In 2009/10, he earns a salary of £7,500 from a part-time job and receives bank interest of £4,000.

Calculate Joe's tax liability for 2009/10.

	Non-savings income £	Savings income £	Total £
Employment income	7,500		
Bank interest £4,000 × 100/80		5,000	
Net income	7,500	5,000	12,500
Less: personal allowance	(6,475)		
Taxable income	1,025	5,000	6,025

	£
Income tax	
Non-savings income	
£1,025 × 20 %	205
Savings income	
£1,415 × 10%	141
£3,585 × 20%	717
Tax liability	1,063

Any dividend income falling within the starting or basic rate bands is taxed at 10%. Dividend income in excess of the basic rate threshold is taxed at 32.5%.

Any tax already suffered and the tax credit on dividend income comes off the tax liability. However, the tax credit on dividend income cannot be repaid.

Activity 1	**(5 minutes)**

An individual has taxable income (all non-savings income) of £50,000 for 2009/10. What is the total income tax?

The remainder of this chapter gives more details of the income tax computation.

2 VARIOUS TYPES OF INCOME

2.1 Classification of income

All income received must be classified according to the nature of the income. This is because different computational rules apply to different types of income. The main types of income are:

- Income from employment, pensions and some social security benefits
- Profits of trades, professions and vocations
- Profits of property businesses
- Savings and investment income, including interest and dividends
- Miscellaneous income.

2.2 Savings income

What is savings income?

Savings income comprises the following.

(a) **Interest** (includes interest from banks, building societies, gilts and debentures and under the accrued income scheme)

Savings income received gross

The following savings income is received gross.

(a) **Interest on National Savings & Investments accounts** (eg. Investment account, Easy Access Savings account)

(b) Interest paid to individuals by listed UK companies on debentures and loan stock

(c) Gilt interest

Savings income received net of 20% tax

The following savings income is received net of 20% tax. **This is called income taxed at source.**

(a) Bank and building society interest paid to individuals (but not National Savings & Investments account interest)

(b) Interest paid to individuals by unlisted UK companies on debentures and loan stocks

The amount received is grossed up by multiplying by 100/80 and is included gross in the income tax computation. The tax deducted at source is deducted in computing tax payable and may be repaid.

Although bank and building society interest paid to individuals is generally paid net of 20% tax, if a recipient is not liable to tax, he can recover the tax suffered, or he can certify in advance that he is a non-taxpayer and receive the interest gross.

2.3 Dividends on UK shares

Dividends on UK shares are received net of a 10% tax credit. This means a dividend of £90 has a £10 tax credit, giving gross income of £100 to include in the income tax computation. The tax credit can be deducted in computing tax payable but it cannot be repaid.

Higher rate taxpayers pay tax at 32½% on their gross dividends and can deduct the 10% tax credit. This is the same as taxing the net dividend at 25%. For example, a higher rate taxpayer receiving a net dividend of £9,000 will pay tax of £2,250, which is £3,250 (£10,000 @ 32½%) less £1,000 (£10,000 @ 10%). This is the same as taking 25% × £9,000.

Stock dividends

Sometimes a company will offer shares in lieu of a cash dividend. A shareholder who takes the shares receives a stock dividend. The amount of the stock dividend is:

(a) the cash alternative, if that equals the market value of the shares offered plus or minus 15%;

(b) the market value of the shares offered, if that differs from the cash alternative by more than 15% or if there is no cash alternative.

The shareholder is treated as receiving a gross dividend of the stock dividend × 100/90, with a tax credit of 10% of the gross dividend.

2.4 Exempt income

Some income is exempt from income tax. Several of these exemptions are mentioned at places in this text where the types of income are described in detail, but you should note the following types of exempt income now.

(a) Scholarships (exempt as income of the scholar. If paid by a parent's employer, a scholarship may be taxable income of the parent)

(b) Betting and gaming winnings, including premium bond prizes

(c) Interest or terminal bonus on National Savings Certificates

(d) Many social security benefits, although the jobseeker's allowance, the state pension and certain incapacity benefits are taxable

(e) Gifts

(f) Damages and payments for personal injury. The exemption applies to both lump sum and periodical payments, including payments made via trusts and payments made by buying annuities. Payments under annuities are made gross (unlike most annuities)

(g) Payments under insurance policies to compensate for loss of income on illness or disability (permanent health insurance) or while out of work (eg policies to pay interest on mortgages), so long as the person benefiting paid the premiums and did not get tax relief for them

(h) The amount by which a pension awarded on a retirement due to a disability caused at work, by a work related illness or by war wounds exceeds the pension that would have been payable if the retirement had been on ordinary ill health grounds. This exemption only applies to pensions paid under non-approved pension schemes.

(i) Interest on amounts repaid to borrowers under the income contingent student loans scheme

(j) Income on investments made though individual savings accounts (ISAs).

Activity 2   **(10 minutes)**

An individual has the following income in 2009/10.

	£
Building society interest received	6,400
Dividends received	7,875
Premium bond prize	5,000

His personal allowance is £6,475. What is his taxable income?

---

3 CHARGES ON INCOME

Charges on income are deducted in computing taxable income.

Definition

> A **charge on income** is a payment by the taxpayer which income tax law allows as a deduction.

Examples of charges on income are:

(a) eligible interest
(b) patent royalties (non-trading)
(c) copyright royalties (non-trading)

3.1 Categories of charges on income

Charges on income paid in money fall into two categories: those from which basic rate (20%) income tax is first deducted by the payer (charges paid net) and those which are paid gross (without any tax deduction). Always deduct the gross figure in the payer's tax computation.

Patent royalties are an example of a charge on income which is paid net. Eligible interest and copyright royalties are paid gross.

In the personal tax computation of someone who **receives** a charge, for example the owner of a patent who gets royalties from someone who exploits the patent you should:

(a) Include the **gross** amount under non-savings income. If the charge is paid gross, the gross amount is the amount received. If it is paid net, the gross amount is the amount received × 100/80.

(b) If the charge was received net, then under the heading 'less tax suffered' (between tax liability and tax payable) include the tax deducted. This is the gross amount × 20%.

3.2 Eligible interest

Interest on a loan is a charge when the loan is used for one of the following qualifying purposes.

(a) The purchase of an interest in a partnership, or contribution to the partnership of capital or a loan. The borrower must be a partner (other than a limited partner), and relief ceases when he ceases to be one.

(b) The purchase of ordinary shares in a close company (other than a close investment holding company) or the loan of money to such a company for use in its business, provided that when the interest is paid, the individual either has (with any associates) a material (more than 5%) interest in the close company, or holds (ignoring associates) some ordinary share capital and works full time as a manager or director of the company. A close company is (broadly) a company controlled by its shareholder-directors or by five or fewer shareholders.

(c) Investment in a co-operative. This provision applies to investment in shares or through loans to the co-operative. The borrower must work for the greater part of his time in the co-operative.

(d) The purchase of shares in an employee-controlled company. The company must be an unquoted trading company resident in the UK with at least 50% of the voting shares held by employees.

(e) The purchase by a partner of plant or machinery used in the business. Interest is allowed only until three years from the end of the tax year in which the loan was taken out. If the plant is used partly for private purposes, then the allowable interest is proportionately reduced.

(f) The purchase by an employee of plant or machinery used by him in the performance of his duties. The interest is allowable only until three years from the end of the tax year in which the loan was taken out.

(g) The replacement of other loans qualifying under (a) to (f) above.

Interest on a loan within (a) to (d) above continues to be allowable if a partnership is succeeded by a new partnership or is incorporated into a co-operative or an employee controlled company, or if shares in a company of one of these kinds are exchanged for shares in a company of another of these kinds, provided that interest on a new loan (to make the loan to or buy the shares in the new entity) would have qualified.

Interest is never allowed if it is payable under a scheme or arrangement of which the expected sole or main benefit was tax relief on the interest. Interest on an overdraft or on a credit card debt does not qualify. Relief under (a) to (d) above is reduced or withdrawn if capital is withdrawn from the business.

3.3 Business traders

A taxpayer paying interest, patent royalties or copyright royalties wholly and exclusively for business purposes should deduct such items in the computation of his taxable profit, instead of as a charge. The interest need not fall into any of the categories outlined above, and it may be on an overdraft or a credit card debt.

If interest is allowable as a deduction when calculating taxable profits, the amount payable (on an accruals basis) is deducted.

3.4 Charges in personal tax computations

The gross amount of any charge is deducted from the taxpayer's income to arrive at Net Income. Deduct charges from non-savings income, then from savings (excl dividend) income and lastly from dividend income.

If a charge has been paid net, the basic rate income tax deducted (20% of the gross charge) is added to any tax liability. The taxpayer obtained tax relief because the charge reduced his income: he cannot keep the basic rate tax as well, but must pay it to HMRC.

If charges paid net exceed total income (ignoring charges paid net) minus allowances deductible from total income, the payer of the charge must pay HMRC the tax withheld when the excess charge was paid. In other words, HMRC ensure that you do not get tax relief for charges if you are not a payer of tax.

EXAMPLE

Three taxpayers have the following Trading profits and allowances for 2009/10. Taxpayers A and B pay a non-trade royalty of £200 (net). Taxpayer C pays a non-trade royalty of £1,280 (net).

	A	B	C
	£	£	£
Trading Profits	8,000	3,000	46,195
Less: charge on income (×100/80)	(250)	(250)	(1,600)
	7,750	2,750	44,595
Less: personal allowance	(6,475)	(6,475)	(6,475)
Taxable income	1,275	–	38,120
Income tax			
20% on £1,275/-/£37,400	255		7,480
40% on -/-/720	—	—	288
	255	–	7,768
Add: 20% tax retained on charge	50	50	320
Tax payable	305	50	8,088

4 ALLOWANCES DEDUCTED FROM NET INCOME

Once taxable income from all sources has been aggregated and any charges on income deducted, the remainder is the taxpayer's net income. Two allowances, the personal allowance and the blind person's allowance, are deducted from Net Income. Like charges, they come off non savings income first, then off savings (excl. dividend) income and lastly off dividend income. The amounts given in the following paragraphs are for 2009/10.

Other allowances are not deducted from Net Income, but reduce tax instead. These allowances are explained below.

4.1 PA: personal allowance

Once taxable income from all sources has been aggregated and any deductible interest deducted, the remainder is the taxpayer's net income. The personal allowance is deducted from net income. Like deductible interest, it is deducted from non savings income first, then from savings income and lastly from dividend income. The amounts given in the following paragraphs are for 2009/10.

All persons (including children) are entitled to the personal allowance of £6,475.

A person aged 65 or over (at any time in the tax year) gets an age allowance of £9,490 instead of the ordinary PA of £6,475.

Where net income exceeds £22,900, cut the age allowance by £1 for every £2 of income over £22,900 until it comes down to £6,475.

EXAMPLE

Jonah is 69 and single. In 2009/10 he has pension income totalling £18,800 plus bank interest received of £4,000. What is Jonah's taxable income?

2009/10	Non savings £	Savings £	Total £
Pension income	18,800		
Interest 4,000 × 100/80		5,000	
Net income	18,800	5,000	23,800
Less PAA (W1)	(9,040)		
Taxable income	9,760	5,000	14,760

W1

PAA 65+	9,490
Less income restriction (23,800 – 22,900) × ½	(450)
	9,040

PAA of £9,040 exceeds basic allowance of £6,475.

Individuals aged 75 or over (at any time in the tax year) get a slightly more generous age allowance of £9,640. In all respects, the higher age allowance works in the same way as the basic age allowance, with the same income limit of £22,900.

Someone who dies in the tax year in which they would have had their 65th or 75th birthday receives the age allowance (for 65 year olds or 75 year olds) for that year.

4.2 BPA: blind person's allowance

A taxpayer who is registered with a local authority as a blind person gets an allowance of £1,890. The allowance is also given for the year before registration, if the taxpayer had obtained the proof of blindness needed for registration before the end of that earlier year.

Activity 3	**(15 minutes)**

Susan has an annual salary of £37,000. She has a loan of £7,000 at 10% interest to buy shares in her employee-controlled company, and another loan of £5,000 at 12% interest to buy double glazing for her house. She receives building society interest of £2,000 a year. What is her taxable income for 2009/10?

5 GIFT AID

5.1 Gift aid donations

Definition

One-off and regular charitable gifts of money qualify for tax relief under the **gift aid scheme** provided the donor gives the charity a gift aid declaration.

Gift aid declarations can be made in writing, electronically through the internet or orally over the phone. A declaration can cover a one-off gift or any number of gifts made after a specified date (which may be in the past).

The gift must not be repayable, and must not confer any more than a minimal benefit on the donor. Gift aid may be used for entrance fees (for example to National Trust properties or historic houses) provided the right of admission applies for at least one year or the visitor pays at least 10% more than the normal admission charge.

5.2 Tax relief for gift aid donations

A gift aid donation is treated as though it is paid net of basic rate tax (20%). Additional tax relief for higher rate taxpayers is given in the personal tax computation by increasing the donor's basic rate band by the gross amount of the gift. To arrive at the gross amount of the gift you must multiply the amount paid by 100/80.

No additional relief is due for basic rate taxpayers. Extending the basic rate band is then irrelevant as taxable income is below the basic rate threshold.

NOTES

EXAMPLE

James earns a salary of £65,180 but has no other income. In 2009/10 he paid £8,000 (net) under the gift aid scheme.

Compute James' income tax liability for 2009/10.

		Non-savings income
		£
Salary/Net income		65,180
Less: personal allowance		(6,475)
Taxable income		58,705
Income tax	£	£
Basic rate band	37,400 × 20%	7,480
Basic rate band (extended)	10,000 × 20%	2,000
Higher rate band	11,305 × 40%	4,522
	58,705	14,002

The basic rate band is extended by the gross amount of the gift (£8,000 × 100/80)

Activity 4   **(10 minutes)**

James earns a salary of £58,000 but has no other income. In 2009/10 he paid £8,000 (net) under the gift aid scheme.

Compute James' income tax liability for 2009/10.

6 FAMILIES

6.1 Spouses and civil partners

Spouses and civil partners are taxed as two separate people. Each spouse/civil partner is entitled to a personal allowance or an age related personal allowance depending on his or her own age and income.

6.2 Joint property

When spouses/civil partners jointly own income-generating property, it is assumed that they are entitled to equal shares of the income. This does not apply to income from shares held in close companies (see later in this Course Book for an explanation of close companies).

If the spouses/civil partners are not entitled to equal shares in the income-generating property (other than shares in close companies), **they may make a joint declaration to HMRC, specifying the proportion to which each is entitled.** These proportions are used to tax each of them separately, in respect of income arising on or after the date of the declaration. For capital gains tax purposes it is always this underlying beneficial ownership that is taken into account.

6.3 Example: income tax planning for spouses/civil partners

Mr Buckle is a higher rate taxpayer who owns a rental property producing £20,000 of property income on which he pays tax at 40%, giving him a tax liability of £8,000. His spouse has no income.

If he transfers only 5% of the asset to his wife, they will be treated as jointly owning the property and will each be taxed on 50% of the income. Mr Buckle's tax liability will be reduced to £4,000. His wife's liability is only £705, giving an overall tax saving of £3,295.

6.4 Minor children

Income which is directly transferred by a parent to his minor child, or is derived from capital so transferred, remains income of the parent for tax purposes. This applies only to parents, however, and tax saving is therefore possible by other relatives. Even where a parent is involved, the child's income is not treated as the parent's if it does not exceed £100 (gross) a year. **The legislation does not apply to income from a Child Trust Fund (CTF).** CTFs are dealt with later in this Course Book.

7 THE LAYOUT OF PERSONAL TAX COMPUTATIONS

7.1 Steps in the income tax computation

Step 1 **The first step in preparing a personal tax computation is to set up three columns**

One column for non-savings income, one for savings income and one for dividend income. Add up income from different sources. The sum of these is known as 'total income'.

Step 2 **Deal with non-savings income first**

Any income in the basic rate band is taxed at 20% and income above the basic rate threshold is taxed at 40%.

Step 3 **Now deal with savings income**

If non-savings income is below the starting rate limit, savings can be taxed at the savings income starting rate of 10% up to starting rate limit. If savings income falls within the basic rate band it is taxed at 20%. Once income is above the higher rate threshold, it is taxed at 40%. In most cases, non-savings income and savings income can be added together and tax calculated on the total, provided that the savings income starting rate does not apply.

Step 4 **Lastly, tax dividend income**

If dividend income falls within the starting or basic rate bands, it is taxed at 10% (never 20%). If, however, the dividend income exceeds the basic rate threshold, it is taxable at 32.5%.

Step 5 Add the amounts of tax together. The resulting figure is the income tax liability.

Step 6 Next, deduct the tax credit on dividends. Although deductible this tax credit cannot be repaid if it exceeds the tax liability calculated so far.

Step 7 Finally deduct the tax deducted at source from savings income and any PAYE. These amounts can be repaid to the extent that they exceed the income tax liability.

7.2 Examples: personal tax computations

(a) Kathe has a salary of £10,000 and receives dividends of £4,500.

	Non-savings income	Dividend income	Total
	£	£	£
Earnings	10,000		
Dividends £4,500 × 100/90		5,000	
Net income	10,000	5,000	15,000
Less personal allowance	(6,475)		
Taxable income	3,525	5,000	8,525

	£
Income tax	
Non savings income	
£3,525 × 20%	705
Dividend income	
£5,000 × 10%	500
Tax liability	1,205
Less tax credit on dividend	(500)
Tax payable	705

Some of the tax payable has probably already been paid on the salary under PAYE.

The dividend income falls within the basic rate band so it is taxed at 10% (*not* 20%).

(b) Jules has a salary of £20,000, business profits of £30,000, net dividends of £6,750 and building society interest of £3,000 net. He is entitled to relief on interest paid of £2,000.

	Non-savings income £	Savings income £	Dividend income £	Total £
Business profits	30,000			
Employment income	20,000			
Dividends £6,750 × 100/90			7,500	
Building society interest £3,000 × 100/80	–	3,750	–	
Total income	50,000	3,750	7,500	
Less interest paid	(2,000)			
Net income	48,000	3,750	7,500	59,250
Less personal allowance	(6,475)			
Taxable income	41,525	3,750	7,500	52,775

Income tax	£
Non savings income	
£37,400 × 20%	7,480
£4,125 × 40%	1,650
Savings income	
£3,750 × 40%	1,500
Dividend income	
£7,500 × 32.5%	2,437
Tax liability	13,067
Less tax credit on dividend income	(750)
Less tax suffered on building society interest	(750)
Tax payable	11,567

Savings income and dividend income fall above the basic rate threshold so they are taxed at 40% and 32.5% respectively.

(c) Jim does not work. He receives net bank interest of £38,000. He is entitled to relief on interest paid of £2,000.

	Savings income £	Total £
Bank interest × 100/80/Total income	47,500	
Less interest paid	(2,000)	
Net income	45,500	45,500
Less personal allowance	(6,475)	
Taxable income	39,025	39,025

	£
Savings income	
£2,440 × 10%	244
£34,960 × 20%	6,992
£1,625 × 40%	650
Tax liability	7,886
Less tax suffered	(9,500)
Tax repayable	(1,614)

Chapter roundup

- The fiscal year is the year that runs from 6 April in one year to 5 April in the next.

- In a personal income tax computation, we bring together income from all sources, splitting the sources into non-savings, savings (excl dividend) and dividend income.

- We deduct charges and then the personal allowance in computing net income.

- Finally, we work out income tax on the taxable income, and take account of tax retained on charges and tax already suffered. We extend the basic rate band by the gross amount of any gift aid donation.

- Husbands, wives and children are all separate taxpayers. There are special rules to prevent parents from exploiting a child's personal allowance.

Quick quiz

1   At what rates is income tax on non-savings income charged?

2   What types of income are taxed at source?

3   How is UK dividend income taxed?

4   What charges on income are paid net?

5   What loan interest is allowable as a charge?

6   What is the amount of personal age allowance available to a 70 year old?

7   How is income from property jointly owned by spouses taxed?

Answers to Quick quiz

1   20% on the first £37,400 of income. 40% on all excess.

2   Interest paid to individuals by banks, building societies, and interest on company loan stocks or debentures.

3   As the top slice of taxable income and always at 10% tax unless it falls into the higher tax band when 32.5% tax is due.

4   Patent royalties.

5   Loans to

- purchase an interest in a partnership
- purchase ordinary shares in a close company
- invest in a co-operative
- purchase shares in an employee controlled company
- purchase plant and machinery

6   £9,490

7   The income is split equally between the spouses unless actual ownership is not 50:50 and a declaration as such is made to HMRC.

Answers to Activities

1

	£
£37,400 × 20%	7,480
£12,600 × 40%	5,040
£50,000	12,520

Note. Taxable income is the amount after deducting personal allowance(s).

2

	Savings (excl dividend) £	Dividend £	Total £
Building society interest £6,400 × 100/80	8,000		
Dividends £7,875 × 100/90		8,750	
Premium bond prize: exempt			
Net Income	8,000	8,750	16,750
Less personal allowance	(6,475)		
Taxable income	1,525	8,750	10,275

3

	Non-savings	Savings (excl dividend)	Total
	£	£	£
Salary	37,000		
Building society interest £2,000 × 100/80		2,500	
	37,000	2,500	
Less charge £7,000 × 10%	(700)		
Net Income	36,300	2,500	38,800
Less personal allowance	(6,475)		
Taxable income	29,825	2,500	32,325

Note. Susan's Net income is £38,800, so even if she is aged 65 or more she will not get any age allowance. The loan to purchase double glazing is not a qualifying loan.

4

	Non-savings
	£
Salary	58,000
Less personal allowance	(6,475)
Taxable income	51,525

Income tax	£		£
Basic rate band	37,400 × 20%		7,480
Basic rate band (extended)	10,000 × 20%		2,000
Higher rate band	4,125 × 40%		1,650
	51,525		11,130

Note. £8,000 × 100/80 = £10,000 extension to basic rate tax band re the gift aid payment.

Chapter 10
TAXATION OF EMPLOYMENT

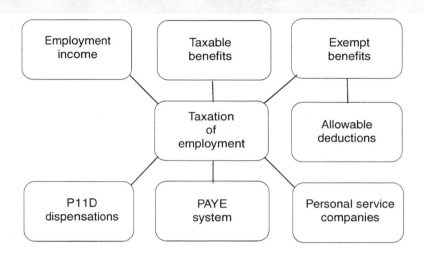

Introduction

The system for the taxation of employment is quite straightforward but includes a large amount of detail, which can at first sight make the system seem complicated. The main thrust of the law here is to ensure that employees pay a fair amount of tax; they cannot be paid in non-monetary ways, for example, and thereby avoid paying tax.

Your objectives

In this chapter you will learn about the following.

(a) Assessable employment income

(b) The difference between employment and self-employment

(c) The basis of assessment (directors and others)

(d) The principal categories of allowable deductions and their scope

(e) The employer's responsibility to collect tax from its employees and how the PAYE system works (including key documents and the net pay scheme)

(f) The information required on the P11D and the P9D

(g) Benefits assessable on all employees and how to compute their value

(h) Benefits assessable only on certain employees and how to compute their value

1 EMPLOYMENT INCOME

1.1 Outline of the charge

Employment income includes income arising from an employment under a contract of service (see below) and the income of office holders, such as directors. The term 'employee' is used in this book to mean anyone who receives employment income (ie both employees and directors).

There are two types of employment income:

- **General earnings**, and
- **Specific employment income.**

General earnings are an employees' earnings (see key term below) plus the 'cash equivalent' of any taxable non-monetary benefits.

Definition

> **'Earnings'** means any salary, wage or fee, any gratuity or other profit or incidental benefit obtained by the employee if it is money or money's worth (something of direct monetary value or convertible into direct monetary value) or anything else which constitutes an emolument of the employment.

'Specific employment income' includes payments on termination of employment and share related income.

The residence and domicile status of an employee determines whether earnings are taxable. If an employee is resident, ordinarily resident and domiciled in the UK, **taxable earnings from an employment in a tax year are the general earnings received in that tax year.**

1.2 When are earnings received?

General earnings consisting of money are treated as received at the earlier of:

- **The time when payment is made**
- **The time when a person becomes entitled to payment of the earnings.**

If the employee is a director of a company, earnings from the company are received on the earliest of:

- The earlier of the two alternatives given in the general rule (above)

- The time when the amount is credited in the company's accounting records

- The end of the company's period of account (if the amount was determined by then)

- The time the amount is determined (if after the end of the company's period of account).

Taxable benefits are generally treated as received when they are provided to the employee.

The receipts basis does not apply to pension income or taxable social security benefits. These sources of income are taxed on the amount accruing in the tax year, whether or not it is received in that year.

Activity 1   **(10 minutes)**

John is a director of X Corp Ltd. His earnings for 2009/10 are:

Salary	£60,000
Taxable benefits	£5,000

For the year ended 31 December 2009 the Board of Directors decide to pay John a bonus of £40,000. This is decided on 1 March 2010 at a board meeting and credited in the company accounts 7 days later.

However John only received the bonus in his April pay on 30 April 2010.

What is John's taxable income from employment for 2009/10?

1.3 Net taxable earnings

Total taxable earnings less total allowable deductions (see below) **are net taxable earnings of a tax year. Deductions cannot usually create a loss: they can only reduce the net taxable earnings to nil.**

1.4 Person liable for tax on employment income

The person liable to tax on employment income is generally the **person to whose employment the earnings relate.** However, if the tax relates to general earnings received after the death of the person to whose employment the earnings relate, the person's personal representatives are liable for the tax. The tax is a liability of the estate.

1.5 Employment and self employment

The distinction between employment (receipts taxable as earnings) and self employment (receipts taxable as trading income) is a fine one. Employment involves a contract of service, whereas self employment involves a contract for services. Taxpayers tend to prefer self employment, because the rules on deductions for expenses are more generous.

Factors which may be of importance include:

- The degree of control exercised over the person doing the work
- Whether he must accept further work
- Whether the other party must provide further work
- Whether he provides his own equipment
- Whether he hires his own helpers
- What degree of financial risk he takes
- What degree of responsibility for investment and management he has
- Whether he can profit from sound management
- Whether he can work when he chooses
- The wording used in any agreement between the parties.

Relevant cases include:

(a) *Edwards v Clinch 1981*

A civil engineer acted occasionally as an inspector on temporary ad hoc appointments.

Held: there was no ongoing office which could be vacated by one person and held by another so the fees received were from self employment not employment.

(b) *Hall v Lorimer 1994*

A vision mixer was engaged under a series of short-term contracts.

Held: the vision mixer was self employed, not because of any one detail of the case but because the overall picture was one of self-employment.

(c) *Carmichael and Anor v National Power plc 1999*

Individuals engaged as visitor guides on a casual 'as required' basis were not employees. An exchange of correspondence between the company and the individuals was not a contract of employment as there was no provision as to the frequency of work and there was flexibility to accept work or turn it down as it arose. Sickness, holiday and pension arrangements did not apply and neither did grievance and disciplinary procedures.

A worker's status also affects national insurance. The self-employed generally pay less than employees.

2 TAXABLE BENEFITS

2.1 Introduction

The Income Tax (Earnings and Pensions) Act 2003 (ITEPA 2003) provides comprehensive legislation covering the taxation of benefits. **The legislation generally applies to all employees. However, only certain parts of it apply to 'excluded employees'**

(a) **An excluded employee is an employee in lower paid employment who is either not a director of a company or is a director but has no material interest in the company** ('material' means control of more than 5% of the ordinary share capital) and either:

(i) **He is full time working director,** or

(ii) **The company is non-profit-making or is established for charitable purposes only.**

(b) **The term 'director' refers to any person who acts as a director or any person in accordance with whose instructions the directors are accustomed to act** (other than a professional advisor).

(c) **Lower paid employment is one where earnings for the tax year are less than £8,500.** To decide whether this applies, add together the **total earnings and benefits that would be taxable if the employee were *not* an excluded employee.**

(d) A number of **specific deductions** must be taken into account to determine lower paid employment. These include **contributions to authorised pension schemes and payroll giving**. However, general deductions from employment income (see later in this chapter) are not taken into account.

(e) Where a car is provided but the employee could have chosen a cash alternative, then the higher of the cash alternative and the car benefit should be used in the computation of earnings to determine whether or not the employee is an excluded employee.

Activity 2   **(10 minutes)**

Tim earns £6,500 per annum working full time as a sales representative at Chap Co Ltd. The company provides the following staff benefits to Tim:

Private health insurance	£300
Company car	£1,500
Expense allowance	£2,000

Tim used £1,900 of the expense allowance on business mileage petrol and on entertaining clients.

Is Tim an excluded employee?

2.2 General business expenses

If business expenses on such items as travel or hotel stays, are reimbursed by an employer, the reimbursed amount is a taxable benefit for employees other than excluded employees. To avoid being taxed on this amount, **an employee must then make a claim to deduct it as an expense** under the rules set out below. **In practice,** however, **many such expense payments are not reported to HMRC and can be ignored because it is agreed in advance that a claim to deduct them would be possible (a P11D dispensation).**

When an individual has to spend one or more nights away from home, his employer may reimburse expenses on items incidental to his absence (for example meals and private telephone calls). **Such incidental expenses are exempt** if:

(a) The expenses of travelling to each place where the individual stays overnight, throughout the trip, are incurred necessarily in the performance of the duties of the employment (or would have been, if there had been any expenses).

(b) The total (for the whole trip) of incidental expenses not deductible under the usual rules is no more than £5 for each night spent wholly in the UK and £10 for each other night. If this limit is exceeded, all of the expenses are taxable, not just the excess. The expenses include any VAT.

This incidental expenses exemption applies to expenses reimbursed, and to benefits obtained using credit tokens and non-cash vouchers.

2.3 Vouchers

If any employee (including an excluded employee):

    (a)   receives cash vouchers (vouchers exchangeable for cash)

    (b)   uses a credit token (such as a credit card) to obtain money, goods or services, or

    (c)   receives exchangeable vouchers (such as book tokens), also called non-cash vouchers

he is taxed on the cost of providing the benefit, less any amount made good.

However, the first 15p per working day of meal vouchers (eg luncheon vouchers) is not taxed. In addition, the first £55 per week of child care vouchers is exempt (see below).

2.4 Accommodation

The taxable value of accommodation provided to an employee (including an excluded employee) is the rent that would have been payable if the premises had been let at an amount equal to their annual value (taken to be their **rateable value**). **If the premises are rented** rather than owned by the employer, then **the taxable benefit is the higher of the rent actually paid and the annual value.** If property does not have a rateable value HMRC estimate a value.

If a property cost the employer more than £75,000, an additional amount is chargeable:

Formula to learn

> (Cost of providing the accommodation − £75,000) × the official rate of interest at the start of the tax year.

Thus with an official rate of 4.75%, the total benefit for accommodation costing £90,000 and with an annual value of £2,000 would be £2,000 + £(90,000 − 75,000) × 4.75% = £2,713.

The 'cost of providing' the living accommodation is the aggregate of the cost of purchase and the cost of any improvements made before the start of the tax year for which the benefit is being computed. It is therefore not possible to avoid the charge by buying an inexpensive property requiring substantial repairs and improving it.

If a property was acquired more than six years before first being provided to the employee, the market value when first provided plus the cost of subsequent improvements is used as the cost of providing the accommodation. However, unless the actual cost plus improvements to the start of the tax year in question exceeds £75,000, the additional charge cannot be imposed, however high the market value. In addition, the additional charge can only be imposed if the employer owns (rather than rents) the property concerned.

There is no taxable benefit in respect of job related accommodation. Accommodation is job related if:

(a) Residence in the accommodation **is necessary for the proper performance of the employee's duties** (as with a caretaker), or

(b) The accommodation is provided **for the better performance of the employee's duties** and the employment is of a kind in which it is **customary for accommodation to be provided** (as with a policeman), or

(c) The **accommodation is provided as part of arrangements in force because of a special threat to the employee's security.**

Directors can only claim exemptions (a) or (b) if:

(i) They have no **material interest** ('material' means over 5%) in the company, and

(ii) Either they are **full time working directors** or the company is **non-profit making or is a charity.**

Any contribution paid by the employee is deducted from the annual value of the property and then from the additional benefit.

If the employee is given a cash alternative to living accommodation, the benefits code still applies in priority to treating the cash alternative as earnings. If the cash alternative is greater than the taxable benefit, the excess is treated as earnings.

2.5 Expenses connected with living accommodation

In addition to the benefit of living accommodation itself, **employees, other than excluded employees, are taxed on related expenses paid by the employer,** such as:

(a) **Heating, lighting or cleaning the premises**
(b) **Repairing, maintaining or decorating the premises**
(c) **The provision of furniture (the annual value is 20% of the cost)**

Unless the accommodation qualifies as 'job related' (as defined above) **the full cost of ancillary services** (excluding structural repairs) **is taxable. If the accommodation is 'job related',** however, **taxable ancillary services are restricted to a maximum of 10% of the employee's 'net earnings'.**

For this purpose, net earnings are all earnings from the employment (excluding the ancillary benefits (a)–(c) above) less any allowable expenses, statutory mileage allowances, contributions to registered occupational pension schemes (but not personal pension plans), and capital allowances.

If there are ancillary benefits other than those falling within (a)–(c) above (such as a telephone) they are taxable in full.

Council tax and water or sewage charges paid by the employer are taxable in full as a benefit unless the accommodation is 'job-related'.

NOTES

Activity 3 (10 minutes)

Mr Quinton has a gross salary in 2009/10 of £28,850. He normally lives and works in London, but he is required to live in a company house in Scotland, which costs £70,000 three years ago, so that he can carry out a two year review of his company's operations in Scotland. The annual value of the house is £650. In 2009/10 the company pays an electricity bill of £550, a gas bill of £400, a gardener's bill of £750 and redecoration costs of £1,800. Mr Quinton makes a monthly contribution of £50 for his accommodation. He also pays £1,450 occupational pension contributions.

Calculate Mr Quinton's taxable employment income for 2009/10.

2.6 Cars

A car provided by reason of the employment to an employee or member of his family or household for private use gives rise to a taxable benefit. This does not apply to excluded employees. **'Private use' includes home to work travel.**

(a) A tax charge arises whether the car is provided by the employer or by some other person. The benefit is computed as shown below, even if the car is taken as an alternative to another benefit of a different value.

(b) The starting point for calculating a car benefit is the list price of the car (plus accessories). **The percentage of the list price that is taxable depends on the car's CO_2 emissions.**

(c) The price of the car is the sum of the following items.

   (i) The list price of the car for a single retail sale at the time of first registration, including charges for delivery and standard accessories. The manufacturer's, importer's or distributor's list price must be used, even if the retailer offered a discount. A notional list price is estimated if no list price was published.

   (ii) The price (including fitting) of all optional accessories provided when the car was first provided to the employee, excluding mobile telephones and equipment needed by a disabled employee. The extra cost of adapting or manufacturing a car to run on road fuel gases is not included.

   (iii) The price (including fitting) of all optional accessories fitted later and costing at least £100 each, excluding mobile telephones and equipment needed by a disabled employee. Such accessories affect the taxable benefit from and including the tax year in which they are fitted. However, accessories which are merely replacing existing accessories and are not superior to the ones replaced are ignored. Replacement accessories which *are* superior are taken into account, but the cost of the old accessory is then deducted.

(d) There is a special rule for classic cars. If the car is at least 15 years old (from the time of first registration) at the end of the tax year, and its market value at the end of the year (or, if earlier, when it ceased to be available to the employee) is over £15,000 and greater than the price found under (c), that market value is used instead of the price. The market value takes account of all accessories (except mobile telephones and equipment needed by a disabled employee).

(e) Capital contributions are payments by the employee in respect of the price of the car or accessories. In any tax year, we take account of capital contributions made in that year and previous years (for the same car). The maximum deductible capital contributions is £5,000; contributions beyond that total are ignored.

(f) If the price or value found under (c) or (d) exceeds £80,000, then £80,000 is used instead of the price or value. This £80,000 is after capital contributions (see (e) above) have been taken into account.

(g) **For cars that emit CO$_2$ of 135g/km (2009/10) or less, the taxable benefit is 15% of the car's list price. This percentage increases by 1% for every 5g/km (rounded down to the nearest multiple of 5) by which CO$_2$ emissions exceed 135g/km up to a maximum of 35%.**

(h) Diesel cars have a supplement of 3% of the car's list price added to the taxable benefit. However, the benefit is discounted for cars that are particularly environmentally friendly. The maximum percentage, however, remains 35% of the list price.

(i) **The benefit is reduced on a time basis where a car is first made available or ceases to be made available during the tax year** or is incapable of being used for a continuous period of not less than 30 days (for example because it is being repaired).

(j) **The benefit is reduced by any payment the user must make for the private use of the car** (as distinct from a capital contribution to the cost of the car). Payments for insuring the car do not count (*IRC v Quigley 1995*). The benefit cannot become negative to create a deduction from the employee's income.

(k) Pool cars are exempt. A car is a pool car if **all** the following conditions are satisfied.

   (i) It is used by more than one employee and is not ordinarily used by any one of them to the exclusion of the others

   (ii) Any private use is merely incidental to business use

   (iii) It is not normally kept overnight at or near the residence of an employee

There are many ancillary benefits associated with the provision of cars, such as insurance, repairs, vehicle licences and a parking space at or near work. No extra taxable benefit arises as a result of these, with the exception of the cost of providing a driver.

2.7 Fuel for cars

Where fuel is provided there is a further benefit in addition to the car benefit.

No taxable benefit arises where either

  (a) **All the fuel provided was made available only for business travel**, or

  (b) **The employee is required to make good, and has made good, the whole of the cost of any fuel provided for his private use.**

Unlike most benefits, a reimbursement of only part of the cost of the fuel available for private use does not reduce the benefit.

The taxable benefit is a percentage of a base figure. The base figure for 2009/10 is £16,900. The percentage is the same percentage as is used to calculate the car benefit (see above).

The fuel benefit is reduced in the same way as the car benefit **if the car is not available for 30 days or more.**

The fuel benefit is also reduced if private fuel is not available for part of a tax year. However, if private fuel later becomes available in the same tax year, the reduction is not made. If, for example, fuel is provided from 6 April 2009 to 30 June 2009, then the fuel benefit for 2009/10 will be restricted to just three months. This is because the provision of fuel has permanently ceased. However, if fuel is provided from 6 April 2009 to 30 June 2009, and then again from 1 September 2009 to 5 April 2010, then the fuel benefit will not be reduced since the cessation was only temporary.

Activity 4	(5 minutes)

An employee was provided with a new car costing £15,000. The car emits 186g/km of CO_2. During 2009/10 the employer spent £900 on insurance, repairs and a vehicle license. The firm paid for all petrol, costing £1,500, without reimbursement. The employee paid the firm £270 for the private use of the car.

Calculate the taxable benefit.

2.8 Vans and heavier commercial vehicles

If a van (of normal maximum laden weight up to 3,500 kg) **is made available for an employee's private use, there is an annual scale charge of £3,000.** The scale charge covers ancillary benefits such as insurance and servicing. Paragraphs 2.6 (i) and (j) above apply to vans as they do to cars.

There is, however, **no taxable benefit where an employee takes a van home** (ie uses the van for home to work travel) but is not allowed any other private use.

If the employer provides **fuel for unrestricted private use**, an additional **fuel charge of £500** applies.

If a commercial vehicle of normal maximum laden weight over 3,500 kg is made available for an employee's private use, but the employee's use of the vehicle is not wholly or mainly private, no taxable benefit arises except in respect of the provision of a driver.

2.9 Statutory mileage allowances

A single authorised mileage allowance for business journeys in an employee's own vehicle applies to all cars and vans. There is no income tax on payments up to this allowance and employers do not have to report mileage allowances up to this amount. The allowance for 2009/10 is 40p per mile on the first 10,000 miles in the tax year with each additional mile over 10,000 miles at 25p per mile. The authorised mileage allowance for employees using their own motor cycle is 24p per mile. For employees using their own pedal cycle it is 20p per mile.

If employers pay less than the statutory allowance, employees can claim tax relief up to that level.

The statutory allowance does not prevent employers from paying higher rates, but any excess will be subject to income tax. There is a similar (but slightly different) system for NICs, covered below.

Employers can make income tax and NIC free payments of up to 5p per mile for each fellow employee making the same business trip who is carried as a passenger. If the employer does not pay the employee for carrying business passengers, the employee cannot claim any tax relief.

EXAMPLE

Sophie uses her own car for business travel. During 2009/10, Sophie drove 15,400 miles in the performance of her duties. Sophie's employer paid her 35p a mile. How is the mileage allowance received by Sophie treated for tax purposes?

	£
Mileage allowance received (15,400 × 35p)	5,390
Less tax free [(10,000 × 40p) + (5,400 × 25p)]	(5,350)
Taxable benefit	40

£5,350 is tax free and the excess amount received of £40 is a taxable benefit.

2.10 Beneficial loans

Introduction

Employment related loans to employees (other than excluded employees) and their relatives give rise to a benefit equal to:

(a) **Any amounts written off** (unless the employee has died), and

(b) **The excess of the interest based on an official rate prescribed by the Treasury, over any interest actually charged ('taxable cheap loan').** Interest payable during the tax year but paid after the end of the tax year is taken into account, but if the benefit is determined before such interest is paid a claim must be made to take it into account.

The following loans are normally not treated as taxable cheap loans for calculation of the interest benefits (but not for the purposes of the charge on loans written off).

(a) A loan on normal commercial terms made in the ordinary course of the employer's money-lending business.

(b) A loan made by an individual in the ordinary course of the lender's domestic, family or personal arrangements.

Calculating the interest benefit

There are two alternative methods of calculating the taxable benefit. The simpler **'average' method** automatically applies unless the taxpayer or HMRC elect for the alternative **'strict' method**. (HMRC normally only make the election where it appears that the 'average' method is being deliberately exploited.) In both methods, the benefit is the interest at the official rate minus the interest payable.

The 'average' method averages the balances at the beginning and end of the tax year (or the dates on which the loan was made and discharged if it was not in existence throughout the tax year) and applies the official rate of interest to this average. If the loan was not in existence throughout the tax year only the number of complete tax months (from the 6th of the month) for which it existed are taken into account.

The 'strict' method is to compute interest at the official rate on the actual amount outstanding on a daily basis.

EXAMPLE

At 6 April 2009 a taxable cheap loan of £30,000 was outstanding to an employee earning £12,000 a year, who repaid £20,000 on 7 December 2009. The remaining balance of £10,000 was outstanding at 5 April 2010. Interest paid during the year was £250. What was the benefit under both methods for 2009/10, assuming that the official rate of interest was 4.75%?

Average method

	£
$4.75\% \times \dfrac{30,000 + 10,000}{2}$	950
Less interest paid	(250)
Benefit	700

Alternative method (strict method)

	£
$£30,000 \times \dfrac{245}{365}$ (6 April - 6 December) × 4.75%	957
$£10,000 \times \dfrac{120}{365}$ (7 December - 5 April) × 4.75%	156
	1,113
Less interest paid	(250)
Benefit	863

HMRC might opt for the alternative method.

The de minimis test

The benefit is not taxable if:

    (a)   The total of all taxable cheap loans to the employee did not exceed £5,000 at any time in the tax year, or

    (b)   The loan is not a qualifying loan and the total of all non-qualifying loans to the employee did not exceed £5,000 at any time in the tax year.

A qualifying loan is one on which all or part of any interest paid would qualify as a charge on income.

When the £5,000 threshold is exceeded, a benefit arises on interest on the whole loan, not just on the excess of the loan over £5,000.

When a loan is written off and a benefit arises, there is no £5,000 threshold: writing off a loan of £1 gives rise to a £1 benefit.

Qualifying loans

If the whole of the interest payable on a qualifying loan is eligible for tax relief as deductible interest, then no taxable benefit arises. If the interest is only partly eligible for tax relief, then the employee is treated as receiving earnings because the actual rate of interest is below the official rate. He is also treated as paying interest equal to those earnings. This **deemed interest paid may qualify as a business expense or as deductible interest in addition to any interest actually paid.**

Activity 5   **(10 minutes)**

Anna, who is single, has an annual salary of £30,000, and two loans from her employer.

(a)   A season ticket loan of £2,300 at no interest

(b)   A loan, 90% of which was used to buy shares in her employee-controlled company, of £54,000 at 1.5% interest

The official rate of interest is to be taken at 4.75%.

What is Anna's tax liability for 2009/10?

2.11   Other assets made available for private use

When assets are made available to employees or members of their family or household, the taxable benefit is the higher of 20% of the market value when first provided as a benefit to any employee, or on the rent paid by the employer if higher. The 20% charge is time-apportioned when the asset is provided for only part of the year. The charge after any time apportionment is reduced by any contribution made by the employee.

Certain assets, such as bicycles provided for journeys to work, are exempt. These are described later in this chapter.

If an asset made available is subsequently acquired by the employee, **the taxable benefit on the acquisition is the** *greater* **of:**

- The **current market value minus the price paid by the employee.**

- The **market value when first provided minus any amounts already taxed (ignoring contributions by the employee) minus the price paid by the employee.**

This rule prevents tax free benefits arising on rapidly depreciating items through the employee purchasing them at their low second-hand value.

There is an exception to this rule for bicycles which have previously been provided as exempt benefits. The taxable benefit on acquisition is restricted to current market value, minus the price paid by the employee.

EXAMPLE

A suit costing £400 is purchased by an employer for use by an employee on 6 April 2008. On 6 April 2009 the suit is purchased by the employee for £30, its market value then being £50.

		£
The benefit in 2008/09 is £400 × 20%		**£80**

The benefit in 2009/10 is £290, being the **greater** of:

		£
(a)	Market value at acquisition by employee	50
	Less price paid	(30)
		20
(b)	Original market value	400
	Less taxed in respect of use	(80)
		320
	Less price paid	(30)
		290

EXAMPLE

Rupert is provided with a new bicycle by his employer on 6 April 2009. The bicycle is available for private use as well as commuting to work. It cost the employer £1,500 when new. On 6 October 2009 the employer transfers ownership of the bicycle to Rupert when it is worth £800. Rupert does not pay anything for the bicycle.

What is the total taxable benefit on Rupert for 2009/10 in respect of the bicycle?

Use benefit	Exempt
Transfer benefit (use MV at acquisition by employee only)	
MV at transfer	£800

2.12 Scholarships

If scholarships are given to members of an employee's family, the **employee is taxable on the cost** unless the scholarship fund's or scheme's payments by reason of people's employments are not more than 25% of its total payments.

2.13 Residual charge

We have seen above how certain specific benefits are taxed. **A 'residual charge' is made on the taxable value of other benefits. In general, the taxable value of a benefit is the cost of the benefit less any part of that cost made good by the employee to the persons providing the benefit.**

The residual charge applies to any benefit provided for an employee or a member of his family or household, by reason of the employment. There is an exception where the employer is an individual and the provision of the benefit is made in the normal course of the employer's domestic, family or personal relationships.

This rule does not apply to taxable benefits provided to excluded employees. **These employees are taxed only on the second hand value of any benefit that could be converted into money.**

3 EXEMPT BENEFITS

Various benefits are exempt from tax. These include:

(a) **Entertainment provided to employees by genuine third parties** (eg seats at sporting/cultural events), even if it is provided by giving the employee a voucher.

(b) **Gifts of goods** (or vouchers exchangeable for goods) from third parties (ie not provided by the employer or a person connected to the employer) if the total cost (incl. VAT) of all gifts by the same donor to the same employee in the tax year is £250 or less. If the £250 limit is exceeded, the full amount is taxable, not just the excess.

(c) **Non-cash awards for long service** if the period of service was at least 20 years, no similar award was made to the employee in the past 10 years and the cost is not more than £50 per year of service.

(d) **Awards under staff suggestion schemes if:**

    (i)   There is a formal scheme, open to all employees on equal terms.

    (ii)   The suggestion is outside the scope of the employee's normal duties.

    (iii)   Either the award is not more than £25, or the award is only made after a decision is taken to implement the suggestion.

    (iv)   Awards over £25 reflect the financial importance of the suggestion to the business, and either do not exceed 50% of the expected net financial benefit during the first year of implementation or do not exceed 10% of the expected net financial benefit over a period of up to five years.

    (v)   Awards of over £25 are shared on a reasonable basis between two or more employees putting forward the same suggestion.

If an award exceeds £5,000, the excess is always taxable.

(e) **The first £8,000 of removal expenses if:**

    (i) The employee does not already live within a reasonable daily travelling distance of his new place of employment, but will do so after moving.

    (ii) The expenses are incurred or the benefits provided by the end of the tax year following the tax year of the start of employment at the new location.

(f) The cost of running a **workplace nursery or play scheme (without limit).** **Otherwise up to £55 a week of childcare is tax free** if the employer contracts with an approved childcare or provides childcare vouchers to pay an approved childcare. The childcare must be available to all employees and the childcare must either be registered or approved home-childcare.

(g) **Sporting or recreational facilities available to employees generally and not to the general public,** unless they are provided on domestic premises, or they consist in an interest in or the use of any mechanically propelled vehicle or any overnight accommodation. Vouchers only exchangeable for such facilities are also exempt, but membership fees for sports clubs are taxable.

(h) **Assets or services used in performing the duties of employment** provided any private use of the item concerned is insignificant. This exempts, for example, the benefit arising on the private use of employer-provided tools.

(i) **Welfare counselling** and similar minor benefits if the benefit concerned is available to employees generally.

(j) **Bicycles or cycling safety equipment provided to enable employees to get to and from work or to travel between one workplace and another.** The equipment must be available to the employer's employees generally. Also, it must be used mainly for the aforementioned journeys.

(k) **Workplace parking**

(l) **Up to £15,000 a year paid to an employee who is on a full-time course lasting at least a year,** with average full-time attendance of at least 20 weeks a year. If the £15,000 limit is exceeded, the whole amount is taxable.

(m) **Work related training and related costs. This includes the costs of** training material and assets either made during training or incorporated into something so made.

(n) **Air miles or car fuel coupons** obtained as a result of business expenditure but used for private purposes.

(o) **The cost of work buses and minibuses or subsidies to public bus services.**

A work bus must have a seating capacity of 12 or more and a works minibus a seating capacity of 9 or more but not more than 12 and be available generally to employees of the employer concerned. The bus or minibus must mainly be used by employees for journeys to and from work and for journeys between workplaces.

(p) Transport/overnight costs where public transport is disrupted by industrial action, late night taxis and travel costs incurred where car sharing arrangements unavoidably breakdown.

(q) The private use of one **mobile phone**. Top up vouchers for exempt mobile phones are also tax free. If more than one mobile phone is provided to an employee for private use only the second or subsequent phone is a taxable benefit valued using 'cost of provision to the employer'.

(r) **Employer provided uniforms** which employees must wear as part of their duties.

(s) The cost of **staff parties** which are open to staff generally provided that the **cost per staff member per year (including VAT) is £150 or less**. The £150 limit may be split between several parties. If exceeded, the full amount is taxable, not just the excess over £150.

(t) **Private medical insurance premiums paid to cover treatment when the employee is outside the UK in the performance of his duties**. Other medical insurance premiums are taxable as is the cost of medical diagnosis and treatment except for routine check ups. Eye tests and glasses for employees using VDUs are exempt.

(u) **The first 15p per day of meal vouchers (eg luncheon vouchers)**.

(v) Cheap loans **that do not exceed £5,000** at any time in the tax year (see above).

(w) **Job related accommodation** (see above).

(x) **Employer contributions towards additional household costs incurred by an employee who works wholly or partly at home**. Payments up to £3 pw (£156 pa) may be made without supporting evidence. Payments in excess of that amount require supporting evidence that the payment is wholly in respect of additional household expenses.

(y) **Meals or refreshments for cyclists** provided as part of official 'cycle to work' days.

(z) **Personal incidental expenses**.

Where a voucher is provided for a benefit which is exempt from income tax the provision of the voucher itself is also exempt.

4 ALLOWABLE DEDUCTIONS

4.1 General principles

Certain expenditure is specifically deductible in computing net taxable earnings:

(a) **Contributions** (within certain limits) **to registered occupational pension schemes** (see earlier in this Course Book).

(b) **Subscriptions to professional bodies** on the list of bodies issued by HMRC (which includes most UK professional bodies), if relevant to the duties of the employment

(c) Payments for certain **liabilities relating to the employment** and for insurance against them (see below)

(d) **Payments to charity made under the payroll deduction scheme** operated by an employer

(e) **Mileage allowance** relief (see above)

Otherwise, **allowable deductions are notoriously hard to obtain. They are limited to:**

- **Qualifying travel expenses** (see below)

- **Other expenses the employee is obliged to incur and pay as holder of the employment which are incurred wholly, exclusively and necessarily in the performance of the duties of the employment**

- **Capital allowances on plant and machinery (other than cars or other vehicles) necessarily provided for use in the performance of those duties.**

4.2 Liabilities and insurance

If a director or employee incurs a liability related to his employment or pays for insurance against such a liability, the cost is a deductible expense. If the employer pays such amounts, there is no taxable benefit.

A liability relating to employment is one which is imposed in respect of the employee's acts or omissions as employee. Thus, for example, liability for negligence would be covered. Related costs, for example the costs of legal proceedings, are included.

For insurance premiums to qualify, the insurance policy must:

(a) Cover only liabilities relating to employment, vicarious liability in respect of liabilities of another person's employment, related costs and payments to the employee's own employees in respect of their employment liabilities relating to employment and related costs.

(b) It must not last for more than two years (although it may be renewed for up to two years at a time), and the insured person must not be not required to renew it.

4.3 Travel expenses

Tax relief is not available for an employee's normal commuting costs. This means relief is not available for any costs an employee incurs in getting from home to his normal place of work. However **employees are entitled to relief for travel expenses which basically are the full costs that they are obliged to incur and pay as holder of the employment in travelling in the performance of their duties or travelling to or from a place which they have to attend in the performance of their duties (other than a permanent workplace).**

4.4 Example: travel in the performance of duties

Judi is an accountant. She often travels to meetings at the firm's offices in the North of England returning to her office in Leeds after the meetings. Relief is available for the full cost of these journeys as the travel is undertaken in the performance of her duties.

Activity 6   **(10 minutes)**

Zoe lives in Wycombe and normally works in Chiswick. Occasionally she visits a client in Wimbledon and travels direct from home. Distances are shown in the diagram below:

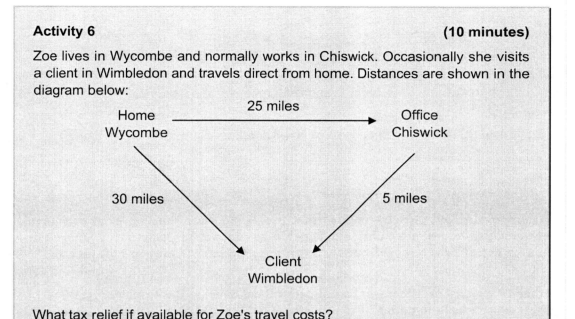

What tax relief if available for Zoe's travel costs?

To prevent manipulation of the basic rule normal commuting will not become a business journey just because the employee stops en-route to perform a business task (eg make a 'phone call'). Nor will relief be available if the journey is essentially the same as the employee's normal journey to work.

4.5   Example: normal commuting

Judi is based at her office in Leeds City Centre. One day she is required to attend a 9.00 am meeting with a client whose premises are around the corner from her Leeds office. Judi travels from home directly to the meeting. As the journey is substantially the same as her ordinary journey to work relief is not available.

Site based employees (eg construction workers, management consultants etc) **who do not have a permanent workplace, are entitled to relief for the costs of all journeys made from home to wherever they are working**. This is because these employees do not have an ordinary commuting journey or any normal commuting costs.

If an employee is seconded to work at another location for some considerable time, then the question arises as to whether the journey from home to that workplace can become normal commuting. There is a 24 month rule.

Tax relief is available for travel, accommodation and subsistence expenses incurred by an employee who is working at a temporary workplace on a secondment expected to last up to 24 months. If a secondment is initially expected not to exceed 24 months, but it is extended, relief ceases to be due from the date the employee becomes aware of the change.

When looking at how long a secondment is expected to last, HMRC will consider not only the terms of the written contract but also any verbal agreement by the employer and other factors such as whether the employee buys a house etc.

NOTES

Activity 7 (10 minutes)

Philip works for Vastbank at its Newcastle City Centre branch. Philip is sent to work full-time at another branch in Morpeth for 20 months at the end of which he will return to the Newcastle branch. Morpeth is about 20 miles north of Newcastle.

What travel costs is Philip entitled to claim as a deduction?

4.6 Other expenses

The word 'exclusively' strictly implies that the expenditure must give no private benefit at all. If it does, none of it is deductible. In practice inspectors may ignore a small element of private benefit or make an apportionment between business and private use.

Whether an expense is 'necessary' is not determined by what the employer requires. The test is whether the duties of the employment could not be performed without the outlay.

- *Sanderson v Durbridge 1955*

  The cost of evening meals taken when attending late meetings was not deductible because it was not incurred in the performance of the duties.

- *Blackwell v Mills 1945*

  As a condition of his employment, an employee was required to attend evening classes. The cost of his textbooks and travel was not deductible because it was not incurred in the performance of the duties.

- *Lupton v Potts 1969*

  Examination fees incurred by a solicitor's articled clerk were not deductible because they were incurred neither wholly nor exclusively in the performance of the duties, but in furthering the clerk's ambition to become a solicitor.

- *Brown v Bullock 1961*

  The expense of joining a club that was virtually a requisite of an employment was not deductible because it would have been possible to carry on the employment without the club membership, so the expense was not necessary.

- *Elwood v Utitz 1965*

  A managing director's subscriptions to two residential London clubs were claimed by him as an expense on the grounds that they were cheaper than hotels.

  The expenditure was deductible as it was necessary in that it would be impossible for the employee to carry out his London duties without being provided with first class accommodation. The residential facilities (which were cheaper than hotel accommodation) were given to club members only.

- *Lucas v Cattell 1972*

  The cost of business telephone calls on a private telephone is deductible, but no part of the line or telephone rental charges is deductible.

LEARNING MEDIA

- *Fitzpatrick v IRC 1994; Smith v Abbott 1994*

  Journalists cannot claim a deduction for the cost of buying newspapers which they read to keep themselves informed, since they are merely preparing themselves to perform their duties.

The cost of clothes for work is not deductible, except that for certain trades requiring protective clothing there are annual deductions on a set scale.

An employee required to work at home may be able to claim a deduction for an appropriate proportion of his or her expenditure on lighting and heating. Employers can pay up to £3 per week without the need for supporting evidence of the costs incurred by the employee (see above). Payments above the £3 limit require evidence of the employee's actual costs.

5 PERSONAL SERVICE COMPANIES

5.1 Application and outline of computation

We looked at the distinction between employment and self employment earlier in this chapter. Taxpayers normally prefer to avoid being classified as employees. Consequently, there are anti-avoidance rules which prevent workers avoiding tax and National Insurance contributions by offering their services through an intermediary, such as a personal service company. **These provisions are commonly known as the IR35 provisions**.

Broadly, the IR35 provisions provide that

(a) if an individual ('the worker') performs, or has an obligation to perform, services for 'a client', and

(b) the performance of those services is referable to arrangements involving a third party (eg the personal service company), rather than referable to a contract between the client and the worker, and

(c) if the services were to be performed by the worker under a contract between himself and the client, he would be regarded as employed by the client

then **a salary payment may be deemed to have been made to the worker at the end of the tax year**. This deemed payment is subject to PAYE and NICs.

The following steps should be followed to compute the amount of the deemed payment.

Step 1 Take 95% of all payments and benefits received in respect of the relevant engagements by the third party.

Step 2 **Add amounts received in respect of the relevant engagements by the worker otherwise than from the third party**, if they are not chargeable as employment income, but would have been so chargeable if the worker had been employed by the client.

Step 3 **Deduct expenses met by the third party** if those expenses would have been deductible had they been paid out of the taxable earnings of the employment by the worker. This also includes expenses paid by the worker and reimbursed by the third party. Mileage allowances up to the statutory amounts are also deductible where a vehicle is provided by the third party.

Step 4 **Deduct capital allowances on expenditure incurred by the third party** if the worker would have been able to deduct them had he incurred the expenditure and had he been employed by the client.

Step 5 **Deduct any 'registered' pension contributions and employer's NICs paid by the third party** in respect of the worker.

Step 6 **Deduct amounts received by the worker from the third party** that are chargeable as employment income but were not deducted under Step 3.

Step 7 Find the amount that together with employer's NIC (see below) on it, is equal to the amount resulting from Step 6 above. This means that you should multiply the amount in Step 6 by $12.8/112.8$ and deduct this amount from the amount in Step 6.

Step 8 The result is the amount of the deemed employment income.

5.2 Effect on company

The deemed employment income is an allowable trading expense for the personal service company and is treated as made on the last day of the tax year.

The personal service company should consider having an accounting date of 5 April, or shortly thereafter.

For example, if accounts are prepared to 5 April the deemed employment income for 2009/10 is deductible in the company in the year to 5 April 2010, whereas with a 31 March year end the deemed payment would be deductible in the year to 31 March 2011.

EXAMPLE

Alison offers technical writing services through a company. During 2009/10 the company received income of £40,000 in respect of relevant engagements performed by Alison. The company paid Alison a salary of £20,000 plus employer's NIC of £1,828. The company also pays £3,000 into an occupational pension scheme in respect of Alison. Alison incurred travelling expenses of £400 in respect of the relevant engagements.

The deemed employment income taxed on Alison is

	£
Income (£40,000 × 95%)	38,000
Less: travel	(400)
pension	(3,000)
salary	(20,000)
employer's NIC on actual salary	(1,828)
	12,772
Less: employer's NIC on deemed payment	
$\frac{12.8}{112.8} \times £12,772$	(1,449)
Deemed employment income	11,323

6 THE PAYE SYSTEM

6.1 Introduction

Cash payments

The objective of the PAYE system is to deduct the correct amount of tax over the year. Its scope is very wide. It applies to most cash payments, other than reimbursed business expenses, and to certain non cash payments.

In addition to wages and salaries, PAYE applies to round sum expense allowances and payments instead of benefits. It also applies to any readily convertible asset.

A readily convertible asset is any asset which can effectively be exchanged for cash. The amount subject to PAYE is the amount that would be taxed as employment income. This is usually the cost to the employer of providing the asset.

Tips paid direct to an employee are normally outside the PAYE system (although still assessable as employment income). An exception may apply in the catering trades where tips are often pooled. Here the PAYE position depends on whether a 'tronc', administered other than by the employer, exists.

It is the employer's duty to deduct income tax from the pay of his employees, whether or not he has been directed to do so by HMRC. **If he fails to do this he** (or sometimes the employee) **must pay over the tax which he should have deducted and the employer may be subject to penalties.** Interest will also run from 14 days after the end of the tax year concerned on any underpaid PAYE. Officers of HMRC can inspect employer's records in order to satisfy themselves that the correct amounts of tax are being deducted and paid over to HMRC.

Benefits

PAYE is not normally operated on benefits; instead the employee's PAYE code is restricted (see below).

However, PAYE must be applied to remuneration in the form of a taxable non-cash voucher if at the time it is provided:

(a) the voucher is capable of being exchanged for readily convertible assets; or

(b) the voucher can itself be sold, realised or traded.

PAYE must normally be operated on cash vouchers and on each occasion when a director/employee uses a credit-token (eg a credit card) to obtain money or goods which are readily convertible assets. However, a cash voucher or credit token which is used to defray expenses is not subject to PAYE.

6.2 How PAYE works

Operation of PAYE

To operate PAYE the employer needs:

(a) deductions working sheets

(b) codes for employees that reflect the tax allowances to which the employees are entitled

(c) tax tables.

The employer works out the amount of PAYE tax to deduct on any particular pay day by using the employee's code number (see below) in conjunction with the PAYE tables. The tables are designed so that tax is normally worked out on a cumulative basis. This means that with each payment of earnings the running total of tax paid is compared with tax due on total earnings to that date. The difference between the tax due and the tax paid is the tax to be deducted on that particular payday.

National insurance tables are used to work out the national insurance due on any payday.

Records

The employer must keep records of each employee's pay and tax at each pay day. The records must also contain details of National Insurance. The employer has a choice of three ways of recording and returning these figures:

(a) he may use the official deductions working sheet (P11)

(b) he may incorporate the figures in his own pay records using a substitute document

(c) he may retain the figures on a computer.

These records will be used to make a return at the end of the tax year.

6.3 Payment under the PAYE system

Under PAYE income tax and national insurance is normally paid over to HMRC monthly, 14 days after the end of each tax month.

If an employer's average monthly payments under the PAYE system are less than £1,500, the employer may choose to pay quarterly, within 14 days of the end of each tax quarter. Tax quarters end on 5 July, 5 October, 5 January and 5 April. Payments can continue to be made quarterly during a tax year even if the monthly average reaches or exceeds £1,500, but a new estimate must be made and a new decision taken to pay quarterly at the start of each tax year. Average monthly payments are the average net monthly payments due to HMRC for income tax and NICs.

6.4 PAYE codes

An employee is normally entitled to various allowances. Under the PAYE system an amount reflecting the effect of a proportion of these allowances is set against his pay each pay day. To determine the amount to set against his pay the allowances are expressed in the form of a code which is used in conjunction with the Pay Adjustment Table (Table A).

An employee's code may be any one of the following:

L   tax code with basic personal allowance
P   tax code with age 65–74 age allowance
Y   tax code with age 75+ age allowance

The codes BR, DO and OT are generally used where there is a second source of income and all allowances have been used in a tax code which is applied to the main source of income.

Generally, a tax code number is arrived at by deleting the last digit in the sum representing the employee's tax free allowances. Every individual is entitled to a personal tax free allowance of £6,475. The code number for an individual who is entitled to this but no other allowance is 647L.

The code number may also reflect other items. For example, **it will be restricted to reflect benefits, small amounts of untaxed income** and **unpaid tax on income from earlier years**. If an amount of tax is in point, it is necessary to gross up the tax in the code using the taxpayer's estimated marginal rate of income tax.

EXAMPLE

Adrian is a 40 year old single man (suffix letter L) who earns £15,000 pa. He has benefits of £560 and his unpaid tax for 2007/08 was £58. Adrian is entitled to a tax free personal allowance of £6,475 in 2009/10.

Adrian is a basic rate taxpayer.

What is Adrian's PAYE code for 2009/10?

	£
Personal allowance	6,475
Benefits	(560)
Unpaid tax £58 × 100/20	(290)
Available allowances	5,625

Adrian's PAYE code is 562L

Codes are determined and amended by HMRC. They are normally notified to the employer on a code list. The employer must act on the code notified to him until amended instructions are received from HMRC, even if the employee has appealed against the code.

By using the code number in conjunction with the tax tables, an employee is generally given 1/52nd or 1/12th of his tax free allowances against each week's/month's pay. However because of the cumulative nature of PAYE, if an employee is first paid in, say, September, that month he will receive six months' allowances against his gross pay. In cases where the employee's previous PAYE history is not known, this could lead to under-deduction of tax. To avoid this, codes for the employees concerned have to be operated on a 'week 1/month1' basis, so that only 1/52nd or 1/12th of the employee's allowances are available each week/month.

6.5 PAYE forms

At the end of each tax year, the employer must provide each employee with a form P60. This shows total taxable earnings for the year, tax deducted, code number, NI number and the employer's name and address. **The P60 must be provided by 31 May following the year of assessment.**

Following the end of each tax year, the employer must send HMRC:

(a) **by 19 May:**

    (i)   **End of year Returns P14** (showing the same details as the P60)

    (ii)   **Form P35** (summary of total tax and NI deducted from all employees)

(b) **by 6 July:**

    (i)   **Forms P11D** (benefits etc for directors and employees paid £8,500+ pa)

    (ii)   **Forms P11D(b)** (return of Class 1A NICs (see later in this Course Book))

    (iii)   **Forms P9D** (benefits etc for other employees)

A copy of the form P11D (or P9D) must also be provided to the employee by 6 July. The details shown on the P11D include the full cash equivalent of all benefits, so that the employee may enter the details on his self-assessment tax return. Specific reference numbers for the entries on the P11D are given to assist with the preparation of the employee's self assessment tax return.

When an employee leaves, a form P45 (particulars of Employee Leaving) must be prepared. This form shows the employee's code and details of his income and tax paid to date and is a four part form. One part is sent to HMRC, and three parts handed to the employee. One of the parts (part 1A) is the employee's personal copy.

If the employee takes up a new employment, he must hand the other two parts of the form P45 to the new employer. The new employer will fill in details of the new employment and send one part to HMRC, retaining the other. The details on the form are used by the new employer to calculate the PAYE due on the next payday. If the employee dies a P45 should be completed, and the whole form sent to HMRC.

If an employee joins with a form P45, the new employer can operate PAYE. If there is no P45 the employer still needs to operate PAYE. **The employee is required to complete a form P46.**

If he declares that the employment is his first job since the start of the tax year and he has not received a taxable state benefit, or that it is now his only job but he previously had another job or received a taxable state benefit, the emergency code

(647L for 2009/10) applies, on a cumulative basis or week 1/month 1 basis respectively. If the employee declares that he has another job or receives a pension the employer must use code BR.

The P46 is sent to HMRC, unless the pay is below the PAYE and NIC thresholds, and the emergency code applies. In this case no PAYE is deductible until the pay exceeds the threshold.

6.6 Penalties

A form P35 is due on 19 May after the end **of the tax year.** In practice, a 7 day extension to the due date of 19 May is allowed.

Where a form P35 is late, a penalty of £100 per month per 50 employees may be imposed. This penalty cannot be mitigated. **This penalty ceases 12 months after the due date and a further penalty of up to 100% of the tax (and NIC) for the year which remains unpaid** at 19 April may be imposed. This penalty can be mitigated. HMRC automatically reduce the penalty by concession to the greater of £100 and the total PAYE/NIC which should be reported on the return.

Where a person has fraudulently or negligently submitted an incorrect form P35 the penalty is 100% of the tax (and NIC) attributable to the error. This penalty can be mitigated.

6.7 PAYE settlement agreements

PAYE settlement agreements (PSAs) are arrangements under which employers can make single payments to settle their employees' income tax liabilities on expense payments and benefits which are minor, irregular or where it would be impractical to operate PAYE.

6 P11D DISPENSATIONS

As we have seen expense payments to P11D employees should be reported to HMRC. They form part of the employee's employment income and a claim must be made to deduct the expenses in computing net employment income.

To avoid this cumbersome procedure **the employer and HMRC can agree for a dispensation to apply to avoid the need to report expenses covered by the dispensation, and the employee then need not make a formal claim for a deduction.**

Dispensations can only apply to genuine business expenses. Some employers only reimburse business expenses, so that a dispensation may be agreed to cover all payments. Other employers may agree to cover a particular category of expenses, such as travel expenses.

A dispensation cannot be given for mileage allowances paid to employees using their own cars for business journeys as these payments are governed by a statutory exemption.

NOTES

Chapter roundup

- Most employees are taxed on benefits under the benefits code. 'Excluded employees' (lower paid/non-directors) are only subject to part of the provisions of the code.

- The benefit in respect of accommodation is its annual value. There is an additional benefit if the property cost over £75,000.

- Employees who have a company car are taxed on a % of the car's list price which depends on the level of the car's CO_2 emissions. The same % multiplied by £16,900 determines the benefit where private fuel is also provided.

- Cheap loans are charged to tax on the difference between the official rate of interest and any interest paid by the employee.

- 20% of the value of assets made available for private use is taxable.

- There is a residual charge for other benefits, usually equal to the cost to the employer of the benefits.

- There are a number of exempt benefits including removal expenses, childcare, meal vouchers and workplace parking.

- Most tax in respect of employment income is deducted under the PAYE system. The objective of the PAYE system is to collect the correct amount of tax over the year. An employee's PAYE code is designed to ensure that allowances etc are given evenly over the year.

- Employers must complete forms P60, P14, P35, P9D, P11D and P45 as appropriate. A P45 is needed when an employee leaves. Forms P9D and P11D record details of benefits. Forms P60, P14 and P35 are year end returns.

Quick quiz

1 What is employment income?

2 What are the conditions for expenses other than travel expenses to be deductible?

3 Give an example of a PAYE code.

4 What accommodation does not give rise to a taxable benefit?

5 How are assets made available for private use (other than vehicles, accommodation and computers) taxed?

Answers to Quick quiz

1 Employment income is income and taxable benefits arising from an employment under a contract of service.

2 To be incurred wholly, exclusively and necessarily in the performance of duties.

3 461L for example.

4 Job-related accommodation.

5 20% × Market value when first provided.

Answers to Activities

1

Salary	£60,000
Taxable benefits	5,000
Bonus (1.3.10)	40,000
Taxable employment Income	105,000

The salary and benefits were paid/made available during 2009/10 and hence taxed in 2009/10. The bonus was paid/made available on 30 April 2010 (2010/11) *but* was determined after the company's year end (31.12.09) by the board meeting on 1 March 2010 (2009/10) – hence taxed in 2009/10.

2 No. Although Tim's taxable income is less than £8,500 this is only after his expense claim. The figure to consider and compare to £8,500 is the £10,300 as shown below.

	£
Salary	6,500
Benefits: health insurance	300
car	1,500
expense allowance	2,000
Earnings to consider if Tim is lower paid	10,300
Less: claim for expenses paid out	(1,900)
Taxable income	8,400

BPP
LEARNING MEDIA

3

	£	£
Salary		28,850
Less occupational pension scheme contributions		(1,450)
Net earnings		27,400
Accommodation benefits		
Annual value: exempt (job related)		
Ancillary services		
Electricity	550	
Gas	400	
Gardener	750	
Redecorations	1,800	
	3,500	
Restricted to 10% of £27,400	2,740	
Less employee's contribution	(600)	
		2,140
Employment income		29,540

4   Round CO_2 emissions figure down to the nearest 5, ie 185 g/km.

Amount by which CO_2 emissions exceed the baseline:

(185 – 135) = 50 g/km

Divide by 5 = 10

Taxable percentage = 15% + 10% = 25%

	£
Car benefit £15,000 × 25%	3,750
Fuel benefit £16,900 × 25%	4,225
	7,975
Less contribution towards use of car	(270)
	7,705

If the contribution of £270 had been towards the petrol the benefit would have been £7,975.

5

	£
Salary	30,000
Season ticket loan not over £5,000	0
Loan to buy shares £54,000 × (4.75 – 1.5 = 3.25%)	1,755
Earnings	31,755
Less deductible interest paid (£54,000 × 4.75% × 90%)	(2,308)
	29,447
Less personal allowance	(6,475)
Taxable income	22,972

Income tax
Tax liability £22,972 × 20%	4,594

6   Zoe is not entitled to tax relief for the costs incurred in travelling between Wycombe and Chiswick since these are normal commuting costs. However, relief is available for all costs that Zoe incurs when she travels from Wycombe to Wimbledon to visit her client.

7   Although Philip is spending all of his time at the Morpeth branch it will not be treated as his normal work place because his period of attendance will be less than 24 months. Thus Philip can claim relief in full for the costs of travel from his home to the Morpeth branch.

NOTES

Chapter 11

INCOME FROM INVESTMENTS AND PROPERTY

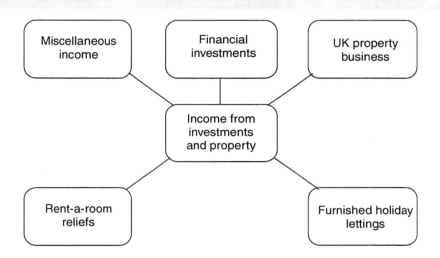

Introduction

The main sources of income from investments are savings. The main source of income from property is rental income which is taxable as property income. 'Property' is usually taken to mean houses or flats, but property income also encompasses rent a room relief, when tax is not payable on a small amount of rent received from letting out a single room.

Your objectives

In this chapter you will learn about the following.

(a)   Investments taxed at source

(b)   Tax free investments

(c)   Miscellaneous income

(d)   Income assessable from a UK Property Business and the basis of assessment (including losses)

(e)   Deductions obtainable for capital allowances, wear and tear, repairs and renewals

(f)   The effect of private use on the deductibility of expenses

(g)   The way the rules are adapted for furnished holiday lettings

(h)   Rent-a-room relief

1 MISCELLANEOUS INCOME

Definition

> **Miscellaneous Income** deals with any income not falling into any other category.

Examples are income or profits from:

- the sale of patents and know how
- income from royalties and other intellectual property
- any other income which is not taxed under any provision

The income arising in a tax year is taxed in that year.

2 OTHER FINANCIAL INVESTMENTS

2.1 Savings income

What is savings income?

Savings income is interest. Interest is paid on bank and building society accounts, on Government securities, such as Treasury Stock, and on company debentures and loan stock.

Interest may be paid net of 20% tax or it may be paid gross.

Savings income received net of 20% tax

The following savings income is received net of 20% tax. **This is called income taxed at source.**

(a) Bank and building society interest paid to individuals (but not National Savings & Investments bank account interest)

(b) Interest paid to individuals by unlisted UK companies on debentures and loan stocks

The amount received is grossed up by multiplying by 100/80 and is included gross in the income tax computation. The tax deducted at source is deducted in computing tax payable and may be repaid.

In examinations you may be given either the net or the gross amount of such income: read the question carefully. If you are given the net amount (the amount received or credited), you should gross up the figure at the rate of 20%. For example, net building society interest of £160 is equivalent to gross income of £160 × 100/80 = £200 on which tax of £40 (20% of £200) has been suffered.

Savings income received gross

Some savings income is received gross, ie without tax having been deducted. Examples are:

(a) National Savings & Investments bank account Interest

(b) Interest on government securities (these are also called 'gilts')

(c) Interest from quoted company debentures and loan stock.

2.2 Dividend income

Dividends on UK shares are received net of a 10% tax credit. This means a dividend of £90 has a £10 tax credit, giving gross income of £100 to include in the income tax computation. The tax credit can be deducted in computing tax payable but it cannot be repaid.

This treatment applies to dividends received from open ended investment companies (OEICs) and to dividend distributions from unit trusts.

2.3 Tax exempt income

Types of tax exempt investments

Income from certain investments is exempt from income tax.

Individual savings accounts

An individual savings account (ISA) is a special tax exempt way of saving. In 2009/10 an individual aged 50 or under can invest £7,200 in ISAs, of which up to £3,600 can be held as cash. Individuals who are aged 50 or over in 2009/10 can invest £10,200 in ISAs, of which up to £5,100 can be held as cash.

Funds invested in ISAs can be used to buy stock market investments, such as shares in quoted companies or OEICs, units in unit trusts, fixed interest investments, or insurance policies.

Dividend income and interest received from ISAs is exempt from income tax, whether it is paid out to the investor or retained and reinvested within the ISA.

Savings certificates

Savings certificates are issued by National Savings and Investments (NS&I). They may be fixed rate certificates or index linked, and are for fixed terms of between two and five years. On maturity the profit is tax exempt. This profit is often called interest.

Premium bonds

Prizes received from premium bonds are exempt from tax.

Activity 1 (10 minutes)

A single taxpayer's only income in 2009/10 is bank deposit interest of £9,600 net. What tax repayment is due?

---

3 UK PROPERTY BUSINESS

3.1 Profits of a UK property business

Income from land and buildings in the UK, including caravans and houseboats which are not moved, is taxed as non-savings income.

(a) **A taxpayer with UK rental income is treated as running a business, his 'UK property business'. All the rents and expenses for all properties are pooled, to give a single profit or loss.** Profits and losses are computed in the same way as trading profits are computed for tax purposes, on an **accruals basis.**

Expenses will often include rent payable where a landlord is himself renting the land which he in turn lets to others. For individuals, interest on loans to buy or improve properties is treated as an expense (on an accruals basis).

Relief is available for irrecoverable rent as an impaired debt.

(b) **Capital allowances are given on plant and machinery used in the UK property business and on industrial buildings, in the same way as they are given for a trading business** with an accounting date of 5 April. Capital allowances are not normally available on plant or machinery used in a dwelling. As someone who lets property furnished cannot claim capital allowances on the furniture he can choose instead between the **renewals basis** and the **10% wear and tear allowance.**

(i) Under the **renewals** basis, there is no deduction for the cost of the first furniture provided, but the cost of replacement furniture is treated as a revenue expense. However, the part of the cost attributable to improvement, as opposed to simple replacement, is not deductible.

(ii) Under the **10% wear and tear** basis, the actual cost of furniture is ignored. Instead, an annual deduction is given of 10% of rents. The rents are first reduced by amounts which are paid by the landlord but are normally a tenant's burden. These amounts include any **water rates** and **council tax** paid by the landlord.

If plant and machinery is used partly in a dwelling house and partly for other purposes a just and reasonable apportionment of the expenditure can be made.

3.2 Losses of UK property business

A loss from a UK property business is carried forward to set against the first future profits from the UK property business. **It may be carried forward until the UK property business ends, but it must be used as soon as possible.**

Activity 2   **(20 minutes)**

Pete over the last few years has purchased several properties in Manchester as 'buy to let' investments.

5 Whitby Ave is let out furnished at £500 per month. A tenant moved in on 1 March 2009 but left unexpectedly on 1 May 2010 having paid rent only up to 31 December 2009. The tenant left no forwarding address.

17 Bolton Rd has been let furnished to the same tenant for a number of years at £800 per month.

A recent purchase, 27 Turner Close has been let unfurnished since 1 August 2009 at £750 per month having been empty whilst Pete redecorated it after its purchase March 2009.

Pete's expenses during 2009/10 are:

	No 5	No 17	No27
	£	£	£
Insurance	250	200	200
Letting agency fees	–	–	100
Repairs	300	40	–
Redecoration	–	–	500

No 27 was in a fit state to let when Pete bought it but he wanted to redecorate the property as he felt this would allow him to achieve a better rental income.

Water rates and council tax are paid by the tenants. Pete made a UK property business loss in 2008/09 of £300.

What is Pete's taxable property income for 2009/10?

3.3 Premiums on leases

When a premium or similar consideration is received on the grant (that is, by a landlord to a tenant) **of a short lease (50 years or less), part of the premium is treated as rent received in the year of grant.** A lease is considered to end on the date when it is most likely to terminate.

The premium taxed as rental income is the whole premium, less 2% of the premium for each complete year of the lease, except the first year using the following formula:

Premium	P
Less: $2\% \times (n-1) \times P$	(a)
Taxable as income	X

This rule does not apply on the **assignment** of a lease (ie one tenant selling his entire interest in the property to another).

3.4 Premiums paid by traders

Where a trader pays a premium for a lease he may deduct an amount from his taxable trading profits in each year of the lease. The amount deductible is the figure treated as rent received by the landlord divided by the number of years of the lease. For example, suppose that B, a trader, pays A a premium of £30,000 for a ten year lease. A is treated as receiving £30,000 – (£30,000 × (10 – 1) × 2%) = £24,600. B can therefore deduct £24,600/10 = £2,460 in each of the ten years. He starts with the accounts year in which the lease starts and apportions the relief to the nearest month.

3.5 Premiums for granting subleases

A tenant may decide to sublet property and to charge a premium on the grant of a lease to the subtenant. This premium is treated as rent received in the normal way (because this is a grant and not an assignment, the original tenant retaining an interest in the property). **Where the tenant originally paid a premium for his own head lease, this deemed rent is reduced by:**

$$\text{Rent part of premium for head lease} \times \frac{\text{duration of sub-lease}}{\text{duration of head lease}}$$

If the relief exceeds the part of the premium for the sub-lease treated as rent (including cases where there is a sub-lease with no premium), the balance of the relief is treated as rent payable by the head tenant, spread evenly over the period of the sub-lease. This rent payable is an expense, reducing the overall profit from the UK property business.

> **Activity 3**   **(10 minutes)**
>
> C granted a lease to D on 1 March 1999 for a period of 40 years. D paid a premium of £16,000. On 1 June 2009 D granted a sublease to E for a period of ten years. E paid a premium of £30,000. Calculate the amount treated as rent out of the premium received by D.

3.6 Real Estate Investment Trusts (REITs)

Property companies may operate as **Real Estate Investment Trusts** (REITs).

REITs can elect for their property income (and gains) to be exempt from corporation tax and must withhold basic rate (20%) tax from distributions paid to shareholders (who cannot own more than 10% of a REIT's shares) out of these profits. These distributions are taxed as property income, not as dividends.

Distributions by REITs out of other income (ie not property income or gains) are taxed as dividends in the normal way.

4 FURNISHED HOLIDAY LETTINGS

There are special rules for furnished holiday lettings. The letting is treated as if it were a trade. This means that, although the income is taxed as income from a UK property business, the provisions which apply to actual trades also apply to furnished holiday lettings, as follows.

(a) Relief for losses is available as if they were trading losses, including the facility to set losses against other income. The usual UK property business loss reliefs do not apply.

(b) Capital allowances are available on furniture: the renewals basis and the 10% wear and tear basis do not apply if capital allowances are claimed.

(c) The income qualifies as relevant UK earnings for pension relief.

(d) Capital gains tax rollover relief, entrepreneurs' relief and relief for gifts of business assets are available (see later in this Text).

Note, however, that the basis period rules for trades do not apply, and the profits or losses must be computed for tax years.

The letting must be of furnished accommodation made on a **commercial basis with a view to the realisation of profit**. The property must also satisfy the following three conditions.

(a) **The availability condition** – the accommodation is available for commercial let as holiday accommodation to the public generally, for **at least 140 days during the year**.

(b) **The letting condition** – the accommodation is commercially let as holiday accommodation to members of the public for **at least 70 days during the year**.

(c) **The pattern of occupation condition** – **not more than 155 days in the year** fall during periods of longer term occupation. Longer term occupation is defined as **a continuous period of more than 31 days during which the accommodation is in the same occupation** unless there are abnormal circumstances.

If someone has furnished holiday lettings and other lettings, **draw up two profit and loss accounts as if they had two separate property businesses.** This is so that the profits and losses treated as trade profits and losses can be identified.

5 RENT A ROOM RELIEF

If an individual lets a room or rooms, furnished, in his or her main residence as living accommodation, then a special exemption may apply.

The limit on the exemption is gross rents (before any expenses or capital allowances) of £4,250 a year. This limit is halved if any other person (eg spouse/civil partner) also received income from renting accommodation in the property.

If gross rents are not more than the limit, the rents are wholly exempt from income tax and expenses are ignored. However, the taxpayer may claim to ignore the exemption, for example to generate a loss by taking into account both rent and expenses.

If gross rents exceed the limit, the taxpayer will be taxed in the ordinary way, ignoring the rent a room scheme, unless he elects for the 'alternative basis'. If he so elects, he will be taxable on gross receipts plus balancing charges less £4,250 (or £2,125 if the limit is halved), with no deductions for expenses or capital allowances.

An election to ignore the exemption or an election for the alternative basis must be made by the 31 January which is 22 months from the end of the tax year concerned.

An election to ignore the exemption applies only for the tax year for which it is made, but an election for the alternative basis remains in force until it is withdrawn or until a year in which gross rents do not exceed the limit.

Activity 4 (10 minutes)

Sylvia owns a house near the sea in Norfolk. She has a spare bedroom and during 2009/10 this was let to a chef working at a nearby restaurant for £85 per week which includes the cost of heating, lighting etc.

Sylvia estimates that each year her lodger costs her an extra:

£50 on gas
£25 on electricity
£50 on insurance

How much property income must Sylvia pay tax on?

Chapter roundup

- Miscellaneous income is taxed in the year of receipt.
- There are several tax exemptions for investment income.
- Income from a UK property is computed for tax years on an accruals basis.
- Special rules apply to income from furnished holiday lettings.
- Rents received from letting a room in the taxpayer's home may be tax free under the rent-a-room scheme.
- Part of a premium received on grant of a short lease is as rent.
- Traders can receive relief for premium payments over the life of the lease.

Quick quiz

1 What income falls within the category Miscellaneous Income?

2 What is the tax treatment of Individual Savings Accounts?

3 When may interest be paid to individuals gross?

4 Describe the renewals basis.

5 What are the advantages of furnished holiday letting income over other UK Property business income?

6 How much income per annum is tax free under the rent a room scheme?

Answers to Quick quiz

1   Income not falling under any other category.

2   ISAs produce tax free income.

3   NS&I bank account interest, gilt interest and interest from quoted company debentures and loan stock may all by paid gross.

4   Under the renewals basis there is no deduction for the cost of the first furniture provided but the cost of replacement furniture is treated as a revenue expense.

5   (i)   Relief for losses are available as if they were trading losses
    (ii)   Capital allowances are available on furniture
    (iii) Capital gains tax reliefs are available

6   £4,250.

Answers to Activities

1

	£
Net Income (bank deposit interest) £9,600 × 100/80	12,000
Less personal allowance	(6,475)
Taxable income	5,525

	£
Income tax on savings (excl dividend) income	
£2,440 × 10%	244
£3,085 × 20% (savings income)	617
Tax suffered £12,000 × 20%	(2,400)
Repayment due	(1,539)

2

	No 5	No 17	No 27
2009/10	£	£	£
Accrued income			
12 × £500	6,000		
12 × £800		9,600	
8 × £750			6,000
Less:			
Insurance	(250)	(250)	(200)
Letting agency			(100)
Impairment (irrecoverable rent)			
3 × £500	(1,500)		
Repairs	(300)	(40)	
Redecoration (note)			(500)
Wear and tear allowance			
£(6,000 – 1,500) × 10%	(450)		
£9,600 × 10%		(960)	
Property Income	3,500	8,350	5,200

	£
Total property income	17,050
Less: loss b/fwd	(300)
Taxable property income for 2009/10	16,750

Note. The redecoration is allowable as the property was already in a usable state. If the redecoration had been needed to put the property into a fit state to be rented, it would not be allowable.

3

	£
Premium received by D	30,000
Less £30,000 × 2% × (10 – 1)	(5,400)
	24,600
Less allowance for premium paid	
(16,000 – (£16,000 × 39 × 2%)) × 10/40	(880)
Premium treated as rent	23,720

4   Sylvia has a choice:

(1)   Total rental income of £85 × 52 = £4,420 exceeds £4,250 limit so taxable income is £170 (ie £4,420 – 4,250) ie rent a room relief claim.

(2)   Alternatively she can be taxed on her actual profit:

	£
Rental income	4,420
Less expenses (50 + 25 +50)	(125)
	4,295

Sylvia should be advised to claim rent a room relief.

Chapter 12
TAX DOCUMENTATION AND PAYMENT OF TAX

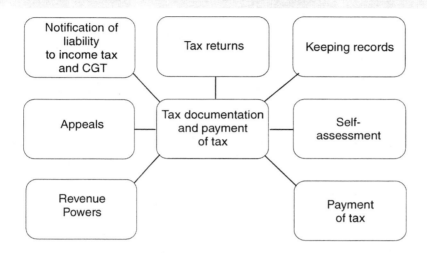

Introduction

The tax practitioner will often effectively 'run' the client's tax affairs on their behalf. This involves keeping the necessary records, filing the appropriate returns (on time) and dealing with the HMRC should there be any disputes. In doing this, the tax practitioner is expected to observe client confidentiality and professionalism at all times.

Your objectives

In this chapter you will learn about the following.

- (a)   Notification of liability to income tax and CGT
- (b)   Tax returns and keeping records
- (c)   Self assessment and claims
- (d)   Payment of income tax and capital gains tax
- (e)   Revenue powers
- (f)   Penalties
- (g)   Appeals

1 NOTIFICATION OF LIABILITY TO INCOME TAX AND CGT

Individuals who are chargeable to income tax or CGT for any tax year and who have not received a notice to file a return are required to give notice of chargeability to an Officer of the Revenue and Customs within six months from the end of the year ie by 5 October 2010 for 2009/10.

A person who has no chargeable gains and who is not liable to higher rate tax does not have to give notice of chargeability if all his income:

(a) Is taken into account under PAYE
(b) Is from a source of income not subject to tax under a self-assessment
(c) Has had (or is treated as having had) income tax deducted at source, or
(d) Is UK dividends.

A penalty may be imposed for late notification (see later in this chapter).

2 TAX RETURNS AND KEEPING RECORDS

2.1 Tax returns

The tax return comprises a Tax Form, together with supplementary pages for particular sources of income. Taxpayers are sent a Tax Form and a number of supplementary pages depending on their known sources of income, together with a Tax Return Guide and various notes relating to the supplementary pages. Taxpayers with new sources of income may have to ask the orderline for further supplementary pages. Taxpayers with simple tax returns may be asked to complete a short four page tax return.

If a return for the previous year was filed electronically the taxpayer may be sent a notice to file a return, rather than the official HMRC form.

Partnerships must file a separate return which includes 'a partnership statement' showing the firm's profits, losses, proceeds from the sale of assets, tax suffered, tax credits, charges on income and the division of all these amounts between partners.

A partnership return must include a declaration of the name, residence and tax reference of each partner, as well as the usual declaration that the return is correct and complete to the best of the signatory's knowledge.

Each partner must then include his share of partnership profits on his personal tax return.

2.2 Time limit for submission of tax returns

Definition

The latest **filing date for a personal tax return** for a tax year (Year 1) is:

- 31 October in the next tax year (Year 2), for a non-electronic return (eg a paper return).

- 31 January in Year 2, for an electronic return (eg made via the internet).

There are **two exceptions to this general rule.**

The **first exception applies if the notice to file a tax return is issued by HMRC to the taxpayer after 31 July in Year 2, but on or before 31 October in Year 2.** In this case, the latest filing date is:

- **the end of 3 months following the notice, for a non-electronic return.**
- **31 January in Year 2, for an electronic return.**

The second exception applies **if the notice to file the tax return is issued to the taxpayer after 31 October in Year 2.** In this case, **the latest filing date is the end of 3 months following the notice.**

EXAMPLE

Advise the following clients of the latest filing date for her personal tax return for 2009/10 if the return is:

(a)   non-electronic; or

(b)   electronic.

Norma	Notice to file tax return issued by HMRC on 6 April 2010
Melanie	Notice to file tax return issued by HMRC on 10 August 2010
Olga	Notice to file tax return issued by HMRC on 12 December 2010

	Non-electronic	*Electronic*
Norma	31 October 2010	31 January 2011
Melanie	9 November 2010	31 January 2011
Olga	11 March 2011	11 March 2011

A partnership return may be filed as a non-electronic return or an electronic return. **The general rule and the exceptions to the general rule for personal returns apply also to partnership returns.**

2.3   Keeping records

All taxpayers must retain all records required to enable them to make and deliver a correct tax return.

Records must be retained until the later of:

(a)   (i)   **5 years after the 31 January following the tax year where the taxpayer is in business** (as a sole trader or partner or letting property). Note that this applies to all of the records, not only the business records, or

          (ii)   **1 year after the 31 January following the tax year otherwise, or**

(b)   Provided notice to deliver a return is given before the date in (a):

          (i)   **The time after which enquiries by HMRC into the return can no longer be commenced,** or

          (ii)   **The date any such enquiries have been completed.**

HMRC can specify a shorter time limit for keeping records where the records are bulky and the information they contain can be provided in another way.

BPP
LEARNING MEDIA

Where a person receives a notice to deliver a tax return after the normal record keeping period has expired, he must keep all records in his possession at that time until no enquiries can be raised in respect of the return or until such enquiries have been completed.

Taxpayers can keep 'information', rather than 'records', but must show that they have prepared a complete and correct tax return. The information must also be able to be provided in a legible form on request. Records can be kept in electronic format.

HMRC can inspect 'in-year' records, i e *before* **a return is submitted, if they believe it is reasonably required to check a tax position.**

3 SELF-ASSESSMENT AND CLAIMS

3.1 Self-assessment

Definition

A self-assessment is a calculation of the amount of taxable income and gains after deducting reliefs and allowances, a calculation of income tax and CGT payable after taking into account tax deducted at source and tax credits on dividends.

If the taxpayer is filing a **paper return (other than a Short Tax Return), he may make the tax calculation on his return or ask HMRC to do so on his behalf.**

If the taxpayer wishes HMRC to make the calculation for Year 1, a paper return must be filed:

- **on or before 31 October in Year 2 or,**
- **if the notice to file the tax return is issued after 31 August in Year 2, within 2 months of the notice.**

If the taxpayer is filing an **electronic return, the calculation of tax liability is made automatically when the return is made online.**

3.2 Amending the self-assessment

The taxpayer may amend his return (including the tax calculation) for Year 1 within twelve months after the filing date. For this purpose the filing date means:

- **31 January of Year 2; or**
- **where the notice to file a return was issued after 31 October in Year 2, the last day of the three month period starting with the issue.**

A return may be amended by the taxpayer at a time when an enquiry is in progress into the return. The amendment does not restrict the scope of an enquiry into the return but may be taken into account in that enquiry. If the amendment made during an enquiry is the amount of tax payable, the amendment does not take effect while the enquiry is in progress.

A return may be amended by HMRC to correct any obvious error or omission in the return (such as errors of principle and arithmetical mistakes) or anything else that an officer has reason to believe is incorrect in the light of information available. The correction must be usually be made within nine months after the day on which the return was actually filed. The taxpayer can object to the correction but must do so within 30 days of receiving notice of it.

3.3 Claims

All claims and elections which can be made in a tax return must be made in this manner if a return has been issued. A claim for any relief, allowance or repayment of tax must be quantified at the time it is made.

In general, the time limit for making a claim is 4 years from the end of tax year. Where different time limits apply these have been mentioned throughout this Course Book.

3.4 Recovery of overpaid tax

If a taxpayer discovers that he has overpaid tax, for example because he has made an error in his tax return, he can make a claim to have the overpaid tax repaid to him. The claim must be made within four years of the end of the tax year to which the overpayment relates.

4 PAYMENT OF INCOME TAX AND CAPITAL GAINS TAX

4.1 Payments on account and final payment

Introduction

The self-assessment system may result in the taxpayer making three payments of income tax and Class 4 NICs.

Date	Payment
31 January in the tax year	1st payment on account
31 July after the tax year	2nd payment on account
31 January after the tax year	Final payment to settle the remaining liability

HMRC issue payslips/demand notes in a credit card type 'Statement of Account' format, but there is no statutory obligation for it to do so and **the onus is on the taxpayer to pay the correct amount of tax on the due date.**

Payments on account

Definition

> **Payments on account** are usually required where the income tax and Class NICs due in the previous year exceeded the amount of income tax deducted at source; this excess is known as **'the relevant amount'**. Income tax deducted at source includes tax suffered, PAYE deductions and tax credits on dividends.

The payments on account are each equal to 50% of the relevant amount for the previous year.

Payments on account of CGT are never required.

Activity 1   **(15 minutes)**

Sue is a self employed writer who paid tax for 2009/10 as follows:

		£
Total amount of income tax charged		9,200
This included:	Tax deducted on savings income	3,200
She also paid:	Class 4 NIC	1,900
	Class 2 NIC	125
	Capital gains tax	4,800

How much are the payments on account for 2010/11?

Payments on account are not required if the relevant amount falls below a de minimis limit of £1,000. Also, payments on account are not required from taxpayers who paid 80% or more of their tax liability for the previous year through PAYE or other deduction at source arrangements.

Reducing payments on account

Payments on account are normally fixed by reference to the previous year's tax liability but if a taxpayer expects his liability to be lower than this **he may claim to reduce his payments on account to:**

    (a) **A stated amount,** or
    (b) **Nil.**

The claim must state the reason why he believes his tax liability will be lower, or nil.

If the taxpayer's eventual liability is higher than he estimated he will have reduced the payments on account too far. Although the payments on account will not be adjusted, the taxpayer will suffer an interest charge on late payment.

A penalty of the difference between the reduced payment on account and the correct payment on account may be levied if the reduction was claimed fraudulently or negligently.

Balancing payment

The balance of any income tax and Class 4 NICs together with all CGT due for a year, is normally payable on or before the 31 January following the year.

Activity 2   **(10 minutes)**

Giles made payments on account for 2009/10 of £6,500 each on 31 January 2010 and 31 July 2010, based on his 2008/09 liability. He then calculates his total income tax and Class 4 NIC liability for 2009/10 at £18,000 of which £2,750 was deducted at source. In addition he calculated that his CGT liability for disposals in 2009/10 is £5,120.

What is the final payment due for 2009/10?

In one case the due date for the final payment is later than 31 January following the end of the year. **If a taxpayer has notified chargeability by 5 October but the notice to file a tax return is not issued before 31 October, then the due date for the payment is three months after the issue of the notice.**

Tax charged in an amended self-assessment is usually payable on the later of:

(a) The normal due date, generally 31 January following the end of the tax year, and

(b) The day following 30 days after the making of the revised self-assessment.

Tax charged on a discovery assessment (see below) is due thirty days after the issue of the assessment.

4.2 Surcharges

Definition

Surcharges are normally imposed in respect of amounts paid late:

Paid	Surcharge
(a) Within 28 days of due date:	none
(b) More than 28 days but not more than six months after the due date:	5%
(c) More than six months after the due date	10%

Surcharges apply to:

(a) Balancing payments of income tax and Class 4 NICs and any CGT under self-assessment or a determination

(b) Tax due on the amendment of a self-assessment

(c) Tax due on a discovery assessment

The surcharge rules do not apply to late payments on account.

No surcharge will be applied where the late paid tax liability has attracted a tax-geared penalty on the failure to notify chargeability to tax, or the failure to submit a return, or on the making of an incorrect return (including a partnership return).

4.3 Interest on late paid tax

Interest is chargeable on late payment of both payments on account and balancing payments. In both cases interest runs from the due date until the day before the actual date of payment.

Interest is charged from 31 January following the tax year (or the normal due date for the balancing payment, in the rare event that this is later), even if this is before the due date for payment on:

(a) Tax payable following an amendment to a self-assessment

(b) Tax payable in a discovery assessment, and

(c) Tax postponed under an appeal which becomes payable.

Since a determination (see below) is treated as if it were a self-assessment, interest runs from 31 January following the tax year.

If a taxpayer claims to reduce his payments on account and there is still a final payment to be made, interest is normally charged on the payments on account as if each of those payments had been the lower of:

(a) the reduced amount, plus 50% of the final income tax liability; and

(b) the amount which would have been payable had no claim for reduction been made.

Activity 3   **(20 minutes)**

Herbert's payments on account for 2009/10 based on his income tax liability for 2008/09 were £4,500 each. However when he submitted his 2008/09 income tax return in January 2010 he made a claim to reduce the payments on account for 2009/10 for £3,500 each. The first payment on account was made on 29 January 2010, and the second on 12 August 2010.

Herbert filed his 2009/10 tax return in December 2010. The returned showed that his tax liabilities for 2009/10 (before deducting payments on account) were income tax and Class 4 NIC: £10,000, capital gains tax: £2,500. Herbert paid the balance of tax due of £5,500 on 19 February 2011.

For what periods and in respect of what amounts will Herbert be charged interest?

Where interest has been charged on late payments on account but the final balancing settlement for the year produces a repayment, all or part of the original interest is repaid.

4.4 Repayment of tax and repayment supplement

Tax is repaid when claimed unless a greater payment of tax is due in the following 30 days, in which case it is set-off against that payment.

Technically, interest (repayment supplement) is paid on overpayments of tax. However, for 2009/10, the rate of repayment supplement is 0%.

5 REVENUE POWERS

5.1 Enquiries into returns

Opening an enquiry

An officer of the Revenue and Customs has a limited period within which to commence enquiries into a return or amendment. **The officer must give written notice of his intention by:**

(a) **The first anniversary of the actual filing date (if the return was delivered on or before the due filing date), or**

(b) **If the return is filed after the due filing date, the quarter day following the first anniversary of the actual filing date. The quarter days are 31 January, 30 April, 31 July and 31 October.**

If the taxpayer amended the return after the due filing date, the enquiry 'window' extends to the quarter day following the first anniversary of the date the amendment was filed. Where the enquiry was not raised within the limit which would have applied had no amendment been filed, the enquiry is restricted to matters contained in the amendment.

The officer does not have to have, or give, any reason for raising an enquiry. In particular the taxpayer will not be advised whether he has been selected at random for an audit. Enquiries may be full enquiries, or may be limited to 'aspect' enquiries.

During the enquiry

In the course of his enquiries **the officer may require the taxpayer to produce documents, accounts or any other information required. The taxpayer can appeal to the Tribunal.**

During the course of his enquiries an officer may amend a self assessment if it appears that insufficient tax has been charged and an immediate amendment is necessary to prevent a loss to the Crown. This might apply if, for example, there is a possibility that the taxpayer will emigrate.

If a return is under enquiry HMRC may postpone any repayment due as shown in the return until the enquiry is complete. HMRC have discretion to make a provisional repayment but there is no facility to appeal if the repayment is withheld.

At any time during the course of an enquiry, the taxpayer may apply to the Tribunal to require the officer to notify the taxpayer within a specified period that the enquiries are complete, unless the officer can demonstrate that he has reasonable grounds for continuing the enquiry.

Closing an enquiry

An officer must issue a notice that the enquiries are complete, state his conclusions and amend the self-assessment, partnership statement or claim accordingly.

If the taxpayer is not satisfied with the officer's amendment he may, within 30 days, appeal to the Tribunal.

Once an enquiry is complete the officer cannot make further enquiries. HMRC may, in limited circumstances, raise a discovery assessment if they believe that there has been a loss of tax (see below).

5.2 Determinations

If notice has been served on a taxpayer to submit a return but the return is not submitted by the due filing date, an officer of HMRC may make a determination of the amounts liable to income tax and CGT and of the tax due. Such a determination must be made to the best of the officer's information and belief, and is then treated as if it were a self-assessment. This enables the officer to seek payment of tax, including payments on account for the following year and to charge interest.

A determination must be made within four year following the end of the relevant tax year.

5.3 Discovery assessments

If an officer of HMRC discovers that profits have been omitted from assessment, that any assessment has become insufficient, or that any relief given is, or has become excessive, an assessment may be raised to recover the tax lost.

If the tax lost results from an error in the taxpayer's return but the return was made in accordance with prevailing practice at the time, no discovery assessment may be made.

A discovery assessment may only be raised where a return has been made if:

(a) There has been **careless or deliberate understatement** by the taxpayer or his agent, or

(b) At the time that enquiries into the return were completed, or could no longer be made, the officer **did not have information** to make him aware of the loss of tax.

Information is treated as available to an officer if it is contained in the taxpayer's return or claim for the year or either of the two preceding years, or it has been provided as a result of an enquiry covering those years, or it has been specifically provided.

The time limit for raising a discovery assessment is four years from the end of the tax year but this is extended to 6 years if there has been careless understatement and 20 years if there has been deliberate understatement. The taxpayer may appeal against a discovery assessment within 30 days of issue.

5.4 Information and inspection powers

Information powers

HMRC has one set of information and inspection powers covering income tax, capital gains tax, corporation tax, VAT and PAYE to ensure taxpayers comply with their obligations, pay the right amount of tax at the right time and claim the correct reliefs and allowances.

HMRC usually informally requests information and documents from taxpayers in connection with their tax affairs. If, however, a taxpayer does not co-operate fully, **HMRC can use its statutory powers to request information and documents** from taxpayers and third parties via a written 'information notice'. HMRC can request both statutory records and supplementary information, such as appointment diaries, notes of board meetings, correspondence and contracts.

HMRC can only issue a taxpayer notice if the information and documents requested are 'reasonably required' for the purpose of checking the taxpayer's tax position. A taxpayer notice may be issued either with or without the approval of the Tribunal.

An information notice issued to a third party must be issued with the agreement of the taxpayer or the approval of the Tribunal, unless the information relates only to the taxpayer's statutory VAT records. The taxpayer to whom the notice relates must receive a summary of the reasons for the third party notice unless the Tribunal believes it would prejudice the assessment or collection of tax.

Tax advisers and auditors cannot be asked to provide information connected with their functions. For example, a tax adviser does not have to provide access to his working papers used in the preparation of the taxpayer's return. In addition, HMRC cannot ask a tax adviser to provide communications between himself and either the taxpayer or his other advisers. This 'professional privilege' does not apply in certain situations, for example, to explanatory material provided to a client in relation to a document already supplied to HMRC.

The taxpayer or third party must provide the information or document requested by the information notice within such period as is reasonably specified within the notice.

The recipient of an information notice has a right of appeal against an information notice unless the Tribunal has approved the issue of the notice.

Inspection powers

An authorised officer of HMRC can enter the business premises of a taxpayer whose liability is being checked and inspect the premises and the business assets and business documents that are on the premises. The power does not extend to any part of the premises used solely as a dwelling. If an information notice has been issued, the documents required in that notice can be inspected at the same time. **The inspection must be reasonably required for the purposes of checking the taxpayer's tax position.**

HMRC will usually agree a time for the inspection with the taxpayer. However, an authorised HMRC officer can carry out the inspection at 'any reasonable time' if either:

(a) **The taxpayer receives at least seven days' written notice,** or

(b) **The inspection is carried out by, or with the approval of, an authorised HMRC officer.**

There is no right of appeal against an inspection notice.

6 PENALTIES

6.1 Penalties for errors

There is a common penalty regime for errors in tax returns, including income tax, NICs, corporation tax and VAT. Penalties range from 30% to 100% of the Potential Lost Revenue. Penalties may be reduced.

A common penalty regime for errors in tax returns for income tax, national insurance contributions, corporation tax and value added tax.

A penalty may be imposed where **a taxpayer makes an inaccurate return** if he has:

- been **careless** because he has not taken reasonable care in making the return or discovers the error later but does not take reasonable steps to inform HMRC; or

- made a **deliberate error** but **does not make arrangements to conceal it**; or

- made a **deliberate error** and **has attempted to conceal it** eg by submitting false evidence in support of an inaccurate figure.

Note that **an error which is made where the taxpayer has taken reasonable care** in making the return and which he **does not discover later, does not result in a penalty.**

In order for a penalty to be charged, the **inaccurate return must result in:**

- **an understatement of the taxpayer's tax liability;** or
- **a false or increased loss for the taxpayer;** or
- **a false or increased repayment of tax to the taxpayer.**

If a return contains more than one error, a penalty can be charged for each error.

The rules also extend to **errors in claims for allowances and reliefs** and in **accounts submitted in relation to a tax liability.**

Penalties for error also apply where **HMRC has issued an assessment estimating a person's liability** where:

- a **return has been issued to that person and has not been returned,** or

- the taxpayer was **required to deliver a return to HMRC but has not delivered it.**

The taxpayer will be charged a penalty where

- the **assessment understates the taxpayer's liability** to income tax, capital gains tax, corporation tax or VAT, and

- the **taxpayer fails to take reasonable steps within 30 days of the date of the assessment** to tell HMRC that there is an under-assessment.

The amount of **the penalty for error is based on the Potential Lost Revenue (PLR)** to HMRC as a result of the error. For example, if there is an understatement of tax, this understatement will be the PLR.

The maximum amount of the penalty for error depends on the type of error:

Type of error	Maximum penalty payable
Careless	30% of PLR
Deliberate not concealed	70% of PLR
Deliberate and concealed	100% of PLR

EXAMPLE

Alex is a sole trader. He files his tax return for 2009/10 on 10 January 2011. The return shows his trading income to be £60,000. In fact, due to carelessness, his trading income should have been stated to be £68,000.

State the maximum penalty that could be charged by HMRC on Alex for his error.

The Potential Lost Revenue as a result of Alex's error is:

£(68,000 – 60,000) = £8,000 x [40% (income tax) + 1% (NICs)]   <u>£3,280</u>

Alex's error is careless so the maximum penalty for error is:

£3,280 x 30%   <u>£984</u>

A penalty for error may be reduced if the taxpayer tells HMRC about the error – this is called a disclosure. The reduction depends on the **circumstances of** the disclosure and the **help that the taxpayer gives to HMRC in relation to the disclosure.**

An **unprompted disclosure is one made at a time when the taxpayer has no reason to believe HMRC has discovered, or is about to discover, the error.** Otherwise, the disclosure will be a **prompted disclosure.** The **minimum penalties** that can be imposed are as follows:

Type of error	Unprompted	Prompted
Careless	0% of PLR	15% of PLR
Deliberate not concealed	20% of PLR	35% of PLR
Deliberate and concealed	30% of PLR	50% of PLR

EXAMPLE

Sue is a sole trader. She files her tax return for 2008/09 on 31 January 2010. The return shows a loss for the year of £(80,000). In fact, Sue has deliberately increased this loss by £(12,000) and has submitted false figures in support of her claim. HMRC initiate a review into Sue's return and in reply Sue then makes a disclosure of the error. Sue is a higher rate taxpayer due to her substantial investment income and she has made a claim to set the loss against general income in 2008/09.

State the maximum and minimum penalties that could be charged by HMRC on Sue for her error.

The potential lost revenue as a result of Sue's error is:

£12,000 x 40%   <u>£4,800</u>

Sue's error is deliberate and concealed so the maximum penalty for error is:

£4,800 x 100%   <u>£4,800</u>

Sue has made a prompted disclosure so the minimum penalty for error is:

£4,800 x 50%   <u>£2,400</u>

The help that the taxpayer gives to HMRC relates to when, how and to what extent the taxpayer:

- **tells HMRC about the error,** making full disclosure and explaining how the error was made;

- **gives reasonable help** to HMRC to enable it **to quantify the error**; and

- **allows access to business and other records** and other relevant documents.

A taxpayer can appeal to the First-Tier Tribunal against :

- the **penalty being charged;**
- the **amount of the penalty.**

6.2 Penalties for late notification of chargeability

A common penalty regime also applies to certain taxes for failures to notify chargeability to, or liability to register for, tax that result in a loss of tax. The taxes affected include income tax, NICs, PAYE, CGT, corporation tax and VAT. Penalties are behaviour related, increasing for more serious failures, and are based on the 'potential lost revenue'.

The minimum and maximum penalties as percentages of PLR are as follows:

Behaviour	Maximum penalty	Minimum penalty with unprompted disclosure		Minimum penalty with prompted disclosure	
Deliberate and concealed	100%	30%		50%	
Deliberate but not concealed	70%	20%		35%	
		>12m	<12m	>12m	<12m
Careless	30%	10%	0%	20%	10%

Note that there is no zero penalty for reasonable care (as there is for penalties for errors on returns – see above), although the penalty may be reduced to 0% if the failure is rectified within 12 months through unprompted disclosure. The penalties may also be reduced at HMRC's discretion in 'special circumstances'. However, inability to pay the penalty is not a 'special circumstance'.

The same penalties apply for failure to notify HMRC of a new taxable activity.

Where the taxpayer's failure is not classed as deliberate, there is no penalty if he can show he has a 'reasonable excuse'. Reasonable excuse does not include having insufficient money to pay the penalty. Taxpayers have a right of appeal against penalty decisions to the First-Tier Tribunal.

6.3 Penalties for late filing

The maximum penalties for delivering a tax return after the filing due date are:

(a) **Return up to 6 months late:** £100

(b) **Return more than 6 months but not more than 12 months late:** £200

(c) **Return more than 12 months late:** £200 + 100% of the tax liability

In addition, the First Tier Tribunal can direct that a maximum penalty of £60 per day be imposed where failure to deliver a tax return continues after notice of the direction has been given to the taxpayer. In this case the additional £100 penalty, imposed under (b) if the return is more than six months late, is not charged.

The fixed penalties of £100/£200 can be set aside by the First Tier Tribunal if they are satisfied that the taxpayer had a reasonable excuse for not delivering the return. If the tax liability shown on the return is less than the fixed penalties, the fixed penalty is reduced to the amount of the tax liability. The tax geared penalty is mitigable by HMRC or the First Tier Tribunal.

A taxpayer only has a reasonable excuse for a late filing if a default occurred because of a factor outside his control. This might be non-receipt of the return by the taxpayer, an industrial dispute in the post office after the return was posted, serious illness of the taxpayer or a close relative, or destruction of records through fire and flood. Illness etc is only accepted as a reasonable excuse if the taxpayer was taking timeous steps to complete the return, and if the return is filed as soon as possible after the illness etc.

6.4 Penalties for failure to keep records

The maximum (mitigable) penalty for each failure to keep and retain records is £3,000 per tax year/accounting period.

7 APPEALS

Disputes between taxpayers and HMRC can be dealt with by an HMRC internal review or by a Tribunal hearing.

7.1 Internal reviews

For direct taxes, appeals must first be made to HMRC, which will assign a 'caseworker'.

For indirect taxes, appeals must be sent directly to the Tribunal, although the taxpayer can continue to correspond with his caseworker where, for example, there is new information.

At this stage the taxpayer may be offered, or may ask for, an **'internal review'**, which will be made by an objective HMRC review officer not previously connected with the case. This is a less costly and more effective way to resolve disputes informally, without the need for a Tribunal hearing. An appeal to Tribunal cannot be made until any review has ended.

The taxpayer must either accept the review offer, or notify an appeal to the Tribunal within 30 days of being offered the review, otherwise the appeal will be treated as settled.

HMRC must usually carry out the review within 45 days, or any longer time as agreed with the taxpayer. The review officer may decide to uphold, vary or withdraw decisions.

After the review conclusion is notified, **the taxpayer has 30 days to appeal to the Tribunal.**

7.2 Tribunal hearings

If there is no internal review, or the taxpayer is unhappy with the result of an internal review, the case may be heard by the Tribunal. The person wishing to make an appeal (the appellant) must send a notice of appeal to the Tribunal. The Tribunal must then give notice of the appeal to the respondent (normally HMRC).

The Tribunal is made up of two 'tiers':

(a) **A First Tier Tribunal and**
(b) **An Upper Tribunal.**

The case will be allocated to one of four **case 'tracks'**:

(a) **Complex cases,** which the Tribunal considers will require lengthy or complex evidence or a lengthy hearing, or involve a complex or important principle or issue, or involves a large amount of money. Such cases will usually be heard by the Upper Tribunal,

(b) **Standard cases, heard by the First Tier Tribunal,** which have detailed case management and are subject to a more formal procedure than basic cases,

(c) **Basic cases, also heard by the First Tier Tribunal,** which will usually be disposed of after a hearing, with minimal exchange of documents before the hearing, and

(d) **Paper cases, dealt with by the First Tier Tribunal,** which applies to straightforward matters such as fixed filing penalties and will usually be dealt with in writing, without a hearing.

A decision of the First Tier Tribunal may be appealed to the Upper Tribunal.

Decisions of the Upper Tribunal are binding on the Tribunals and any affected public authorities. A decision of the Upper Tribunal may be appealed to the Court of Appeal.

Chapter roundup

- Individuals who do not receive a tax return must notify their chargeability to income tax or CGT.

- Tax returns must usually be filed by 31 October (paper) or 31 January (electronic) following the end of the tax year.

- If a paper return is filed the taxpayer can ask HMRC to compute the tax due. Electronic returns have tax calculated automatically.

- Two payments on account and a final balancing payment of income tax and Class 4 NICs are due. All capital gains tax is due on 31 January following the end of the tax year.

- HMRC can enquire into tax returns. Strict procedural rules govern enquiries.

- HMRC have powers to request documents from taxpayers and third parties. HMRC also has powers to inspect business premises.

- There is a common penalty regime for errors in tax returns, including income tax, NICs, corporation tax and VAT. Penalties range from 30% to 100% of the Potential Lost Revenue. Penalties may be reduced.

- A common penalty regime also applies to late notification of chargeability.

- Disputes between taxpayers and HMRC can be dealt with by an HMRC internal review or by a Tribunal hearing.

Quick quiz

1 By when must a taxpayer who has a new source of income give notice of his chargeability to capital gains tax due in 2009/10?

2 By when must a taxpayer file a non-electronic tax return for 2009/10?

3 What are the normal payment dates for income tax?

4 What surcharges are due in respect of income tax payments on account that are paid two months late?

5 What is the maximum penalty for failure to keep records?

6 Which body hears tax appeals?

Answers to Quick quiz

1   Within six months of the end of the year, ie by 5 October 2010

2   By 31 October 2010 or, if the return is issued after 31 July 2010, by the end of 3 months following the issue of the notice to file the return.

3   Two payments on account of income tax are due on 31 January in the tax year and on the 31 July following. A final balancing payment is due on 31 January following the tax year.

4   None. Surcharges do not apply to late payment of payment on account.

5   £3,000

6   The Tax Tribunal which consists of the First-Tier Tribunal and the Upper Tribunal

Answers to Activities

1

	£
Income tax:	
Total income tax charged for 2009/10	9,200
Less tax deducted for 2009/10	(3,200)
	6,000
Class 4 NIC	1,900
'Relevant amount'	7,900
Payments on account for 2010/11:	
31 January 2011 £7,900 × ½	3,950
31 July 2011 As before	3,950

There is no requirement to make payments on account of capital gains tax nor Class 2 NIC.

2   Income tax and Class 4 NIC: £18,000 – £2,750 – £6,500 – £6,500 = £2,250. CGT = £5,120.

Final payment due on 31 January 2011 for 2009/2010 £2,250 + £5,120 = £7,370

3   Herbert made an excessive claim to reduce his payments on account, and will therefore be charged interest on the reduction. The payments on account should have been £4,500 each based on the original 2008/09 liability (not £5,000 each based on the 2009/10 liability). Interest will be charged as follows:

(a)   First payment on account
    (i)   On £3,500 – nil – paid on time
    (ii)   On £1,000 from due date of 31 January 2010 to day before payment, 18 February 2011

(b)   Second payment on account
    (i)   On £3,500 from due date of 31 July 2010 to day before payment, 11 August 2010
    (ii)   On £1,000 from due date of 31 July 2010 to day before payment, 18 February 2011

(c)   Balancing payment
    (i)   On £3,500 from due date of 31 January 2011 to day before payment, 18 February 2011

Chapter 13
THE TAXATION OF BUSINESSES

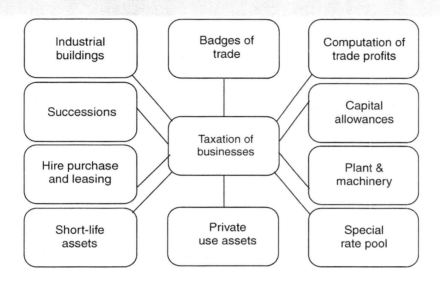

Introduction

We are now moving away from the taxation of the individual, most notably taxation of the employee, to the taxation of businesses. It is important to be able to establish exactly what constitutes 'a business'. One important feature of business taxation is the use of capital allowances, which may be treated as trading expenditure and thus reduce taxable profits.

Your objectives

In this chapter you will learn about the following.

- (a) The nature of a trade with reference to the 'Badges of Trade'
- (b) The principles of deductible and non-deductible expenditure
- (c) How to prepare adjusted profit computations (including capital allowances)
- (d) The principles relating to capital allowances on plant and machinery including the definition of plant, private use assets, short-life assets, hire purchase and leasing
- (e) The eligibility to claim capital allowances on cars and assets acquired by hire purchase or lease
- (f) How to prepare capital allowance computations (plant and machinery)
- (g) The principles relating to capital allowances on industrial buildings as they relate to general industrial buildings and hotels
- (h) How to prepare basic capital allowance computations (industrial buildings) including acquisitions and disposals

NOTES

1 THE BADGES OF TRADE

1.1 Introduction

Before a tax charge can be imposed it is necessary to establish the existence of a trade.

Definition

A trade is defined in the legislation only in an unhelpful manner as including every trade, manufacture, adventure or concern in the nature of a trade. It has therefore been left to the courts to provide guidance. This guidance is often summarised in a collection of principles known as the **'badges of trade'**. These are set out below. **Profits from professions and vocations are taxed in the same way as profits from a trade.**

1.2 The subject matter

Whether a person is trading or not may sometimes be decided by examining the subject matter of the transaction. Some assets are commonly held as investments for their intrinsic value: an individual buying some shares or a painting may do so in order to enjoy the income from the shares or to enjoy the work of art. A subsequent disposal may produce a gain of a capital nature rather than a trading profit. But **where the subject matter of a transaction is such as would not be held as an investment** (for example 34,000,000 yards of aircraft linen (*Martin v Lowry 1927*) or 1,000,000 rolls of toilet paper (*Rutledge v CIR 1929*)), **it is presumed that any profit on resale is a trading profit.**

1.3 The frequency of transactions

Transactions which may, in isolation, be of a capital nature will be interpreted as trading transactions where their **frequency indicates the carrying on of a trade.** It was decided that whereas normally the purchase of a mill-owning company and the subsequent stripping of its assets might be a capital transaction, where the taxpayer was embarking on the same exercise for the fourth time he must be carrying on a trade (*Pickford v Quirke 1927*).

1.4 The length of ownership

The courts may infer adventures in the nature of trade where items purchased are sold soon afterwards.

1.5 Supplementary work and marketing

When work is done to make an asset more marketable, or steps are taken to find purchasers, the courts will be more ready to ascribe a trading motive. When a group of accountants bought, blended and recasked a quantity of brandy they were held to be taxable on a trading profit when the brandy was later sold (*Cape Brandy Syndicate v CIR 1921*).

1.6 A profit motive

The absence of a profit motive will not necessarily preclude a tax charge as trading income, but its presence is a strong indication that a person is trading. The purchase and resale of £20,000 worth of silver bullion by the comedian Norman Wisdom, as a hedge against devaluation, was held to be a trading transaction (*Wisdom v Chamberlain 1969*).

1.7 The way in which the asset sold was acquired

If goods are acquired deliberately, trading may be indicated. If goods are acquired unintentionally, for example by gift or inheritance, their later sale is unlikely to be trading.

1.8 The taxpayer's intentions

Where a transaction is clearly trading on objective criteria, **the taxpayer's intentions are irrelevant**. If, however, a transaction has (objectively) a dual purpose, the taxpayer's intentions may be taken into account. An example of a transaction with a dual purpose is the acquisition of a site partly as premises from which to conduct another trade, and partly with a view to the possible development and resale of the site.

This test is not one of the traditional badges of trade, but it may be just as important.

2 THE COMPUTATION OF TRADE PROFITS

2.1 The adjustment of profits

The net profit before taxation shown in the accounts is the starting point in computing the taxable trade profits. Many adjustments may be required to calculate the taxable amount.

Here is an illustrative adjustment.

		£	£
Net profit per accounts			140,000
Add:	expenditure charged in the accounts which is not deductible		
	for tax purposes	50,000	
	income taxable as trade profits which has not been included		
	in the accounts	30,000	
			80,000
			220,000
Less:	profits included in the accounts but which are not taxable		
	as trade profits	40,000	
	expenditure which is deductible for tax purposes but has not		
	been charged in the accounts	20,000	
			(60,000)
Trade profits as adjusted for tax purposes			160,000

You may refer to deductible and non-deductible expenditure as allowable and disallowable expenditure respectively. The two sets of terms are interchangeable.

2.2 Accounting policies

The fundamental concept is that the profits of the business must be calculated in accordance wwith generally accepted accounting practice (GAAP). These profits are subject to any adjustment specifically required for income tax purposes.

2.3 Capital allowances

Under the Capital Allowances Act 2001 (CAA 2001) **capital allowances are treated as trade expenses and balancing charges are treated as trade receipts** (see later in this Course Book).

2.4 Non-deductible expenditure

Certain expenses are specifically disallowed by the legislation. These are covered below. If however a deduction is specifically permitted this overrides the disallowance.

Capital expenditure

Capital expenditure is not deductible. This denies a deduction for depreciation or amortisation. The most contentious items of expenditure will often be repairs (revenue expenditure) **and improvements** (capital expenditure).

- The cost of restoration of an asset by, for instance, replacing a subsidiary part of the asset is revenue expenditure. Expenditure on a new factory chimney replacement was allowable since the chimney was a subsidiary part of the factory (*Samuel Jones & Co (Devondale) Ltd v CIR 1951*). However, in another case a football club demolished a spectators' stand and replaced it with a modern equivalent. This was held not to be repair, since repair is the restoration by renewal or replacement of subsidiary parts of a larger entity, and the stand formed a distinct and *separate* part of the club (*Brown v Burnley Football and Athletic Co Ltd 1980*).

- The cost of initial repairs to improve an asset recently acquired to make it fit to earn profits is disallowable capital expenditure. In *Law Shipping Co Ltd v CIR 1923* the taxpayer failed to obtain relief for expenditure on making a newly bought ship seaworthy prior to using it.

- The cost of initial repairs to remedy normal wear and tear of recently acquired assets is allowable. *Odeon Associated Theatres Ltd v Jones 1971* can be contrasted with the *Law Shipping* judgement. Odeon were allowed to charge expenditure incurred on improving the state of recently acquired cinemas.

Capital allowances may, however, be available as a deduction for capital expenditure from trading profits.

Two exceptions to the 'capital' rule are worth noting.

(a)   The costs of **registering patents and trade marks** are deductible.

(b)   Incidental costs of obtaining loan finance, **or of attempting to obtain or redeeming it, are deductible other than a discount on issue or a premium on redemption (which are really alternatives to paying interest).**

Expenditure not wholly and exclusively for the purposes of the trade

Expenditure is not deductible if it is not for trade purposes (the remoteness test), or if it reflects more than one purpose (the duality test). The private proportion of payments for motoring expenses, rent, heat and light and telephone expenses of a proprietor is not deductible. If an exact apportionment is possible relief is given on the business element. Where the payments are to or on behalf of employees, the full amounts are deductible but the employees are taxed under the benefits code.

The remoteness test is illustrated by the following cases.

- *Strong & Co of Romsey Ltd v Woodifield 1906*

  A customer injured by a falling chimney when sleeping in an inn owned by a brewery claimed compensation from the company. The compensation was not deductible: 'the loss sustained by the appellant was not really incidental to their trade as innkeepers and fell upon them in their character not of innkeepers but of householders'.

- *Bamford v ATA Advertising Ltd 1972*

  A director misappropriated £15,000. The loss was not allowable: 'the loss is not, as in the case of a dishonest shop assistant, an incident of the company's trading activities. It arises altogether outside such activities'.

- Expenditure which is wholly and exclusively to benefit the trades of several companies (for example in a group) but is not wholly and exclusively to benefit the trade of one specific company is not deductible (*Vodafone Cellular Ltd and others v Shaw 1995*).

- *McKnight (HMIT) v Sheppard (1999)* concerned expenses incurred by a stockbroker in defending allegations of infringements of Stock Exchange regulations. It was found that the expenditure was incurred to prevent the destruction of the taxpayer's business and that as the expenditure was incurred for business purposes it was deductible. It was also found that although the expenditure had the effect of preserving the taxpayer's reputation, that was not its purpose, so there was no duality of purpose.

The **duality test** is illustrated by the following cases.

- *Caillebotte v Quinn 1975*

  A self-employed carpenter spent an average of 40p per day when obliged to buy lunch away from home but just 10p when he lunched at home. He claimed the excess 30p. It was decided that the payment had a dual purpose and was not deductible: a taxpayer 'must eat to live not eat to work'.

- *Mallalieu v Drummond 1983*

  Expenditure by a lady barrister on black clothing to be worn in court (and on its cleaning and repair) was not deductible. The expenditure was for the dual purpose of enabling the barrister to be warmly and properly clad as well as meeting her professional requirements.

- *McLaren v Mumford 1996*

  A publican traded from a public house which had residential accommodation above it. He was obliged to live at the public house but he also had another house which he visited regularly. It was held that the private element of the expenditure incurred at the public house on electricity, rent, gas, etc was not incurred for the purpose of earning profits, but for serving the non-business purpose of satisfying the publican's ordinary human needs. The expenditure, therefore had a dual purpose and was disallowed.

However, the cost of overnight accommodation when on a business trip may be deductible and reasonable expenditure on an evening meal and breakfast in conjunction with such accommodation is then also deductible.

Impaired trade receivables (bad debts)

Only impairment debts incurred wholly and exclusively for the purposes of the trade are deductible for taxation purposes. Thus loans to employees written off are not deductible unless the business is that of making loans, or it can be shown that the writing-off of the loan was earnings paid out for the benefit of the trade. If a trade debt is released as part of a voluntary arrangement under the Insolvency Act 1986, or a compromise or arrangement under s 425 Companies Act 1985, the amount realised is deductible as an impaired debt.

Under FRS 26 Financial Instruments: Measurement, a review of all trade receivables should be carried out to assess their fair value at the balance sheet date, and any impairment debts written off. As a specific provision, no adjustment to the accounts profit is needed for impairment review.

Unpaid remuneration

If earnings for employees are charged in the accounts but are not paid within nine months of the end of the period of account, the cost is only deductible for the period of account in which the earnings are paid. When a tax computation is made within the nine month period, it is initially assumed that unpaid earnings will not be paid within that period. The computation is adjusted if they are so paid.

Earnings are treated as paid at the same time as they are treated as received for employment income purposes.

Similar rules apply to employee benefit contributions.

Entertaining and gifts

The general rule is that expenditure on entertaining and gifts is non-deductible. This applies to amounts reimbursed to employees for specific entertaining expenses and gifts, and to round sum allowances which are exclusively for meeting such expenses.

There are specific exceptions to the general rule:

- **Entertaining for and gifts to employees are normally deductible** although where gifts are made, or the entertainment is excessive, a charge to tax may arise on the employee under the benefits legislation.

- **Gifts to customers not costing more than £50 per donee per year are allowed if they carry a conspicuous advertisement for the business and are not food, drink, tobacco or vouchers exchangeable for goods.**

- Gifts to charities may also be allowed although many will fall foul of the 'wholly and exclusively' rule above. If a gift aid declaration is made in respect of a gift, tax relief will be given under the gift aid scheme, not as a trading expense.

Lease charges for expensive cars

There is a restriction on the leasing costs of a car with CO$_2$ emissions exceeding 160 g/km. 15% of the leasing costs will be disallowed in the calculation of taxable profits.

Interest payments

Interest which is allowed as deductible interest is not also allowed as a trading expense.

National insurance contributions

No deduction is allowed for any national insurance contributions **except for employer's contributions**. For the purpose of your exam, these are Class 1 secondary contributions and Class 1A contributions (Class 1B contributions are not examinable). National insurance contributions for self employed individuals are dealt with later in this chapter.

Penalties and interest on tax

Penalties and interest on late paid tax are not allowed as a trading expense. Tax includes income tax, capital gains tax, VAT and stamp duty land tax.

Crime related payments

A payment is not deductible if making it constitutes an offence by the payer. This covers protection money paid to terrorists, bribes and similar payments made overseas which would be criminal payments if they were made in the UK. Statute also prevents any deduction for payments made in response to blackmail or extortion.

2.5 Deductible expenditure

Most expenses will be deductible under the general rule that expenses incurred wholly and exclusively for the purpose of the trade are not disallowed. Some expenses which might otherwise be disallowed under the 'wholly or exclusively' rule, or under one or other of the specific rules discussed above are, however, specifically allowed by the legislation. These are covered in paragraphs 2.5.1–2.5.12.

Pre-trading expenditure

Expenditure incurred before the commencement of trade is deductible, if it is incurred within seven years of the start of trade and it is of a type that would have been deductible had the trade already started. **It is treated as a trading expense incurred on the first day of trading.**

Incidental costs of obtaining finance

Incidental costs of obtaining loan finance, or of attempting to obtain or redeeming it, are deductible other than a discount on issue or a premium on redemption (which are

really alternatives to paying interest). This deduction for incidental costs does not apply to companies because they obtain a deduction for the costs of borrowing in a different way.

We will look further at corporation tax in Chapter 15.

Short leases

A trader may deduct an annual sum in respect of the amount liable to income tax on a lease premium which he paid to his landlord. Normally, the amortisation of the lease will have been deducted in the accounts (and must be added back as capital expenditure).

Renewals

Where a tool is replaced or altered then the cost of the renewal or alteration may be deducted as an expense in certain instances. These are that:

- A deduction would only be prohibited because the expenditure is capital expenditure, and

- No deduction can be given under any other provisions, such as under the capital allowances legislation.

Restrictive covenants

When an employee leaves his employment he may accept a limitation on his future activities in return for a payment. **Provided the employee is taxed on the payment as employment income the payment is a deductible trading expense.**

Secondments

The **costs of seconding employees to charities or educational establishments are deductible.**

Contributions to agent's expenses

Many employers run payroll giving schemes for their employees. **Any payments made to the agent who administers the scheme towards running expenses are deductible.**

Counselling and retraining expenses

Expenditure on providing counselling and retraining for leaving employees is allowable.

Redundancy

Redundancy payments made when a trade ends are deductible on the earlier of the day of payment and the last day of trading. If the trade does not end, they can be deducted as soon as they are provided for, so long as the redundancy was decided on within the period of account, the provision is accurately calculated and the payments are made within nine months of the end of the period of account. **The deduction extends to additional payments of up to three times the amount of the redundancy pay on cessation of trade.**

Personal security expenses

If there is a particular security threat to the trader because of the nature of the trade, **expenditure on his personal security is allowable.**

Contributions to local enterprise organisations/urban regeneration companies

This allows a deduction for donations made to a local enterprise agency, a training and enterprise council, a Scottish local enterprise company, a business link organisation or an urban regeneration company. If any benefit is received by the trade from the donation, this must be deducted from the allowable amount.

Patents, trade marks and copyrights

The costs of **registering patents and trade marks** are deductible for trades only (not professions or vocations). Copyright arises automatically and so does not have to be registered. **Patent royalties and copyright royalties paid in connection with a trade are deductible as trading expenses.**

2.6 Trading income

There are also statutory rules governing whether certain receipts are taxable or not. These are discussed in below.

Capital receipts

As may be expected, capital receipts are not included in trading income. They may, of course, be taken into account in the capital allowances computation, or as a capital gain.

However, compensation received in one lump sum for the loss of income is likely to be treated as income (*Donald Fisher (Ealing) Ltd v Spencer 1989*).

In some trades, (eg petrol stations and public houses), a wholesaler may pay a lump sum to a retailer in return for the retailer only supplying that wholesaler's products for several years (an **exclusivity agreement**). If the payment must be used for a specific capital purpose, it is a capital receipt. If that is not the case, it is an income receipt. If the sum is repayable to the wholesaler but the requirement to repay is waived in tranches over the term of the agreement, each tranche is a separate income receipt when the requirement is waived.

Debts released

If the trader incurs a deductible expense but does not settle the amount due to the supplier, then if the creditor releases the debt other than under a statutory arrangement, the amount released must be brought into account as trading income.

Takeover of trade

If a trader takes over a trade from a previous owner, then if he receives any amounts from that trade which related to a period before the takeover they must be brought into account unless the previous owner has already done so.

NOTES

Insurance receipts

Insurance receipts which are revenue in nature, such as for loss of profits, are trading receipts. Otherwise the receipt must be brought in as trading income if, and to the extent that, any deduction has been claimed for the expense that the receipt is intended to cover.

Gifts of trading stock to educational establishments or schools

When a business makes a gift of equipment manufactured, sold or used in the course of its trade to an educational establishment or for a charitable purpose, nothing need be brought into account as a trading receipt or (if capital allowances had been obtained on the asset) as disposal proceeds, so full relief is obtained for the cost.

2.7 Excluded income

Income taxed in another way

Although the accounts may include other income, such as interest, such income is not trading income. It will instead be taxed under the specific rules for that type of income, such as the rules for savings income.

Certain types of income are specifically exempt from tax, and should be excluded from trade profits.

2.8 Application of general rules

These general rules can be applied to particular types of expenditure and income that you are likely to come across.

Appropriations

Salary or interest on capital paid to a proprietor are not deductible.

Subscriptions and donations

The general 'wholly and exclusively' rule determines the deductibility of expenses. Subscriptions and donations are not deductible unless the expenditure is for the benefit of the trade. The following are the main types of subscriptions and donations you may meet and their correct treatments.

(a) Trade subscriptions (such as to a professional or trade association) are generally deductible.

(b) Charitable donations are deductible only if they are small and to local charities. Tax relief may be available for donations under the gift aid scheme. In the latter case they are not a deductible trading expense.

(c) Political subscriptions and donations are generally not deductible.

(d) Where a donation represents the most effective commercial way of disposing of stock (for example, where it would not be commercially effective to sell surplus perishable food), the donation can be treated as for the benefit of the trade and the disposal proceeds taken as £Nil. In other cases, the amount credited to the accounts in respect of a donation of stock should be its market value.

238

Legal and professional charges

Legal and professional charges relating to capital or non-trading items are not deductible. These include charges incurred in acquiring new capital assets or legal rights, issuing shares, drawing up partnership agreements and litigating disputes over the terms of a partnership agreement.

Charges are deductible if they relate directly to trading. Deductible items include:

- Legal and professional charges incurred defending the taxpayer's title to fixed assets

- Charges connected with an action for breach of contract

- Expenses of the **renewal** (not the original grant) of a lease for less than 50 years

- Charges for trade debt collection

- Normal charges for preparing accounts/assisting with the self assessment of tax liabilities

Accountancy expenses arising out of an enquiry into the accounts information in a particular year's return are not allowed where the enquiry reveals discrepancies and additional liabilities for the year of enquiry, or any earlier year, which arise as a result of negligent or fraudulent conduct.

Where, however, the enquiry results in no addition to profits, or an adjustment to the profits for the year of enquiry only and that assessment does not arise as a result of negligent or fraudulent conduct, the additional accountancy expenses are allowable.

Goods for own use

The usual example is when a proprietor takes goods for his own use. In such circumstances the normal selling price of the goods is added to the accounting profit. In other words, the proprietor is treated for tax purposes as having made a sale to himself (*Sharkey v Wernher 1955*). This rule does not apply to supplies of services, which are treated as sold for the amount (if any) actually paid (but the cost of services to the trader or his household is not deductible).

Other items

The following is a list of various other items that you may meet.

Item	Treatment	Comment
Educational courses for staff	Allow	
Educational courses for proprietor	Allow	If to update existing knowledge or skills, not if to acquire new knowledge or skills
Removal expenses (to new business premises)	Allow	Only if not an expansionary move
Travelling expenses to the trader's place of business	Disallow	*Ricketts v Colquhoun 1925*: unless an itinerant trader (*Horton v Young 1971*)
Compensation for loss of office and ex gratia payments	Allow	If for benefit of trade: *Mitchell v B W Noble Ltd 1927*

Item	Treatment	Comment
Pension contributions (to schemes for employees and company directors)	Allow	Special contributions may be spread over the year of payment and future years
Parking fines	Allow	For employees using their employer's cars on business.
	Disallow	For proprietors/directors
Damages paid	Allow	If not too remote from trade: *Strong and Co v Woodifield 1906*
Preparation and restoration of waste disposal sites	Allow	Spread preparation expenditure over period of use of site. Pre-trading expenditure is treated as incurred on the first day of trading. Allow restoration expenditure in period of expenditure
Dividends on trade investments	Deduct	Taxed as savings income
Rental income from letting part of premises	Deduct	Taxed as income of a UK property business unless it is the letting of surplus business accommodation.

In the exam you could be given a profit and loss account and asked to calculate 'taxable trade profits'. You must look at every expense in the accounts to decide if it is (or isn't) 'tax deductible'. This means that you must become familiar with the many expenses you may see and the correct tax treatment. Look at the above paragraphs again noting what expenses are (and are not) allowable for tax purposes. Similarly you must decide whether income included in the accounts should be included in the taxable trade profits, or whether it should be excluded.

Activity 1   **(15 minutes)**

Here is the profit and loss account of S Pring, a trader

	£	£
Gross operating profit	30,000	
Taxed interest received	860	
		30,860
Wages and salaries	7,000	
Rent and rates	2,000	
Depreciation	1,500	
Impairment of trade receivables	150	
Entertainment expenses	750	
Patent royalties	1,200	
Bank interest	300	
Legal expenses on acquisition of new factory	250	
		(13,150)
Net profit		17,710

(a) Salaries include £500 paid to Mrs Pring who works full time in the business.

(b) No staff were entertained.

(c) Taxed interest and patent royalties are shown gross.

Compute the taxable trade profits.

2.9 The cessation of trades

Post cessation receipts and expenses

Post-cessation receipts (including any releases of debts incurred by the trader) **are chargeable to income tax as miscellaneous income**.

If they are received in the tax year of cessation or the next six tax years, the trader can elect that they be treated as received on the day of cessation. The time limit for electing is the 31 January which is 22 months after the end of the tax year of receipt.

Certain post cessation expenses paid within seven years of discontinuance may be relieved against other income. The expenses must relate to costs of remedying defective work or goods, or legal expenses of or insurance against defective work claims. Relief is also available for trade receivable that subsequently prove to be impaired.

Valuing trading stock on cessation

When a trade ceases, the closing stock must be valued. The higher the value, the higher the profit for the final period of trading.

NOTES

If the stock is sold to a UK trader who will deduct its cost in computing his taxable profits, it is valued under the following rules.

(a)   If the seller and the buyer are unconnected, take the actual price.

(b)   If the seller and the buyer are connected (see below), take what would have been the price in an arm's length sale.

(c)   However, if the seller and the buyer are connected, the arm's length price exceeds both the original cost of the stock and the actual transfer price, and both the seller and the buyer make an election, then take the greater of the original cost of the stock and the transfer price. The time limit for election for unincorporated business is the 31 January which is 22 months after the end of the tax year of cessation (for companies, it is two years after the end of the accounting period of cessation).

In all cases covered above, the value used for the seller's computation of profit is also used as the buyer's cost.

Definition

An individual is **connected** (connected person) with his spouse (or civil partner), with the relatives (brothers, sisters, ancestors and lineal descendants) of himself and his spouse (or civil partner), and with the spouses (or civil partners) of those relatives. In-laws and step family are included; uncles, aunts, nephews, nieces and cousins are not. He is also connected with his business partners (except in relation to bona fide commercial arrangements for the disposal of partnership assets), and with their spouses (or civil partners) and relatives (see diagram below).

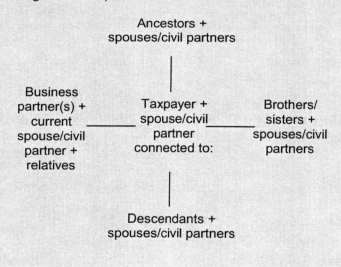

If the stock is not transferred to a UK trader who will be able to deduct its cost in computing his profits, then it is valued at its open market value as at the cessation of trade.

3 CAPITAL ALLOWANCES IN GENERAL

Capital expenditure cannot be deducted in computing taxable trade profits, but it *may* attract capital allowances. Capital allowances are treated as a trading expense and are deducted in arriving at taxable trade profits. Balancing charges, effectively negative allowances, are added in arriving at those profits.

Capital expenditure on plant and machinery qualifies for capital allowances. Expenditure on industrial buildings may also qualify for allowances.

Both unincorporated businesses and companies are entitled to capital allowances. For completeness, in this chapter we will look at the rules for companies alongside those for unincorporated businesses.

For unincorporated businesses, capital allowances are calculated for periods of account. These are simply the periods for which the trader chooses to make up accounts. For companies, capital allowances are calculated for accounting periods.

For capital allowances purposes, expenditure is generally deemed to be incurred when the obligation to pay becomes unconditional. This will often be the date of a contract, but if for example payment is due a month after delivery of a machine, it would be the date of delivery. However, amounts due more than four months after the obligation becomes unconditional are deemed to be incurred when they fall due.

4 PLANT AND MACHINERY – QUALIFYING EXPENDITURE

4.1 Introduction

Capital expenditure on plant and machinery qualifies for capital allowances if the plant or machinery is used for a qualifying activity, such as a trade. 'Plant' is not defined by the legislation, although some specific exclusions and inclusions are given. The word 'machinery' may be taken to have its normal everyday meaning.

4.2 The statutory exclusions

Buildings

Expenditure on a building and on any asset which is incorporated in a building or is of a kind normally incorporated into buildings does not qualify as expenditure on plant, but see below for exceptions.

In addition to complete buildings, **the following assets count as 'buildings', and are therefore not plant.**

- Walls, floors, ceilings, doors, gates, shutters, windows and stairs
- Mains services, and systems, of water, electricity and gas
- Waste disposal, sewerage and drainage systems
- Shafts or other structures for lifts etc.

Structures

Expenditure on structures and on works involving the alteration of land **does not qualify as expenditure on plant,** but see below for exceptions.

A 'structure' is a fixed structure of any kind, other than a building.

Exceptions

Over the years a large body of case law has been built up under which plant and machinery allowances have been given on certain types of expenditure which might be thought to be expenditure on a building or structure. Statute therefore gives a list of various assets which *may* still be plant. These are:

- Any machinery not within any other item in this list

- Electrical (including lighting), cold water, gas and sewerage systems:

    - Provided mainly to meet the particular requirements of the trade, or

    - Provided mainly to serve particular machinery or plant used for the purposes of the trade

- Space or water heating systems and powered systems of ventilation

- Manufacturing and display equipment

- Cookers, washing machines, refrigeration or cooling equipment, sanitary ware, furniture and furnishings

- Lifts etc

- Sound insulation provided mainly to meet the particular requirements of the trade

- Computer, telecommunication and surveillance systems

- Sprinkler equipment, fire alarm and burglar alarm systems

- Strong rooms in bank or building society premises, safes

- Partition walls, where movable and intended to be moved

- Decorative assets provided for the enjoyment of the public in the hotel, restaurant or similar trades, advertising hoardings

- Glasshouses which have, as an integral part of their structure, devices which control the plant growing environment automatically

- Swimming pools (including diving boards, slides) and structures for rides at amusement parks

- Caravans provided mainly for holiday lettings

- Movable buildings intended to be moved in the course of the trade

- Expenditure on altering land for the purpose only of installing machinery or plant

- Dry docks and jetties

- Pipelines, and also underground ducts or tunnels with a primary purpose of carrying utility conduits

- Silos provided for temporary storage and storage tanks, slurry pits and silage clamps

- Fish tanks, fish ponds and fixed zoo cages

- A railway or tramway

Items falling within the above list of exclusions will only qualify as plant if they fall within the meaning of plant as established by case law. This is discussed below.

Land

Land or an interest in land does not qualify as plant and machinery. For this purpose 'land' excludes buildings, structures and assets which are installed or fixed to land in such a way **as to become** part of the land for general legal purposes.

4.3 The statutory inclusions

Certain expenditure is specifically deemed to be expenditure on plant and machinery.

The following are deemed to be on plant and machinery.

- Expenditure incurred by a trader in complying with fire regulations for a building which he occupies

- Expenditure by a trader on thermal insulation of an industrial building

- Expenditure by a trader in meeting statutory safety requirements for sports ground

- Expenditure (by an individual or a partnership, not by a company) on *security assets* provided to meet a special threat to an individual's security that arises wholly or mainly due to the particular trade concerned. Cars, ships, aircraft and dwellings are specifically excluded from the definition of a security asset

On disposal, the sale proceeds for the above are deemed to be zero, so no balancing charge (see below) can arise.

Capital expenditure on computer software (both programs and data) **qualifies as expenditure on plant and machinery**:

(a) Regardless of whether the software is supplied in a tangible form (such as a disk) or transmitted electronically, and

(b) Regardless of whether the purchaser acquires the software or only a licence to use it.

Disposal proceeds are brought into account in the normal way, except that if the fee for the grant of a licence is taxed as income of the licensor, no disposal proceeds are taken into account in computing the licensee's capital allowances.

Where someone has incurred expenditure qualifying for capital allowances on computer software (or the right to use software), and receives a capital sum in exchange for allowing someone else to use the software, that sum is brought into account as disposal proceeds. However, the cumulative total of disposal proceeds is not allowed to exceed the original cost of the software, and any proceeds above this limit are ignored for capital allowances purposes (although they may lead to chargeable gains).

If software is expected to have a useful economic life of less than two years, its cost may be treated as revenue expenditure.

NOTES

For companies the rules for computer software are overridden by the rules for intangible fixed assets unless the company elects otherwise.

4.4 Case law

The original case law **definition of plant** (applied in this case to a horse) is '**whatever apparatus is used by a businessman for carrying on his business: not his stock in trade which he buys or makes for sale; but all goods and chattels, fixed or movable, live or dead, which he keeps for permanent employment in the business**' (*Yarmouth v France 1887*).

Subsequent cases have refined the original definition and have largely been concerned with the **distinction between plant actively used in the business (qualifying) and the setting in which the business is carried on (non-qualifying). This is the 'functional' test.** Some of the decisions have now been enacted as part of statute law, but they are still relevant as examples of the principles involved.

The whole cost of excavating and installing a swimming pool was allowed to the owners of a caravan park. *CIR v Barclay Curle & Co 1969* was followed: the pool performed **the function** of giving 'buoyancy and enjoyment' to the persons using the pool (*Cooke v Beach Station Caravans Ltd 1974*) (actual item now covered by statute).

A barrister succeeded in his claim for his law library: 'Plant includes a man's tools of his trade. It extends to what he uses day by day in the course of his profession. It is not confined to physical things like the dentist's chair or the architect's table' (*Munby v Furlong 1977*).

Office partitioning was allowed. Because it was movable it was not regarded as part of the setting in which the business was carried on (*Jarrold v John Good and Sons Ltd 1963*) (actual item now covered by statute).

A ship used as a floating restaurant was regarded as a 'structure in which the business was carried on rather than apparatus employed ... ' (Buckley LJ). No capital allowances could be obtained (*Benson v Yard Arm Club 1978*). The same decision was made in relation to a football club's spectator stand. The stand performed no function in the actual carrying out of the club's trade (*Brown v Burnley Football and Athletic Co Ltd 1980*).

At a motorway service station, false ceilings contained conduits, ducts and lighting apparatus. **They did not qualify because they did not perform a function in the business. They were merely part of the setting in which the business was conducted** (*Hampton v Fortes Autogrill Ltd 1979*).

Light fittings, decor and murals can be plant. A company carried on business as hoteliers and operators of licensed premises. The function of the items was the creation of an atmosphere conducive to the comfort and well being of its customers (*CIR v Scottish and Newcastle Breweries Ltd 1982*) (decorative assets used in hotels etc, now covered by statute).

On the other hand, it has been held that when an attractive floor is provided in a restaurant, the fact that the floor performs the function of making the restaurant attractive to customers is not enough to make it plant. It functions as premises; the cost therefore does not qualify for capital allowances (*Wimpy International Ltd v Warland 1988*).

General lighting in a department store is not plant, as it is merely setting. Special display lighting, however, can be plant (*Cole Brothers Ltd v Phillips 1982*).

BPP
LEARNING MEDIA

Free-standing decorative screens installed in the windows of a branch of a building society qualified as plant. Their function was not to act a part of the setting in which the society's business was carried on; it was to attract local custom, and accordingly the screens formed part of the apparatus with which the society carried on its business (*Leeds Permanent Building Society v Proctor 1982*).

In *Bradley v London Electricity plc 1996* an electricity substation was held not to be plant because it functioned as premises in which London Electricity carried on a trading activity rather than apparatus with which the activity was carried out.

5 ALLOWANCES ON PLANT AND MACHINERY

5.1 Pooling expenditure

Most expenditure on plant and machinery is put into a pool of expenditure (the main pool) on which capital allowances may be claimed, including cars with CO_2 emissions of 160g/km or less acquired on or after 6 April 2009 (1 April 2009 for companies). An addition increases the pool whilst a disposal decreases it.

Exceptionally the following items are not put into the main pool:

    (a)   assets dealt with in the special rate pool

    (b)   assets with private use by the trader

    (c)   short life assets where an election has been made.

Each of these items is dealt with in further detail later in this chapter.

Expenditure on plant and machinery by a person about to begin a trade is treated as incurred on the first day of trading. Assets previously owned by a trader and then brought into the trade (at the start of trading or later) are treated as bought for their market values at the times when they are brought in.

5.2 Annual investment allowance

Businesses can claim an **Annual Investment Allowance (AIA) on the first £50,000 spent on plant or machinery,** including assets in the main pool, but not including motor cars. Expenditure on motorcycles does qualify for the AIA.

Where the period of account is more or less than a year, the maximum allowance is proportionately increased or reduced.

Main pool expenditure which qualifies for the AIA but is in excess of £50,000 will qualify for a first year allowance if the expenditure is made between 6 April 2009 and 5 April 2010 (1 April 2009 and 31 March 2010 for companies) (see further below).

If there is no first year allowance available on the excess expenditure, for example of the expenditure is made in March 2009 or in May 2011, **the balance of expenditure after the AIA is transferred to the main pool immediately and will be eligible for writing down allowances in the same period.**

5.3 First year allowances and enhanced capital allowances

A first year allowance (FYA) at the rate of 40% is available on the balance of expenditure on plant and machinery (excluding cars and special rate pool expenditure) not covered by the Annual Investment Allowance. A FYA at the rate of 100% is available on low emission cars. Enhanced capital allowances (ECAs) are available on green technologies. FYAs and ECAs are never pro-rated in short periods of account.

FYA on plant and machinery

There is a temporary first year allowance (FYA) of 40% available on expenditure on most plant and machinery between 6 April 2009 and 5 April 2010 (between 1 April 2009 and 31 March 2010 for companies). Expenditure on motor cars and assets in the special rate pool (see further below) does not qualify for this FYA.

The FYA is applied after the AIA. Any remaining balance will be added to the main pool.

It is important to note that the remaining balance after applying the FYA is transferred to the main pool AFTER writing down allowances have been calculated on any pool balance brought forward. This is because the temporary FYA is given instead of writing down allowances.

FYA on low emission cars

Definition

> A **low emission car** is one which has **CO_2 emissions of 110g/km or less.**

A 100% FYA is available for expenditure incurred on low emission motor cars registered between 17 April 2002 and 31 March 2013.

If the FYA is not claimed in full, the balance of expenditure is transferred to the main pool.

Enhanced capital allowances (ECAs)

Capital expenditure on new (ie not second hand) energy and water saving plant and machinery ('green technologies') qualifies for 100% ECAs. Companies can surrender ECAs for a tax credit of 10%. this is idealt with in more detail when we look at companies later in this Course Book.

Short periods of account

FYAs and ECAs are nor reduced pro-rata in a short period of account, unlike the AIA and writing down allowances.

5.4 Writing down allowances

Most expenditure on plant and machinery qualifies for a WDA at 20% every 12 months.

Definition

A **writing down allowance (WDA)** is given on main pool expenditure **at the rate of 20% a year** (on a reducing balance basis). The WDA is calculated on the written down value (WDV) of pooled plant, after adding the current period's additions and taking out the current period's disposals.

When plant is sold, proceeds, **limited to a maximum of the original cost**, are taken out of the pool. Provided that the trade is still being carried on, the pool balance remaining is written down in the future by WDAs, even if there are no assets left.

EXAMPLE: CAPITAL ALLOWANCES (1)

Elizabeth has a tax written down value on her main pool of plant and machinery of £16,000 on 6 April 2009. In the year to 5 April 2010 she bought a car with CO_2 emissions of 130g/km for £8,000 (no non-business use) and she disposed of plant (which originally cost £4,000) for £6,000.

Calculate the maximum capital allowances claim for the year.

	Main pool £	Allowances £
Pool value b/f	16,000	
Addition (not qualifying for AIA or FYA)	8,000	
Less: Disposal (limited to cost)	(4,000)	
	20,000	
WDA @ 20%	(4,000)	(4,000)
TWDV c/f	16,000	
Maximum capital allowances claim		4,000

EXAMPLE: CAPITAL ALLOWANCES (2)

Julia is a sole trader making up accounts to 5 April each year. At 5 April 2009, the tax written down value on her main pool is £20,000.

In the year to 5 April 2010, Julia bought the following assets:

1 June 2009	Machine	£40,000
12 November 2009	Van	£17,500
10 February 2009	Car for salesman (CO2 emissions 150g/km)	£9,000

She disposed of plant on 15 December 2009 for £12,000 (original cost £16,000).

Calculate the maximum capital allowances claim that Julia can make for the year ended 5 April 2010.

	AIA/FYA £	Main pool £	Allowances £
y/e 5 April 2010			
TWDV b/f		20,000	
Additions qualifying for AIA/FYA			
1.6.09 Machine	40,000		
12.11.09 Van	17,500		
	57,500		
AIA	(50,000)		50,000
	7,500		
FYA @ 40%	(3,000)		3,000
Additions not qualifying for AIA/FYA			
10.2.10 Car		9,000	
Disposal			
15.12.09 Plant		(12,000)	
		17,000	
WDA @ 20%		(3,400)	3,400
		13,600	
Transfer balance to pool	(4,500)	4,500	
TWDV c/f		18,100	
Maximum capital allowances			56,400

EXAMPLE: CAPITAL ALLOWANCES BEFORE AND AFTER 6 APRIL 2009

Marcus is a sole trader making up accounts to 31 December each year. At 1 January 2009, the tax written down value on his main pool is £30,000.

In the year to 31 December 2009, Marcus bought the following assets:

| 1 February 2009 | Plant | £60,000 |
| 15 September 2009 | Machinery | £22,500 |

He made no disposals in the year to 31 December 2009.

Calculate the maximum capital allowances claim that Marcus can make for the year ended 31 December 2009.

	AIA/FYA £	Main pool £	Allowances £
y/e 31 December 2009			
TWDV b/f		30,000	
Additions qualifying for AIA only (N1)			
1.2.09 Machinery	60,000		
AIA	(50,000)		50,000
	10,000		
Transfer balance to pool	(10,000)	10,000	
		40,000	
Additions qualifying for AIA/FYA (N2)			
15.9.09 Plant	22,500		
FYA @ 40%	(9,000)		9,000
	13,500		
WDA @ 20%		(8,000)	8,000
		32,000	
Transfer balance to pool	(13,500)	13,500	
TWDV c/f		45,500	
Maximum capital allowances			67,000

Notes

1   The best use of the AIA is to set it against expenditure which only qualifies for this allowance and not for the FYA, thus leaving excess expenditure eligible for the FYA @ 40% instead of the WDA @ 20%.

2   Technically this expenditure is eligible for both these allowances, although in this case the AIA has already been used as explained in note 1. You may have a situation where there not all of the AIA has been used up against expenditure only qualifying for the AIA. You would deal with the remaining AIA in the same way as in the previous example by setting it off against expenditure qualifying for both the AIA and FYA before applying the FYA.

NOTES

5.5 Short and long periods of account

WDAs are 20% × number of months/12:

(a) For unincorporated businesses where the period of account is longer or shorter than 12 months

(b) For companies where the accounting period is shorter than 12 months (a company's accounting period for tax purposes is never longer than 12 months), or where the trade concerned started in the accounting period and was therefore carried on for fewer than 12 months.

EXAMPLE: SHORT PERIOD OF ACCOUNT

Venus is a sole trader and has made up accounts to 30 April each year. At 30 April 2009, the tax written down value of her main pool was £80,000. She decides to make up her next set of accounts to 31 December 2009.

In the period to 31 December 2009, the following acquisitions were made:

1 May 2009	Plant	£60,000
10 July 2009	Car (CO_2 emissions 130 g/km)	£9,000
3 August 2009	Car (CO_2 emissions 105 g/km)	£11,000

Venus disposed of plant on 1 November 2009 for £20,000 (original cost £28,000).

Calculate the maximum capital allowances that Venus can claim for the period ending 31 December 2009.

	AIA/FYA @ 40% £	FYA @ 100% £	Main pool £	Allowances £
p/e 31 December 2009				
TWDV b/f			80,000	
Additions qualifying for AIA and FYA				
1.5.09 Plant	60,000			
AIA £50,000 × 8/12	(33,333)			33,333
	26,667			
FYA on balance @ 40%	(10,667)			10,667
Additions qualifying for FYA only				
3.8.09 Car (low emission)		11,000		
Less: 100% FYA		(11,000)		11,000
c/f	16,000	0	80,000	55,000
Additions not qualifying for AIA or FYA				
10.7.09 Car			9,000	
Disposals				
1.11.09 Plant			(20,000)	
			69,000	
WDA @ 20% × 8/12			(9,200)	9,200
			59,800	
Transfer balance to pool	(16,000)		16,000	
Transfer balance to pool		0	0	
TWDVs c/f			75,800	
Maximum allowances claim				64,200

Note that the annual investment allowance and the writing down allowance are reduced for the short period of account, but the first year allowance is given in full.

EXAMPLE: LONG PERIOD OF ACCOUNT

Oscar started trading on 1 July 2009 and made up his first set of accounts to 31 December 2010. He bought the following assets:

10 July 2009	Plant	£60,000
10 October 2009	Car for business use only	£11,000
	(CO$_2$ emissions 140g/km)	
12 February 2010	Plant	£80,000

Calculate the maximum capital allowances claim that Oscar can make for the period ended 31 December 2010.

	AIA/FYA £	Main pool £	Allowances £
p/e 31 December 2010			
Additions qualifying for AIA/FYA			
10.7.09 Plant	60,000		
12.2.10 Plant	80,000		
	140,000		
AIA £50,000 × 18/12	(75,000)		75,000
	65,000		
FYA @ 40%	(26,000)		26,000
Additions not qualifying for AIA/FYA			
1.10.09 Car		11,000	
WDA @ 20% × 18/12		(3,300)	3,300
		7,700	
Transfer balance to main pool	(39,000)	39,000	
TWDV c/f		46,700	
Maximum capital allowances			104,300

Note that the annual investment allowance and the writing down allowance are increased for the long period of account, but the FYA is given in full.

5.6 Small balance on main pool

A writing down allowance equal to unrelieved expenditure in the main pool can be claimed where this is **£1,000 or less**. If the maximum WDA is claimed, the main pool will then have a nil balance carried forward.

EXAMPLE: SMALL BALANCE ON MAIN POOL

Alan has traded for many years, making up accounts to 30 April each year. At 1 May 2009, the tax written down value of his main pool was £15,000.

On 1 October 2009, he sold some plant and machinery for £14,200 (original cost £16,000).

Calculate the maximum capital allowances claim that Alan can make for the period ending 30 April 2010.

	Main pool	Allowances
	£	£
y/e 30 April 2010		
TWDV b/f	15,000	
Disposal	(14,200)	
	800	
WDA (small pool)	(800)	800
TWDV c/f	nil	
Maximum capital allowances		800

Note the tax planning opportunities available. If plant is bought just before an accounting date, allowances become available as soon as possible. Alternatively, it may be desirable to claim less than the maximum allowances to even out annual taxable profits and avoid a higher rate of tax in later years.

5.7 Balancing charges and allowances

Balancing charges occur when the disposal value deducted exceeds the balance remaining in the pool. The charge equals the excess and is effectively a negative capital allowance, increasing profits. Most commonly this happens when the trade ceases and the remaining assets are sold. It may also occur, however, whilst the trade is still in progress.

Balancing allowances on the main and special pools of expenditure arise only when the trade ceases. The balancing allowance is equal to the remaining unrelieved expenditure after deducting the disposal value of all the assets. Balancing allowances may also arise on single pool items (see below) whenever those items are disposed of.

Activity 2   **(20 minutes)**

Bradley has been trading for many years, preparing accounts to 31 December. He ceases trading on 31 August 2010. The written down value of the general pool at 1 January 2009 was £25,260 and the written down value of the expensive motor car (40% private use by Bradley) was £21,225.

Bradley made the following purchases and sales of plant and machinery in the last 20 months to 31 August 2010:

		£
7 June 2006	Bought machinery	1,620
12 May 2007	Bought machinery	1,740
31 August 2007	Sold all pool items (all less than original cost)	25,295
31 August 2007	Sold car	16,500

What is balancing adjustment is required on cessation?

---

6 SPECIAL RATE POOL

The special rate pool contains expenditure on thermal insulation, long life assets, features integral to a building and cars with CO2 emissions over 160g/km. The AIA can be used against such expenditure except cars. The WDA is 10%.

6.1 Operation of the special rate pool

Expenditure on thermal insulation, long life assets, features integral to a building, and cars with CO_2 emissions over 160g/km acquired on or after 6 April 2009 (1 April 2009 for companies), is not dealt with in the main pool but in a special rate pool.

The Annual Investment Allowance can apply to expenditure on such assets except on cars. The taxpayer can decide how to allocate the AIA. It will be more tax efficient to set the allowance against special rate pool expenditure in priority to main pool expenditure where there is expenditure on assets in both pools in the period. Expenditure in excess of the AIA is added to the special rate pool and will be eligible for writing down allowance in the same period in which the expenditure is incurred.

The writing down allowance for the special rate pool is 10% for a twelve month period. As with the writing down allowance on the main pool, this is adjusted for short and long periods of account. Where the tax written down balance of the special rate pool is £1,000 or less, a writing down allowance can be claimed of up to £1,000. This is in addition to any similar claim in relation to the main pool.

6.2 Long life assets

Definition

> **Long life assets** are assets with an expected working life of 25 years or more.

The **long life asset rules only apply to businesses whose total expenditure on assets with an expected working life of 25 years or more in a chargeable period is more than £100,000**. If the expenditure exceeds £100,000, the whole of the expenditure enters the special rate pool. For this purpose all expenditure incurred under a contract is treated as incurred in the first chargeable period to which that contract relates.

The £100,000 limit is reduced or increased proportionately in the case of a chargeable period of less or more than 12 months.

The following are **not** treated as long life assets:

(a) **Plant and machinery in dwelling houses, retail shops, showrooms, hotels and offices**

(b) **Cars**

6.3 Integral features

Features which are integral to a building include the following:

- **electrical and lighting systems**
- **cold water systems**
- **space or water heating systems**
- **powered systems of ventilation, cooling or air conditioning**
- **lifts and escalators**

When a building is sold, the vendor and purchaser can make a joint election to determine how the sale proceeds are apportioned between the building and its integral features.

EXAMPLE

Lucy has been trading for many years, making up accounts to 5 April each year. The tax written down value of her main pool at 5 April 2009 was £110,000. In the year to 5 April 2010, Lucy had the following expenditure:

10 June 2009	General plant costing £45,000
12 December 2009	Lighting system in shop £40,000
15 January 2010	Car for business use only (CO_2 emissions 175 g/km) £25,000
26 January 2010	Delivery van £15,000
4 March 2010	Lifts £20,000

The maximum capital allowances claim that Lucy can make for the year to 5 April 2010 is:

	AIA/FYA £	Main pool £	Special rate pool £	Allowances £
y/e 5 April 2010				
TWDV b/f		110,000		
Additions qualifying for AIA only				
12.12.09 Lighting	40,000			
4.3.10 Lifts	20,000			
	60,000			
AIA	(50,000)			50,000
Transfer balance to special rate pool	10,000		10,000	
c/f			10,000	50,000
Additions qualifying for FYA				
(AIA already used)				
10.6.09 Plant	45,000			
26.1.10 Van	15,000			
	60,000			
FYA @ 40%	(24,000)			24,000
Additions not qualifying for AIA/FYA				
15.1.10 Car			25,000	
			35,000	
WDA @ 20%		(22,000)		22,000
WDA @ 10%			(3,500)	3,500
		88,000		
Transfer balance to main pool	36,000	36,000		
TWDVs c/f		124,000	31,500	
Allowances				99,500

7 PRIVATE USE ASSETS

An asset (for example, a car) **which is used partly for private purposes by a sole trader or a partner is put into its own pool** (single asset pool).

Capital allowances are calculated on the full cost. The WDA is 20% for cars with CO_2 emissions up to 160 g/km and 10% for cars with CO_2 emissions above 160g/km. The WDA for other assets is 20%.

However, only the business use proportion of the allowances is allowed as a deduction from trading profits. This restriction applies to the AIA, FYAs, WDAs, balancing allowances and balancing charges (there are no FYAs on cars).

An asset with some private use by an employee (not the owner of the business) suffers no such restriction. The employee may be taxed under the benefits code so the business receives capital allowances on the full cost of the asset.

NOTES

EXAMPLE

Jacinth has been in business as a sole trader for many years, making up accounts to 31 March. On 1 November 2009 she bought computer equipment for £2,700 which she uses 75% in her business and 25% privately. She has already used the AIA against other expenditure in the year to 31 December 2009.

Calculate the maximum capital allowance that Jacinth can claim in respect to the computer equipment in the year to 31 March 2010 and the year to 31 March 2011.

	Computer equipment £	Allowances @ 75% £
y/e 31 March 2010		
Acquisition	2,700	
FYA @ 40%	(1,080)	810
TWDV c/f	1,620	
Maximum capital allowance on computer equipment		810
y/e 31 March 2011		
WDA @ 20%	(324)	243
TWDV c/f	1,296	
Maximum capital allowance on computer equipment		243

8   MOTOR CARS

8.1   Motor cars acquired before April 2009

Each motor car acquired before 6 April 2009 (1 April 2009 for companies) which cost more than £12,000 (sometimes called 'expensive' cars) is dealt with in a single asset pool. This means that a separate record of allowances and WDV is kept for each such car and when it is sold a balancing allowance or charge arises.

Expensive cars are eligible for writing down allowances at 20% regardless of their CO_2 emissions. However, the maximum WDA is £3,000 a year. The limit is £3,000 × months/12 in periods of account which are not 12 months long.

Motor cars acquired before 6 April 2009 which cost £12,000 or less were pooled in the main pool, unless there was private use by a sole trader or partner.

EXAMPLE

Niall is a sole trader making up accounts to 5 April each year. His business already owns four cars, used only for business purposes:

Car 1: This car was acquired for £24,000 and had a tax written down value at 6 April 2009 of £18,000. The car has CO_2 emissions of 150g/km.

Car 2: This car cost £19,000 and had a tax written down value at 6 April 2009 of £13,000. The car has CO_2 emissions of 180g/km.

Car 3: This car cost £15,000 and had a tax written down value at 6 April 2009 of £9,000. The car has CO_2 emissions of 140g/km. It was sold on 10 December 2009 for £7,500.

Car 4: This car cost £9,000. It is included in the main pool which had a total tax written down value at 6 April 2009 of £33,000. The car has CO_2 emissions of 120g/km. It was sold on 10 March 2010 for £6,600.

There were no acquisition and no other disposals of assets in the year ended 5 April 2010.

Calculate the maximum capital allowances that Niall can claim for the year ended 5 April 2010.

	Main pool	Car 1 £	Car 2 £	Car 3 £	Allowances £
y/e 5 April 2010					
TWDVs b/f	33,000	18,000	13,000	9,000	
Disposals					
10.12.09 Car 3				(7,500)	
Balancing allowance				1,500	1,500
10.3.10 Car 4	(6,600)				
	26,400				
WDA @ 20%	(5,280)				5,280
WDA @ 20% (max)		(3,000)			3,000
WDA @ 20%			(2,600)		2,600
TWDVs c/f	21,120	15,000	10,400		
Maximum allowances claim					12,380

Notes

1 The writing down allowance for Car 3 is 20% even though it has CO_2 emissions of 180g/km. This is because it was acquired before 6 April 2009. If it had been acquired on or after 6 April 2009, it would only have been eligible for a writing down allowance of 10% (see further below).

2 The disposal of Car 4 does not result in a balancing event because it is part of the main pool. Contrast this treatment with the disposal of Car 3 which does lead to a balancing allowance.

A motor car with private use by a sole trader or partner is always dealt with in a single asset pool, regardless of cost. Such cars acquired before 6 April 2009 will be eligible for writing down allowances at 20%, subject to a maximum of £3,000 per year. Only the business use proportion of the allowances is allowed as a deduction from trading profit, but the full allowance is deducted in calculating the car's tax written down value carried forward.

8.2 Motor cars acquired from April 2009

As we have already seen, motor cars acquired from 6 April 2009 (1 April 2009 for companies) are categorised in accordance with their CO_2 emissions:

(a) **Cars emitting over 160g/km**: expenditure is added to the special rate pool,

(b) **Cars emitting between 111 and 160 g/km**: expenditure is added to the main pool,

(c) **Cars emitting 110 g/km or less**: expenditure eligible for 100% first year allowance, if allowance not claimed in full, excess added to main pool.

Cars with an element of private use continue to be kept separate from the main and special pools and are dealt with in single asset pools. They are entitled to a WDA of 20% (car with CO_2 emissions between 111 and 160 g/km) or 10% (car with CO_2 emissions over 160 g/km). There is no maximum WDA for such cars.

EXAMPLE

Quodos started to trade on 1 July 2009, making up accounts to 31 December 2009 and each 31 December thereafter. On 1 August 2009 he bought a car for £17,000 with CO_2 emissions of 130 g/km. The private use proportion is 10%. The car was sold in July 2012 for £4,000. Calculate the capital allowances, assuming:

(a) The car was used by an employee, or
(b) The car was used by Quodos.

(a)	Car £	Allowances £
1.7.09 – 31.12.09		
Purchase price	17,000	
WDA 20% × 6/12 x £17,000	(1,700)	1,700
	15,300	
1.1.10 – 31.12.10		
WDA 20% x £15,300	(3,060)	3,060
	12,240	
1.1.11 – 31.12.11		
WDA 20% x £12,240	(2,448)	2,448
	9,792	
1.1.12 – 31.12.12		
Proceeds	(4,000)	
Balancing allowance	5,792	5,792

The private use of the car by the employee has no effect on the capital allowances due to Quodos.

BPP
LEARNING MEDIA

(b)

	Car	Allowances 90%
	£	£

1.7.09 – 31.12.09
Purchase price — 17,000
WDA 20% × 6/12 x £17,000 — (1,700) — 1,530
15,300

1.1.10 – 31.12.10
WDA 20% x £15,300 — (3,060) — 2,754
12,240

1.1.11 – 31.12.11
WDA 20% x £12,240 — (2,448) — 2,203
9,792

1.1.12 – 31.12.12
Proceeds — (4,000)
Balancing allowance — 5,792 — 5,213

As the private use is by the proprietor, Quodos, only 90% of the WDAs and balancing allowance are available.

8.3 Motor cars: summary table

	Main pool WDA @ 20%	Special rate pool WDA @ 10%	Single asset pool WDA @ 20%	Single asset pool WDA @ 10%
Car acquired before 6.4.09 (1.4.09 for companies)				
Cost less than £12,000, no private use	•			
Cost £12,000 or more, no private use			• max £3,000	
Cost less than £12,000, private use (sole trader or partner only)			•	
Cost £12,000 or more, private use (sole trader or partner only)			• max £3,000	
Car acquired on or after 6.4.09 (1.4.09 for companies)				
CO_2 emissions 111g/km – 160g/km, no private use	•			

	Main pool WDA @ 20%	Special rate pool WDA @ 10%	Single asset pool WDA @ 20%	Single asset pool WDA @ 10%
CO_2 emissions over 160g/km, no private use		•		
CO_2 emissions 111g/km – 160g/km, private use (sole trader or partner only)			•	
CO_2 emissions over 160g/km, private use (sole trader or partner only)				•

9   SHORT-LIFE ASSETS

A trader can elect that specific items of plant be kept separately from the main pool. The election is irrevocable. For an unincorporated business, the time limit for electing is the 31 January which is 22 months after the end of the tax year in which the period of account of the expenditure ends. (For a company, it is two years after the end of the accounting period of the expenditure.) **Any asset subject to this election is known as a 'short life asset', and the election is known as a 'de-pooling election'.**

Provided that the asset is disposed of within four years of the end of the accounting period in which it was bought, it is a **short life asset** and a balancing charge or allowance arises on its disposal.

If the asset is not disposed of within this time period, its tax written down value is added to the main pool at the end of that time.

The election should be made for assets likely to be sold for less than their tax written down values within four years. It should not usually be made for assets likely to be sold within four years for more than their tax written down values. (These are, of course, only general guidelines based on the assumption that a trader will want to obtain allowances as quickly as possible. There may be other considerations, such as a desire to even out annual taxable profits.)

The Annual Investment Allowance can be set against short life assets. The taxpayer can decide how to allocate the AIA. It will be more tax efficient to set the allowance against main pool expenditure in priority to short life asset expenditure. The FYA is also available for short life assets where relevant.

> **Activity 3**   **(10 mins)**
>
> Caithlin bought a machine for business use on 1 May 20039 for £12,000 and elected for de-pooling. She did not claim the AIA in respect of this asset. Her accounting year end is 30 April. Calculate the capital allowances due if:
>
> (a)   The asset is scrapped for £300 in August 2013.
>
> (b)   The asset is scrapped for £200 in August 2014.

Short-life asset treatment cannot be claimed for motor cars or plant used partly for non-trade purposes.

10   HIRE PURCHASE AND LEASING

Capital allowances are available on assets acquired by hire purchase or lease.

10.1   Assets on hire purchase or long term leases

Any asset (including a car) bought on hire purchase (HP) is treated as if purchased outright for the cash price. Therefore:

(a)   The buyer normally obtains **capital allowances on the cash price** when the agreement begins.

(b)   He may write off the **finance charge as a trade expense** over the term of the HP contract.

Long term leases (those with a term of 5 or more years), are treated in the same way as HP transactions.

10.2   Assets on long term leases

Under a long term lease, the lessee merely hires the asset over a period. The hire charge can normally be deducted in computing trade profits. If an expensive car (one costing over £12,000) is leased, the maximum allowable deduction from trading profits for lease rentals is limited, as described earlier.

A long term lessor of plant normally obtains the benefit of capital allowances although there are anti-avoidance provisions which deny or restrict capital allowances on certain finance leases. Leasing is thus an activity which attracts tax allowances and which can be used to defer tax liabilities where the capital allowances given exceed the rental income. For individuals, any losses arising from leasing are available for offset against other income only if the individual devotes substantially all of his time to the conduct of a leasing business.

11   SUCCESSIONS

Balancing adjustments arise on the cessation of a business. No writing down allowances are given, but the final proceeds (limited to cost) on sales of plant are compared with the tax WDV to calculate balancing allowances or charges.

Balancing charges may be avoided where the trade passes from one connected person to another. If a succession occurs both parties must elect if the avoidance of the balancing adjustments is required. **An election will result in the plant being transferred at its tax written down value for capital allowances purposes.** The predecessor can write down the plant for the period prior to cessation and the successor can write it down from the date of commencement. The election must be made within two years of the date of the succession.

If no election is made on a transfer of business to a connected person, assets are deemed to be sold at their market values.

As we saw earlier, an individual is connected with his spouse, his or his spouse's brothers, sisters, ancestors and lineal descendants, with their spouses, with business partners and their spouses and relatives, and with a company he controls. 'Spouses' includes civil partners.

Where a person succeeds to a business under a will or on intestacy, then even if he was not connected with the deceased he may elect to take over the assets at the lower of their market value and their tax written down value.

For both connected persons transfers and transfers on death, where the elections are made, the limit on proceeds to be brought into account on a later sale of an asset is the original cost of the asset, not the deemed transfer price.

12   INDUSTRIAL BUILDINGS ALLOWANCE

12.1   General definition

A special type of capital allowance (an **industrial buildings allowance** or IBA) is available in respect of **expenditure on industrial buildings**. It is being phased out over the next few years and will be abolished from 2010/11.

The allowance is available to:

- Traders
- Landlords who let qualifying buildings to traders.

Traders can choose whether to segregate expenditure on long life assets in buildings and claim plant and machinery allowances (see above) or whether to claim industrial buildings allowances on the expenditure. Since industrial buildings allowance is being phased out it would be better to claim plant and machinery allowances in such a case.

Definition

> **Industrial buildings** include:
>
> (a)   All factories and ancillary premises used in:
>
>   (i)   A manufacturing business
>   (ii)   A trade in which goods and materials are subject to any process
>   (iii)   A trade in which goods or raw materials are stored
>
> (b)   Staff welfare buildings (such as workplace nurseries and canteens, but not directors' restaurants) where the trade is qualifying

(c) Sport pavilions in any trade

(d) Buildings in use for a transport undertaking, agricultural contracting, mining or fishing

(e) Roads operated under highway concessions. The operation of such roads is treated as a trade for capital allowances purposes. The operator is treated as occupying the roads.

The key term in (a) (ii) above is 'the subjection of goods to any process'.

- The unpacking, repacking and relabelling of goods in a wholesale cash and carry supermarket did not amount to a 'process' but was a mere preliminary to sale (*Bestway Holdings Ltd v Luff 1998*).

- The mechanical processing of cheques and other banking documents was a process but pieces of paper carrying information were not 'goods' and thus the building housing the machinery did not qualify (*Girobank plc v Clarke 1998*).

Estate roads on industrial estates qualify, provided that the estate buildings are used wholly or mainly for a qualifying purpose.

Dwelling houses, retail shops, showrooms and offices are not industrial buildings (although see below for exception.)

Drawing offices (ie those used for technical product and manufacturing planning) which serve an industrial building are regarded as industrial buildings themselves (*CIR v Lambhill Ironworks Ltd 1950*).

Warehouses used for storage often cause problems in practice. A warehouse used for storage which is merely a transitory and necessary incident of the conduct of the business is not an industrial building. Storage is only a qualifying purpose if it is an end in itself.

Any building is an industrial building if it is constructed for the welfare of employees of a trader whose trade is a qualifying one (that is, the premises in which the trade is carried on are industrial buildings).

Sports pavilions provided for the welfare of employees qualify as industrial buildings. In this case, it does not matter whether the taxpayer is carrying on a trade in a qualifying building or not. Thus a retailer's sports pavilion would qualify for IBAs.

12.2 Hotels

Allowances on hotels are given as though they were industrial buildings.

Definition

For a building to qualify as a **'hotel'** for industrial buildings allowance purposes:

(a) It much have at least ten letting bedrooms

(b) It must have letting bedrooms as the whole or main part of the sleeping accommodation

> (c) It must offer ancillary services including at least:
>
> (i) Breakfast
> (ii) Evening meals
> (iii) The cleaning of rooms
> (iv) The making of beds
>
> (d) It must be open for at least four months during the April to October season.

12.3 Eligible expenditure

Capital allowances are computed on the amount of eligible expenditure incurred on qualifying buildings. The eligible expenditure is:

- The original cost of a building if built by the trader, or

- The purchase price if the building was acquired from a person trading as a builder.

If the building was acquired other than from a person trading as a builder, the eligible expenditure is the lower of the purchase price and the original cost incurred by the person incurring the construction expenditure.

If a building is sold more than once before being brought into use, the last buyer before the building is brought into use obtains the allowances. If, in such cases, the building was first sold by someone trading as a builder, the eligible expenditure is the lower of the price paid by the first buyer and the price paid by the last buyer.

In all cases where a building is sold before use and artificial arrangements have increased the purchase price, it is reduced to what it would have been without those arrangements.

Where part of a building qualifies as an industrial building and part does not, the whole cost qualifies for IBAs, provided that the cost of the non-qualifying part is not more than 25% of the total expenditure. If the non-qualifying part of the building does cost more than 25% of the total, its cost must be excluded from the capital allowances computation.

Difficulties arise where non-qualifying buildings (particularly offices and administration blocks) are joined to manufacturing areas. In *Abbott Laboratories Ltd v Carmody 1968* a covered walkway linking manufacturing and administrative areas was not regarded as creating a single building. The administrative area was treated as a separate, non-qualifying building.

The cost of land is disallowed but expenditure incurred in preparing land for building does qualify. The cost of items which would not be included in a normal commercial lease (such as rental guarantees) also does not qualify.

Professional fees, for example architects' fees, incurred in connection with the construction of an industrial building qualify. The cost of repairs to industrial buildings also qualifies, provided that the expenditure is not deductible as a trading expense.

EXAMPLE: IBAs AND ELIGIBLE EXPENSES

Sue purchased an industrial building for £2,500,000. This cost was made up of:

	£
Factory	2,100,000
Land	400,000
	2,500,000

The costs attributable to showrooms and offices within the factory were £400,000 and £200,000 respectively.

What is the expenditure qualifying for industrial buildings allowances?

The showrooms and offices are non-qualifying parts of the building. As the cost of the non qualifying parts, £600,000, is more than 25% of the total expenditure on the building (£2,100,000), industrial buildings allowances are not available on it. The cost of the land is not qualifying expenditure.

The qualifying expenditure for industrial buildings allowance purposes is therefore £1,500,000 (£2,100,000 – £600,000).

12.4 Writing down allowances

A writing down allowance (WDA) is given to the person holding the 'relevant interest'. Broadly, the relevant interest is the interest of the first acquirer of the industrial building and may be a freehold or leasehold interest.

Where a long lease (more than 50 years) has been granted on an industrial building, the grant may be treated as a sale so that allowances may be claimed by the lessee rather than the lessor. A claim must be made by the lessor and lessee jointly, within two years of the start of the lease. The election allows allowances to be claimed on industrial buildings where the lessor is not subject to tax (as with local authorities).

The WDA is given for a period provided that the industrial building was in use as such on the last day of the period concerned.

The WDA is 2% (2009/10) of the eligible expenditure incurred by the taxpayer.

The allowance is calculated on a straight line basis (in contrast to WDAs on plant and machinery which are calculated on the reducing balance), starting when the building is brought into use.

The WDA is 2% × months/12 if the period concerned is not 12 months long.

Buildings always have a **separate computation for each building**. They are never pooled.

NOTES

Activity 4   **(15 mins)**

Mark has been a sole trader for many years, making up accounts to 5 April each year.

On 12 September 2009, he bought a new industrial building from a builder at a cost of £800,000 which he brought into use immediately.

The total cost can be analysed as follows:

	£
Land	200,000
Preparing land	50,000
Architect's fees	40,000
Factory	150,000
Storage warehouse	100,000
Staff canteen	90,000
Offices	170,000
Total expenditure	800,000

Calculate the industrial buildings allowance available to Mark for the year ended 5 April 2010.

12.5 Sales of industrial buildings

Until 21 March 2007, the disposal of an industrial building gave rise to a balancing adjustment (ie a balancing change or a balancing allowance).

In preparation for the eventual abolition of industrial buildings allowance, **no balancing adjustments apply for disposals from 21 March 2007 onwards**.

BPP
LEARNING MEDIA

Chapter roundup

- The badges of trade can be used to decide whether or not a trade exists. If one does exist, the accounts profits need to be adjusted in order to establish the taxable profits.

- Expenditure which is not incurred wholly and exclusively for trade purposes is disallowable.

- Capital allowances are available on plant and machinery and industrial buildings.

- Statutory rules generally exclude specified items from treatment as plant, rather than include specified items as plant.

- There are several cases on the definition of plant. To help you to absorb them, try to see the function/setting theme running through them

- With capital allowances computations, the main thing is to get the layout right. Having done that, you will find that the figures tend to drop into place.

- Businesses are entitled to an annual investment allowance (AIA) of £50,000 for a 12 month period of account.

- A first year allowance (FYA) at the rate of 40% is available on the balance of expenditure on plant and machinery (excluding cars and special rate pool expenditure) not covered by the Annual Investment Allowance. A FYA at the rate of 100% is available on low emission cars. Enhanced capital allowances (ECAs) are available on green technologies. FYAs and ECAs are never pro-rated in short periods of account.

- Most expenditure on plant and machinery qualifies for a WDA at 20% every 12 months.

- The special rate pool contains expenditure on thermal insulation, long life assets, features integral to a building and cars with CO_2 emissions over 160g/km. The AIA can be used against such expenditure. The WDA is 10%.

- An asset which is used privately by a trader is dealt with in a single asset pool and the capital allowances are restricted.

- Motor cars acquired before 6 April 2009 (1 April 2009 for companies) which cost more than £12,000 are dealt with in a single asset pool. The maximum WDA on such cars is £3,000 for a 12 month period.

- Motor cars acquired from 6 April 2009 (1 April 2009 for companies) are generally dealt with in the special rate pool (cars emitting over 160g/km) or the main pool, unless there is private use by the trader.

- Short life asset elections can bring forward the allowances due on an asset.

- Capital allowances are available on assets acquired by hire purchase or lease.

- Balancing adjustments are calculated when a business ceases. If the business is transferred to a connected person, the written down value can be transferred instead.

- Industrial buildings allowances broadly equal to the fall in value of the building whilst it was being used industrially are available to the trader.

- An allowance, normally at the rate of 2% per annum, is given if a building is in industrial use on the last day of the period of account concerned.

Quick quiz

1 List the six traditional badges of trade.

2 What pre-trading expenditure is deductible?

3 In which period of account are earnings paid 12 months after the end of the period for which they are charged deductible?

4 What is the maximum allowable amount of redundancy pay on the cessation of a trade?

5 For what periods are capital allowance for unincorporated businesses calculated?

6 Are writing down allowances pro-rated in a six month period of account?

7 Are first year allowances pro-rated in a six month period of account?

8 When may balancing allowances arise?

9 Within what period must an asset be disposed of if it is to be treated as a short life asset?

10 List four types of building which do not qualify for industrial building allowance.

11 When are drawing offices industrial buildings?

12 What are the conditions for a hotel to qualify for allowances?

13 What is the writing down allowance for industrial buildings?

14 Lucas makes up accounts for a 15 month period to 30 June 2010. What Annual Investment Allowance is he entitled to?

15 Paula makes up accounts to 5 April each year. She buys a car in August 2009 costing £20,000 for use in her business. Her private use of the car is 30%. the CO_2 emissions of the car are 170g/km. What WDA is available on the car for the year ended 5 April 2010?

Answers to Quick quiz

1   The subject matter
     The frequency of transactions
     The length of ownership
     Supplementary work and marketing
     A profit motive
     The way in which goods were acquired

2   Pre-trading expenditure is deductible if it is incurred within seven years of the start of the trade and is of a type that would have been deductible if the trade had already started.

3   In the period in which they are paid

4   3 × statutory amount

5   Periods of account

6   Yes. In a six month period, writing down allowance are pro-rated by multiplying by 6/12.

7   No. First year allowances are given in full in a short period of account.

8   Balancing allowances may arise in respect of pooled expenditure only when the trade ceases. Balancing allowances may arise on non-pooled items whenever those items are disposed of.

9   Within four years of the end of the period of account (or accounting period) in which it was bought.

10   Dwelling houses, retail shops, showrooms and offices.

11   Drawing offices are industrial buildings if they serve an industrial building.

12   (a)   It must have ten letting bedrooms

     (b)   It must have letting bedrooms as the whole or main part of the sleeping accommodation

     (c)   It must offer ancillary services including at least

          (i)   Breakfast
          (ii)   Evening meals
          (iii) The cleaning of rooms
          (iv)   The making of beds

     (d)   It must be open for at least four months during the April to October letting season.

13   2%

14   £50,000 × 15/12 = £62,500.

15   £20,000 × 10% (CO_2 emissions of the car exceed 160g/km) = £2,000.
     The WDA is £2,000 × 70% = £1,400.

Answers to Activities

1

	£	£
Profit per accounts		17,710
Add: Depreciation	1,500	
Entertainment expenses	750	
Legal expenses	250	
		2,500
		20,210
Less interest received (to tax as savings income)		(860)
Taxable trade profits		19,350

2

	FYAs	General pool	Car (60%)	Allowances
	£	£	£	£
1.1.09 – 31.12.09				
WDV b/f		25,260	21,225	
WDA @ 20%		(5,052)		5,052
WDA @ £3,000 (restricted)			(3,000) × 60%	1,800
Addition 7.6.09	1,620			
AIA	(1,620)			1,620
WDV c/f		20,208	18,225	
Total allowances				8,472
1.1.10 – 31.8.10				
Addition 12.5.10		1,287		
Disposals		(25,295)	(16,500)	
No WDA in year of cessation		(3,800)	1,725	
Balancing charge		3,800		(3,800)
Balancing allowance			(1,725)	1,035
Total balancing charge (taxable as profits)				(2,765)

3

(a)
	£
Year to 30.4.10	
Cost	12,000
FYA 40%	(4,800)
	7,200
Year to 30.4.11	
WDA 20%	(1,440)
	5,760
Year to 30.4.12	
WDA 20%	(1,152)
	4,608
Year to 30.4.13	
WDA 20%	(922)
	3,686
Year to 30.4.14	
Disposal proceeds	(300)
Balancing allowance	3,386

(b)   If the asset is still in use at 30 April 2014, WDAs up to 30.4.13 will be as above. In the year to 30.4.14, a WDA can be claimed of 20% × £3,686 = £737. The tax written down value of £3,686 − £737 = £2,949 will be added to the main pool at the beginning of the next period of account. The disposal proceeds of £200 will be deducted from the main pool in that period's capital allowances computation. No balancing allowance will arise and the main pool will continue.

4

Eligible expenditure

	£
Preparing land	50,000
Architect's fees	40,000
Factory	150,000
Storage warehouse	100,000
Staff canteen	90,000
Eligible expenditure	430,000

The cost of land is never eligible expenditure.

The cost of the offices is not eligible expenditure because it exceeds 25% of the total cost (excluding land) as £(800,000 − 200,000) x 25% = £150,000.

Industrial buildings allowance y/e 5 April 2010
£430,000 x 2%	£8,600

NOTES

Chapter 14

TRADE PROFITS – BASIS PERIODS AND LOSSES

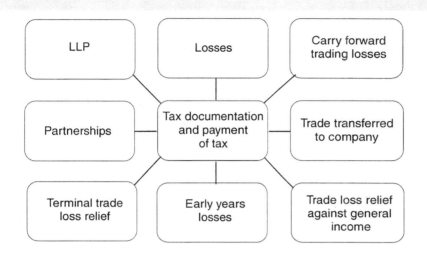

Introduction

Businesses are able to make use of favourable tax provisions in their starting and closing years, and also if they are making losses on an ongoing basis. The impact of losses may be carried both forward and back to subsequent and previous accounting periods, thus smoothing over the tax liability.

This chapter also introduces the tax implications of a group of people trading together as a partnership.

Accounting for partnerships is covered in Unit 10 of the HNC/HND qualification.

Your objectives

In this chapter you will learn about the following.

- (a) The basis of assessment for a continuing business
- (b) The principles which apply on commencement and cessation
- (c) How to compute Taxable Trade profits in a tax year.
- (d) How to calculate overlap relief and its subsequent use
- (e) The loss reliefs available to a sole trader who is neither commencing nor ceasing a business
- (f) The alternative loss reliefs in an income tax computation
- (g) The loss reliefs available on commencement and the implications
- (h) The loss reliefs available on cessation
- (i) The way in which the rules for sole traders are adapted to deal with partnerships

(j)   The capital allowances for a partnership (include assets owned individually by partners)

(k)   The position when there is a change in profit-sharing arrangements

(l)   Outline the position of new partners, ongoing partners, retiring partners

(m)   Trade Profit assessments for individual partners

(n)   Basic adjustments for notional profits/losses

1   INTRODUCTION

A tax year runs from 6 April to 5 April, but most businesses do not have periods of account ending on 5 April. **Thus there must be a link between a period of account of a business and a tax year.** The procedure is to **find a period to act as the basis period for a tax year. The profits for a basis period are taxed in the corresponding tax year.** If a basis period is not identical to a period of account, the profits of periods of account are time-apportioned as required on the assumption that profits accrue evenly over a period of account. We will apportion to the nearest month for exam purposes.

We will now look at the basis period rules that apply in the opening, continuing and closing years of a business when there is no change of accounting date. Special rules are needed when the trader changes his accounting date. We will look at these rules in the next section.

The first tax year is the year during which the trade commences. For example, if a trade commences on 1 June 2009 the first tax year is 2009/10.

1.2   The first tax year

The **basis period for the first tax year runs from the date the trade starts to the next 5 April** (or to the date of cessation if the trade does not last until the end of the tax year).

So continuing the above example a trader commencing in business on 1 June 2009 will be taxed on profits arising from 1 June 2009 to 5 April 2010 in 2009/10, their first tax year.

1.3   The second tax year

(a)   **If the accounting date falling in the second tax year is at least 12 months after the start of trading, the basis period is the 12 months to that accounting date.**

(b)   **If the accounting date falling in the second tax year is less than 12 months after the start of trading, the basis period is the first 12 months of trading.**

(c)   **If there is no accounting date falling in the second tax year,** because the first period of account is a very long one which does not end until a date in the third tax year, **the basis period for the second tax year is the year itself (from 6 April to 5 April).**

The following flowchart may help you determine the basis period for the second tax year.

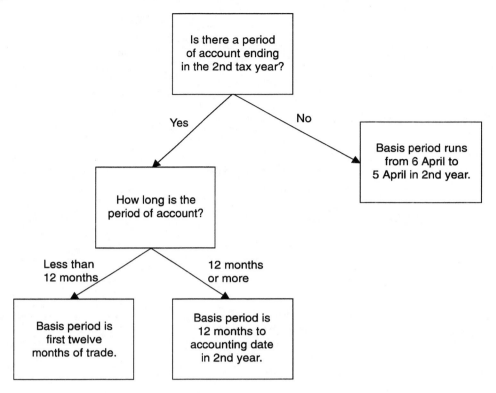

1.4 Examples: the first and second tax year

(a)   John starts to trade on 1 January 2010 making up accounts to 31 December 2010.

1st tax year: 2009/10 – tax profits 1.1.10 – 5.4.10

2nd tax year: 2010/11

- Is there a period of account ending in 2010/11?

  Yes – Y.E. 31.12.10 ends 31.12.10.

- How long is the period of account?

  12 months or more ie 12 months (exactly) to 31.12.10.

- So in 2010/11 tax profits of 12 months to 31.12.10.

(b)   Janet starts to trade on 1 January 2010 making up accounts as follows:

   6 months to 30 June 2010
   12 months to 30 June 2011.

1st tax year: 2009/10 – tax profits 1.1.10 – 5.4.10

2nd tax year: 2010/11.

- Is there a period of account ending in 2010/11?

  Yes – p.e. 30.6.10 ends 30.6.10

- How long is the period of account?

  Less than 12 months ie 6 months long.

- So in 2010/11 tax profits of first 12 months of trade ie 1.1.10 – 31.12.10, ie
  p.e. 30.6.10 profits

  plus

  6/12 of y.e 30.6.11 profits

(c) Jodie starts to trade on 1 March 2010 making up a 14 month set of accounts to 30 April 2011.

1st tax year: 2009/10 – tax profits 1.3.10 – 5.4.10

2nd tax year: 2010/11

- Is there a period of account ending in 2010/11?

  No (p.e. 30.4.11 ends in 2011/12)

- So in 2010/11 tax profits of 6.4.10– 5.4.11

  ie 12/14 × 14 months ended 30 April 2011.

1.5 The third tax year

(a) **If there is an accounting date falling in the second tax year, the basis period for the third tax year is the period of account ending in the third tax year.**

(b) If there is no accounting date falling in the second tax year, the basis period for the third tax year is the 12 months to the accounting date falling in the third tax year.

1.6 Later tax years

For later tax years, except the year in which the trade ceases, **the basis period is the period of account ending in the tax year**. This is known as the **current year basis of assessment**.

1.7 The final year

(a) If a trade starts and ceases in the same tax year, the basis period for that year is the whole lifespan of the trade.

(b) If the final year is the second year, the basis period runs from 6 April at the start of the second year to the date of cessation. This rule overrides the rules that normally apply for the second year.

(c) If the final year is the third year or a later year, **the basis period runs from the end of the basis period for the previous year to the date of cessation.** This rule overrides the rules that normally apply in the third and later years.

1.8 Overlap profits

Definition

Profits which have been taxed more than once are called **overlap profits**.

When a business starts, some profits may be taxed twice because the basis period for the second year includes some or all of the period of trading in the first year or because the basis period for the third year overlaps with that for the second year, or both.

Overlap profits may be deducted on a change of accounting date (see below). Any overlap profits unrelieved when the trade ceases are deducted from the final year's taxable profits. Any deduction of overlap profits may create or increase a loss. The usual loss reliefs (covered later in this Text) are then available.

1.9 Example: accounting date in 2nd year at least 12 months

Jenny trades from 1 July 2004 to 31 December 2009, with the following results.

Period	Profit £
1.7.04 – 31.8.05	7,000
1.9.05 – 31.8.06	12,000
1.9.06 – 31.8.07	15,000
1.9.07 – 31.8.08	21,000
1.9.08 – 31.8.09	18,000
1.9.09 – 31.12.09	5,600
	78,600

The profits to be taxed in each tax year from 2004/05 to 2009/10. and the total of these taxable profits are calculated as follows.

Year	Basis period	Working	Taxable profit £
2004/05	1.7.04 – 5.4.05	£7,000 × 9/14	4,500
2005/06	1.9.04 – 31.8.05	£7,000 × 12/14	6,000
2006/07	1.9.05 – 31.8.06		12,000
2007/08	1.9.06 – 31.8.07		15,000
2008/09	1.9.07 – 31.8.08		21,000
2009/10	1.9.08 – 31.12.09	£(18,000 + 5,600 – 3,500)	20,100
			78,600

The overlap profits are those in the period 1 September 2004 to 5 April 2005, a period of seven months. They are £7,000 × 7/14 = £3,500. Overlap profits are either relieved on a change of accounting date (see below) or are deducted from the final year's taxable profit when the business ceases. In this case the overlap profits are deducted when the business ceases. Over the life of the business, the total taxable profits equal the total actual profits.

Activity 1   **(20 minutes)**

Peter trades from 1 September 2004 to 30 June 2009, with the following results.

Period	Profit
	£
1.9.04 – 30.4.05	8,000
1.5.05 – 30.4.06	15,000
1.5.06 – 30.4.07	9,000
1.5.07 – 30.4.08	10,500
1.5.08 – 30.4.09	16,000
1.5.09 – 30.6.09	950
	59,450

Show the profits to be taxed in each year from 2004/05 to 2009/10, the total of these taxable profits and the overlap profits.

1.10 Example: no accounting date in the second year

Thelma starts to trade on 1 March 2008. Her first accounts, covering the 16 months to 30 June 2009, show a profit of £36,000. The taxable profits for the first three tax years and the overlap profits are as follows.

Year	Basis period	Working	Taxable profits
			£
2007/08	1.3.08 – 5.4.08	£36,000 × 1/16	2,250
2008/09	6.4.08 – 5.4.09	£36,000 × 12/16	27,000
2009/10	1.7.08 – 30.6.09	£36,000 × 12/16	27,000

The overlap profits are the profits from 1 July 2008 to 5 April 2009: £36,000 × 9/16 = £20,250.

1.11 The choice of an accounting date

A new trader should consider which accounting date would be best. There are **three factors to consider** from the point of view of taxation.

- **If profits are expected to rise, a date early in the tax year** (such as 30 April) will delay the time when rising accounts profits feed through into rising taxable profits, whereas a date late in the tax year (such as 31 March) will accelerate the taxation of rising profits. This is because with an accounting date of 30 April, the taxable profits for each tax year are mainly the profits earned in the previous tax year. With an accounting date of 31 March the taxable profits are almost entirely profits earned in the current year.

- If the accounting date in the second tax year is less than 12 months after the start of trading, the taxable profits for that year will be the profits earned in the first 12 months. If the accounting date is at least 12 months from the start of trading, they will be the profits earned in the 12 months to that date. **Different profits may thus be taxed twice (the overlap profits)**, and if profits are fluctuating this can make a considerable difference to the taxable profits in the first few years. **It may be many years before relief for the overlap profits is obtained.**

- **The choice of an accounting date affects the profits shown in each set of accounts,** and this may affect the taxable profits.

2 LOSSES – AN OVERVIEW

2.1 Trade losses in general

This chapter considers how losses are calculated and how a loss-suffering taxpayer can use a loss to reduce his tax liability. Most of the chapter concerns the trade losses in respect of trades, professions and vocations.

The rules in this chapter apply only to individuals, trading alone or in partnership. Loss reliefs for companies are completely different and are covered later in this Text.

When computing taxable trade profits, profits may turn out to be negative, that is a loss has been made in the basis period. **A loss is computed in exactly the same way as a profit,** making the same adjustments to the accounts profit or loss.

If there is a loss in a basis period, the taxable trade profits for the tax year based on that basis period are nil.

2.2 The computation of the loss

The trade loss for a tax year is the trade loss in the basis period for that tax year. However, **if basis periods overlap then a loss in the overlap period is a trade loss for the earlier tax year only.**

2.3 Example: computing the trading loss

Here is an example of a trader who starts to trade on 1 July 2009 and makes losses in opening years.

Period of account	Loss £
1.7.09 – 31.12.09	9,000
1.1.10 – 31.12.10	24,000

Tax year	Basis period	Working	Trade loss for the tax year £
2009/10	1.7.09 – 5.4.10	£9,000 + (£24,000 × 3/12)	15,000
2010/11	1.1.10 – 31.12.10	£24,000 – (£24,000 × 3/12)	18,000

EXAMPLE

Losses and profit

The same rule against using losses twice applies when losses are netted off against profits in the same basis period. Here is an example, again with a commencement on 1 July 2009 but with a different accounting date.

Period of account			(Loss)/profit
			£
1.7.09 – 30.4.10			(10,000)
1.5.10 – 30.4.11			24,000

			Trade
Tax year	Basis period	Working	(Loss)/Profit
			£
2009/10	1.7.09 – 5.4.10	£(10,000) × 9/10	(9,000)
2010/11	1.7.09 – 30.6.10	£(10,000) × 1/10 + £24,000 × 2/12	3,000

3 CARRY FORWARD TRADE LOSS RELIEF

A trade loss not relieved in any other way must be **carried forward to set against the first available trade profits of the same trade** in the calculation of net trading income. Losses may be carried forward for any number of years.

EXAMPLE

Carrying forward losses

B has the following results.

Year ending	£
31 December 2007	(6,000)
31 December 2008	5,000
31 December 2009	11,000

B's net trading income, assuming that he claims carry forward loss relief, are:

	2007/08		2008/09		2009/10
	£		£		£
Trade profits	0		5,000		11,000
Less carry forward loss relief	(0)	(i)	(5,000)	(ii)	(1,000)
Profits	0		0		10,000

Loss memorandum			£
Trading loss, y/e 31.12.07			6,000
Less: claim in y/e 31.12.08 (08/09)		(i)	(5,000)
claim in y/e 31.12.09 (bal of loss) (09/10)		(ii)	(1,000)
			0

4 TRADE TRANSFERRED TO COMPANY

Although carry forward loss relief is restricted to future profits of the same business, this is extended to cover income received from a company to which the business is transferred.

The amount carried forward is the total unrelieved trading losses of the business.

The set off is against income derived from the company including dividends, interest and salary. Set-off the loss against non-savings income or savings income and then against dividend income.

The consideration for the transfer of the business must be wholly or mainly in the form of shares (at least 80%) which must be retained by the vendor throughout any tax year in which the loss is relieved .

5 TRADE LOSS RELIEF AGAINST GENERAL INCOME

Where a loss relief claim is made, trade losses can be set against general income and then gains in the current and/or prior year.

5.1 Introduction

Instead of carrying a trade loss forward against future trade profits, it may be relieved against general income.

5.2 Relieving the loss

Relief is against the income of the tax year in which the loss arose. In addition or instead, relief may be claimed **against the income of the preceding year.**

If there are losses in two successive years, and relief is claimed against the first year's income both for the first year's loss and for the second year's loss, relief is given for the first year's loss before the second year's loss.

A claim for a loss must be made by the 31 January which is 22 months after the end of the tax year of the loss: so by 31 January 2012 for a loss in 2009/10.

The taxpayer cannot choose the amount of loss to relieve: thus the loss may have to be set against income part of which would have been covered by the personal allowance. However, the taxpayer can choose whether to claim full relief in the current year and then relief in the preceding year for any remaining loss, or the other way round.

Set the loss against non-savings income, then against savings income and finally against dividend income.

Relief is available by carry forward for any loss not relieved against general income.

NOTES

> **Activity 2** (10 minutes)
>
> Janet has a loss in her period of account ending 31 December 2009 of £25,000. Her other income is £18,000 part time employment income a year, and she wishes to claim loss relief against general income for the year of loss and then for the preceding year. Her trading income in the previous year was £nil. Show her taxable income for each year, and comment on the effectiveness of the loss relief. Assume that tax rates and allowances for 2009/10 have always applied.

5.3 Capital allowances

The trader may adjust the size of the total loss relief claim by not claiming all the capital allowances he is entitled to: a reduced claim will increase the balance carried forward to the next year's capital allowances computation. This may be a useful **tax planning point where the effective rate of relief for capital allowances in future periods will be greater than the rate of tax relief for the loss relief.**

5.4 Trading losses relieved against capital gains

Where relief is claimed against general income of a given year, the taxpayer may include **a further claim to set the loss against his chargeable gains for the year** less any allowable capital losses for the same year or for previous years. This amount of net gains is computed and the annual exempt amount.

The trading loss is first set against general income of the year of the claim, and only any excess of loss is set against capital gains. The taxpayer cannot specify the amount to be set against capital gains, so the annual exempt amount may be wasted. We include an example here for completeness. You will study chargeable gains later in this book and we suggest that you come back to this example at that point.

> **Activity 3** (20 minutes)
>
> Sibyl had the following results for 2009/10.
>
> | | £ |
> |---|---|
> | Loss available for loss relief against general income | 27,000 |
> | Income | 19,500 |
> | Capital gains less current year capital losses | 11,000 |
> | Annual exempt amount for capital gains tax purposes | 10,100 |
> | Capital losses brought forward | 5,000 |
>
> Show how the loss would be relieved against income and gains.

5.5 Restrictions on trade loss relief against general income

Relief cannot be claimed against general income unless a business is conducted on a commercial basis with a view to the realisation of profits throughout the basis period for the tax year; this condition applies to all types of business.

There is also a limit on the amount of loss relief that a trader can claim against general income if he is a non-active trader. A non-active trader is one who spends less than 10 hours a week personally engaged in trade activities. The limit is £25,000 per tax year.

This restriction applies also to early years trading loss relief (see later in this chapter).

5.6 Temporary extension to carry back loss relief

There is a temporary extension to carry back loss relief where a loss arises in 2008/09 or 2009/10. In order to make a claim for the extended relief, **the taxpayer must make a claim for trade loss relief either in the year of the loss and/or the preceding year, or be unable to make any claim because he does not have any other income in both years.**

Any remaining losses are carried back three years before the year of the loss against trading income only, later years being relieved first. The extended claim is for a **maximum of £50,000 in total of losses from 2009/10 against trading income in 2007/08 and 2006/07.** There is **no restriction against trading income in 2008/09** where the claim against general income is only made for 2009/10.

EXAMPLE

Nicola's trading results are as follows.

Year ended 5 April	Trading profit/(loss) £
2007	25,000
2008	33,000
2009	5,000
2010	(74,000)

Her other income (all non-savings income) is as follows.

	£
2006/07	3,000
2007/08	7,000
2008/09	4,000
2009/10	12,000

Nicola claims loss relief against general income in 2009/10 and 2008/09 and then extended carry back loss relief as far as possible.

Nicola's taxable income for 2006/07 to 2009/10 inclusive is as follows:

	2006/07 £	2007/08 £	2008/09 £	2009/10 £
Trading income	25,000	33,000	5,000	0
Less carry back loss relief	(17,000)	(33,000)	(0)	(0)
	8,000	0	5,000	0
Other income	3,000	7,000	4,000	12,000
	11,000	7,000	9,000	12,000
Less loss relief against general income	(0)	(0)	(9,000)	(12,000)
Net income	11,000	7,000	0	0
Less personal allowance	(6,475)	(6,475)	(6,475)	(6,475)
Taxable income	4,525	525	0	0

Note that the total loss relief available in 2007/08 and 2006/07 from the loss in 2009/10 is £50,000. Therefore the loss relief for 2006/07 is £(50,000 – 33,000) = £17,000.

The remaining loss of £(74,000– 12,000 – 9,000 – 33,000 – 17,000) = £3,000 is carried forward to be set against the first available trading profits from 2010/11 onwards.

5.7 The choice between loss reliefs

When a trader has a choice between loss reliefs, he should aim to obtain relief both quickly and at the highest possible tax rate. However, do consider that losses relieved against income which would otherwise be covered by the personal allowance are wasted.

If the extended loss relief against trading income is available, consider whether it would be better in the year preceding the loss to make a claim against general income or only against trading income.

Another consideration is that a trading loss cannot be set against the capital gains of a year unless relief is first claimed against general income of the same year. It may be worth making the claim against income and wasting the personal allowance in order to avoid a CGT liability.

EXAMPLE

Felicity's trading results are as follows.

Year ended 30 September	Trading profit/(loss) £
2007	1,900
2008	(21,000)
2009	13,000

Her other income (all non-savings income) is as follows.

	£
2007/08	2,200
2008/09	28,500
2009/10	15,000

Show the most efficient use of Felicity's trading loss. Assume that the personal allowance has been £6,475 throughout.

Relief could be claimed against general income for 2007/08 and/or 2008/09, with any unused loss being carried forward. Relief in 2007/08 would be against general income of £(1,900 + 2,200) = £4,100, all of which would be covered by the personal allowance anyway, so this claim should not be made and neither should a claim be made for extended carry back loss relief for the same reason. A claim against general income should be made for 2008/09 as this saves tax quicker than a carry forward claim in 2009/10 would. The final results will be as follows:

	2007/08	2008/09	2009/10
	£	£	£
Trading income	1,900	0	13,000
Less carry forward loss relief	(0)	(0)	(0)
	1,900	0	13,000
Other income	2,200	28,500	15,000
	4,100	28,500	28,000
Less loss relief against general income	(0)	(21,000)	(0)
Net income	4,100	7,500	28,000
Less personal allowance	(6,475)	(6,475)	(6,475)
Taxable income	0	1,025	21,525

Before recommending loss relief against general income consider whether it will result in the waste of the personal allowance. Such waste is to be avoided if at all possible.

6 EARLY TRADE LOSSES RELIEF

Early trade losses relief is available for **trading losses incurred in the first four tax years of a trade**.

Relief is obtained by **setting the allowable loss against general income in the three years preceding the year of loss,** applying the loss to the earliest year first. Thus a loss arising in 2009/10 may be set off against income in 2006/07, 2007/08 and 2008/09 in that order.

A claim for early trade losses relief applies to all three years automatically, provided that the loss is large enough. The taxpayer cannot choose to relieve the loss against just one or two of the years, or to relieve only part of the loss. However, the taxpayer could reduce the size of the loss by not claiming the full capital allowances available to him. This will result in higher capital allowances in future years.

Claims for the relief must be made by the 31 January which is 22 months after the end of the tax year in which the loss is incurred.

EXAMPLE

Mr A is employed as a dustman until 1 January 2008. On that date he starts up his own business as a scrap metal merchant, making up his accounts to 30 June each year. His earnings as a dustman are:

	£
2004/05	5,000
2005/06	6,000
2006/07	7,000
2007/08 (nine months)	6,000

His trading results as a scrap metal merchant are:

	Profit/ (Loss) £
Six months to 30 June 2008	(3,000)
Year to 30 June 2009	(1,500)
Year to 30 June 2010	(1,200)

Assuming that loss relief is claimed as early as possible, show the net income for each of the years 2004/05 to 2010/11 inclusive.

Since reliefs are to be claimed as early as possible, early trade loss relief is applied. The losses available for relief are as follows.

			Years against which relief is available
	£	£	
2007/08 (basis period 1.1.08 – 5.4.08)			
3 months to 5.4.08 £(3,000) × 3/6		(1,500)	2004/05 to 2006/07
2008/09 (basis period 1.1.08 – 31.12.08)			
3 months to 30.6.08			
(omit 1.1.08 – 5.4.08: overlap) £(3,000) × 3/6	(1,500)		
6 months to 31.12.08 £(1,500) × 6/12	(750)		
		(2,250)	2005/06 to 2007/08
2009/10 (basis period 1.7.08 – 30.6.09)			
6 months to 30.6.09			
(omit 1.7.08 – 31.12.08: overlap) £(1,500) × 6/12		(750)	2006/07 to 2008/09
2010/11 (basis period 1.7.09 – 30.6.10)			
12 months to 30.6.10		(1,200)	2007/08 to 2009/10

The net income is as follows.

	£	£
2004/05		
Original	5,000	
Less 2007/08 loss	(1,500)	
		3,500
2005/06		
Original	6,000	
Less 2008/09 loss	(2,250)	
		3,750
2006/07		
Original	7,000	
Less 2009/10 loss	(750)	
		6,250
2007/08		
Original	6,000	
Less 2010/11 loss	(1,200)	
		4,800

The taxable trade profits for 2007/08 to 2010/11 are zero because there were losses in the basis periods.

7 TERMINAL TRADE LOSS RELIEF

7.1 The relief

Trade loss relief against general income will often be insufficient on its own to deal with a loss incurred in the last months of trading. For this reason there is a special relief, **terminal trade loss relief, which allows a loss on cessation to be carried back for relief against taxable trading profits in previous years.**

7.2 Computing the terminal loss

A terminal loss is **the loss of the last 12 months of trading.**

It is built up as follows.

£

(a) The actual trade loss for the tax year of cessation (calculated from 6 April to the date of cessation)   X

(b) The actual trade loss for the period from 12 months before cessation until the end of the penultimate tax year   <u>X</u>

Total terminal trade loss   <u><u>X</u></u>

If the result of either (a) or (b) is a profit rather than a loss, it is treated as zero.

Any unrelieved overlap profits are included within (a) above.

If any loss cannot be included in the terminal loss (eg because it is matched with a profit) it can be relieved instead against general income.

7.3 Relieving the terminal loss

The loss is relieved against trade profits only.

Relief is given in the tax year of cessation and the three preceding years, later years first.

EXAMPLE

Set out below are the results of a business up to its cessation on 30 September 2009.

	Profit/(loss)
	£
Year to 31 December 2006	2,000
Year to 31 December 2007	400
Year to 31 December 2008	300
Nine months to 30 September 2009	(1,950)

Overlap profits on commencement were £450. These were all unrelieved on cessation.

Show the available terminal loss relief, and suggest an alternative claim if the trader had had other non-savings income of £10,000 in each of 2008/09 and 2009/10. Assume that 2009/10 tax rates and allowances apply to all years.

NOTES

The terminal loss comes in the last 12 months, the period 1 October 2008 to 30 September 2009. This period is split as follows.

2008/09   Six months to 5 April 2009
2009/10   Six months to 30 September 2009

The terminal loss is made up as follows.

Unrelieved trading losses		£	£
2009/10			
6 months to 30.9.09	£(1,950) × 6/9		(1,300)
Overlap relief	£(450)		(450)
2008/09			
3 months to 31.12.08	£300 × 3/12	75	
3 months to 5.4.09	£(1,950) × 3/9	(650)	
			(575)
			(2,325)

Taxable trade profits will be as follows.

Year	Basis period	Profits £	Terminal loss relief £	Final taxable profits £
2006/07	Y/e 31.12.06	2,000	1,625	375
2007/08	Y/e 31.12.07	400	400	0
2008/09	Y/e 31.12.08	300	300	0
2009/10	1.10.08 – 30.9.09	0	0	0
			2,325	

If the trader had had £10,000 of other income in 2008/09 and 2009/10, we could consider loss relief claims against general income for these two years, using the loss of £(1,950 + 450) = £2,400 for 2009/10.

The final results would be as follows. (We could alternatively claim loss relief in 2008/09.)

	2006/07 £	2007/08 £	2008/09 £	2009/10 £
Trade profits	2,000	400	300	0
Other income	0	0	10,000	10,000
	2,000	400	10,300	10,000
Less loss relief against general income	0	0	0	(2,400)
Net income	2,000	400	10,300	7,600

Another option would be to make a claim against general income for the balance of the loss not relieved as a terminal loss £(2,400 – 2,325) = £75 in either 2008/09 or 2009/10.

However, as there is only taxable income in 2008/09 and 2009/10 the full claim against general income is more tax efficient.

BPP
LEARNING MEDIA

8 PARTNERSHIPS

8.1 Introduction

A partnership is treated like a sole trader when computing its profits. Partners' salaries and interest on capital are not deductible expenses and must be added back in computing profits, because they are a form of drawings.

Once the partnership's profits for a period of account have been computed, they are shared between the partners according to the profit sharing arrangements for that period of account.

8.2 The tax positions of individual partners

Each partner is taxed like a sole trader who runs a business which:

- Starts when he joins the partnership

- Finishes when he leaves the partnership

- Has the same periods of account as the partnership (except that a partner who joins or leaves during a period will have a period which starts or ends part way through the partnership's period)

- Makes profits or losses equal to the partner's share of the partnership's profits or losses

8.3 Changes in profit sharing ratios

The profits for a period of account are allocated between the partners according to the profit sharing agreement. If the salaries, interest on capital and profit sharing ratio change during the period of account the profits are time apportioned to the periods before and after the change and allocated accordingly. The constituent elements are then added together to give each partner's share of profits for the period of account.

8.4 Changes in membership

When a trade continues but partners join or leave (including cases when a sole trader takes in partners or a partnership breaks up leaving only one partner as a sole trader), **the special rules for basis periods in opening and closing years do not apply to the people who were carrying on the trade both before and after the change. They carry on using the period of account ending in each tax year as the basis period for the tax year ie the current year basis. The commencement rules only affect joiners, and the cessation rules only affect leavers.**

However, when no one same individual carries on the trade both before and after the change, as when a partnership transfers its trade to a completely new owner or set of owners, the cessation rules apply to the old owners and the commencement rules apply to the new owners.

8.5 Loss reliefs

Partners are entitled to the same loss reliefs as sole traders. The reliefs are:

(a) **Carry forward against future trading profits.** If the business is transferred to a company this is extended to carry forward against future income from the company.

(b) **Set off against general income of the same and/or preceding year.** This claim can be extended to set off against capital gains and in 2009/10 against trading profits in the preceding three years.

(c) **For a new partner, losses in the first four tax years of trade can be set off against general income of the three preceding years.** This is so even if the actual trade commenced many years before the partner joined.

(d) **For a ceasing partner, terminal loss relief is available** when he is treated as ceasing to trade. This is so even if the partnership continues to trades after he leaves.

Different partners may claim loss reliefs in different ways.

EXAMPLE

Loss relief restriction

Laura, Mark and Norman form a partnership and each contribute £10,000. Laura and Mark run the trade full time. Norman is employed elsewhere and plays little part in running the trade. Profits and losses are to be shared 45:35:20 to L:M:N. The partnership makes a loss of £60,000 of which £12,000 is allocated to Norman.

Norman may only use £10,000 of loss against general income (plus against capital gains) or early trade loss relief. £2,000 is carried forward, for example to be relieved against future profits.

8.6 Assets owned individually

Where the partners own assets (such as their cars) individually, a capital allowances computation must be prepared for each partner in respect of the assets he owns (not forgetting any adjustment for private use). **The capital allowances must go into the partnership's tax computation.**

EXAMPLE

A partnership

Alice and Bertrand start a partnership on 1 July 2006, making up accounts to 31 December each year. On 1 May 2008, Charles joins the partnership. On 1 November 2009, Charles leaves. On 1 January 2010, Deborah joins. The profit sharing arrangements are as follows.

	Alice	Bertrand	Charles	Deborah
1.7.06 – 31.1.07				
Salaries (per annum)	£3,000	£4,500		
Balance	3/5	2/5		
1.2.07 – 30.4.08				
Salaries (per annum)	£3,000	£6,000		
Balance	4/5	1/5		
1.5.08 – 31.10.09				
Salaries (per annum)	£2,400	£3,600	£1,800	
Balance	2/5	2/5	1/5	
1.11.09 – 31.12.10				
Salaries (per annum)	£1,500	£2,700		
Balance	3/5	2/5		
1.1.10 onwards				
Salaries (per annum)	£1,500	£2,700		£600
Balance	3/5	1/5		1/5

Profits as adjusted for tax purposes are as follows.

Period	Profit £
1.7.06 – 31.12.06	22,000
1.1.07 – 31.12.07	51,000
1.1.08 – 31.12.08	39,000
1.1.09 – 31.12.09	15,000
1.1.10 – 31.12.10	18,000

When approaching the question, we must first share the trade profits for the periods of account between the partners, remembering to adjust the salaries for periods of less than a year.

	Total £	Alice £	Bertrand £	Charles £	Deborah £
1.7.06 – 31.12.06					
Salaries	3,750	1,500	2,250		
Balance	18,250	10,950	7,300		
Total (P/e 31.12.06)	22,000	12,450	9,550		
1.1.07 – 31.12.07					
January					
Salaries	625	250	375		
Balance	3,625	2,175	1,450		
Total	4,250	2,425	1,825		
February to December					
Salaries	8,250	2,750	5,500		
Balance	38,500	30,800	7,700		
Total	46,750	33,550	13,200		
Total for y/e 31.12.07	51,000	35,975	15,025		
1.1.08 – 31.12.08					
January to April					
Salaries	3,000	1,000	2,000		
Balance	10,000	8,000	2,000		
Total	13,000	9,000	4,000		
May to December					
Salaries	5,200	1,600	2,400	1,200	
Balance	20,800	8,320	8,320	4,160	
Total	26,000	9,920	10,720	5,360	

NOTES

	Total £	Alice £	Bertrand £	Charles £	Deborah £
Total for y/e 31.12.08	39,000	18,920	14,720	5,360	
1.1.09 – 31.12.09					
January to October					
Salaries	6,500	2,000	3,000	1,500	
Balance	6,000	2,400	2,400	1,200	
Total	12,500	4,400	5,400	2,700	
November and December					
Salaries	700	250	450		
Balance	1,800	1,080	720		
Total	2,500	1,330	1,170		
Total for y/e 31.12.09	15,000	5,730	6,570	2,700	
1.1.10 – 31.12.10					
Salaries	4,800	1,500	2,700		600
Balance	13,200	7,920	2,640		2,640
Total for y/e 31.12.10	18,000	9,420	5,340		3,240

The next stage is to work out the basis periods and hence the taxable trade profits for the partners. All of them are treated as making up accounts to 31 December, but Alice and Bertrand are treated as starting to trade on 1 July 2006, Charles as trading only from 1 May 2008 to 31 October 2009 and Deborah as starting to trade on 1 January 2010. Applying the usual rules gives the following basis periods and taxable profits.

Alice

Year	Basis period	Working	Taxable profits £
2006/07	1.7.06 – 5.4.07	£12,450 + (£35,975 × 3/12)	21,444
2007/08	1.1.07 – 31.12.07		35,975
2008/09	1.1.08 – 31.12.08		18,920
2009/10	1.1.09 – 31.12.09		5,730

Note that for 2006/07 we take Alice's total for the year ended 2007 and apportion that, because the partnership's period of account runs from 1 January to 31 December 2007. Alice's profits for 2006/07 are *not* £12,450 + £2,425 + (£33,550 × 2/11) = £20,975.

Alice will have overlap profits for the period 1 January to 5 April 2007 (£35,975 × 3/12 = £8,994) to deduct when she ceases to trade.

Bertrand

Year	Basis period	Working	Taxable profits £
2006/07	1.7.06 – 5.4.07	£9,550 + (£15,025 × 3/12)	13,306
2007/08	1.1.07 – 31.12.07		15,025
2008/09	1.1.08 – 31.12.08		14,720
2009/10	1.1.09 – 31.12.09		6,570

Bertrand's overlap profits are £15,025 × 3/12 = £3,756.

Charles

Year	Basis period	Working	Taxable profits £
2008/09	1.5.08 – 5.4.09	£5,360 + (£2,700 × 3/10)	6,170
2009/10	6.4.09 – 31.10.09	£2,700 × 7/10	1,890

BPP
LEARNING MEDIA

Because Charles ceased to trade in his second tax year of trading, his basis period for the second year starts on 6 April and he has no overlap profits.

Deborah

Year	Basis period	Working	Taxable profits £
2009/10	1.1.10– 5.4.10	£3,240 × 3/12	810

8.7 Partnership investment income

A partnership may have non-trading income, such as interest on the partnership's bank deposit account or dividends on shares, or non-trading losses. **Such items are kept separate from trading income, but they** (and any associated tax credits) **are shared between the partners in a similar way to trading income.** That is, the following steps are applied.

Step 1 Find out which period of account the income arose in

Step 2 Share the income between the partners using the profit sharing arrangements for that period. If partners have already been given their salaries and interest on capital in sharing out trading income, do not give them those items again in sharing out non-trading income

Step 3 For income not taxed at source attribute each partner's share of the income to tax years using the same basis periods as are used to attribute his share of trading profits to tax years. When working out the basis periods for untaxed income (which excludes income taxed at source and dividends) or for non-trading losses, we always have a commencement when the partner joins the partnership and a cessation when he leaves, even if he carried on the trade as a sole trader before joining or after leaving. If the relief for overlap untaxed income on leaving the firm exceeds the partner's share of untaxed income for the tax year of leaving, the excess is deducted from his total income for that year

Step 4 For income taxed at source assume that income accrued evenly over the accounting period and time apportion on an actual basis into tax years (6 April to 5 April)

9 LIMITED LIABILITY PARTNERSHIPS

It is possible to form a limited liability partnership. The difference between a limited liability partnership (LLP) and a normal partnership is that **in a LLP the liability of the partners is limited to the capital they contributed.**

The partners of a LLP are taxed on virtually the same basis as the partners of a normal partnership (see above). However, the amount of loss relief that a partner can claim against general income or by early years trade loss relief when the claim is against non-partnership income is restricted to the capital he contributed and is subject to an overall cap of £25,000. This rule is not restricted to the first four years of trading and the rules apply to all partners whether or not involved in the running of the trade.

Chapter roundup

- Basis periods are used to link periods of account to tax years.

- In opening and closing years, special rules are applied so that a new trader can start to be taxed quickly, and a retiring trader need not be taxed long after his retirement.

- On a change of accounting date, special rules apply for fixing basis periods.

- Trade losses may be relieved against future profits of the same trade, against general income and against capital gains.

- A trade loss carried forward must be set against the first available trade profits of the same trade.

- Where a loss relief claim is made, trade losses can be set against general income and then gains in the current and/or prior year.

- It is possible to carry back losses for three years against trading income where a trading loss arises in 2009/10.

- It is important for a trader to choose the right loss relief, so as to save tax at the highest possible rate and so as to obtain relief reasonably quickly.

- If a business is transferred to a company, a loss of unincorporated business can be set against income received from the company.

- In opening years, a special relief involving the carry back of losses against general income is available. Losses arising in the first four tax years of a trade may be set against general income in the three years preceding the loss making year, taking the earliest year first.

- On the cessation of a trade, a loss arising in the last 12 months of trading may be set against trade profits of the tax year of cessation and the previous 3 years, taking the last year first.

- Capital losses arising on certain unquoted shares can be set against general income of the year of the loss and then against general income of the preceding year.

- A partnership is simply treated as a source of profits and losses for trades being carried on by the individual partners. Divide profits or losses between the partners according to the profit sharing ratio in the period of account concerned. If any of the partners are entitled to a salary or interest on capital, apportion this first, not forgetting to pro-rate in periods of less than 12 months.

- The commencement and cessation rules apply to partners individually when they join or leave.

- Limited liability partnerships are taxed on virtually the same basis as normal partnerships but loss relief is restricted for all partners.

Quick quiz

1 What is the basis period for the tax year in which a trade commenced?

2 On what two occasions may overlap profits potentially be relieved?

3 Against what income may trade losses carried forward be set off?

4 When a loss is to be relieved against total income, how are losses linked to particular tax years?

5 Against which years' total income may a loss be relieved against general income for a continuing business which has traded for many years?

6 For which losses is early years trade loss relief available?

7 In which years may relief for a terminal loss be given?

8 How are partnership trading profits divided between the individual partners?

9 What loss reliefs are partners entitled to?

10 Janet and John are partners sharing profits 60:40. For the years ended 30 June 2009 and 2010 the partnership made profits of £100,000 and £150,000 respectively. What are John's taxable trading profits in 2009/10?

11 Pete and Doug have been joint partners for many years. On 1 January Dave joins the partnership and it is agreed to share profits 40:40:20. For the year ended 30 June 2009 profits are £100,000.

    What is Doug's share of these profits?

Answers to Quick quiz

1 Date of commencement to 5 April in that year.

2 On a change of accounting date where a basis period resulting from the change exceeds 12 months or on the cessation of a business.

3 Against trade profits from the same trade.

4 The loss for a tax year is the loss in the basis period for that year. However, if basis periods overlap, a loss in the overlap period is a loss of the earlier tax year only.

5 The year in which the loss arose and/or the preceding year. If the loss arises in 2009/10 it is also possible to carry it back three years against trading income.

6 Losses incurred in the first four tax years of a trade.

7 In the year of cessation and then in the three preceding years, later years first.

8 Profits are divided in accordance with the profit sharing ratio that existed during the period of account in which the profits arose.

9 Partners are entitled to the same loss reliefs as sole traders. These are loss relief against general income, early years trade loss relief, carry forward loss relief, terminal loss relief, and loss relief on transfer of a trade to a company.

10 £40,000
    2009/10: ye 30 June 2009
    £100,000 × 40% = £40,000.

11 £45,000

		Pete £	Doug £	Dave £
Y/e 30 June 2009				
1.7.08 – 31.12.08				
6m × £100,000				
£50,000 50:50		25,000	25,000	
1.1.09 – 30.6.09				
6m × £100,000				
£50,000 40:40:20		20,000	20,000	10,000
		45,000	45,000	10,000

Answers to activities

1

Year	Basis period	Working	Taxable profits £
2004/05	1.9.04 – 5.4.05	£8,000 × 7/8	7,000
2005/06	1.9.04 – 31.8.05	£8,000 + (£15,000 × 4/12)	13,000
2006/07	1.5.05 – 30.4.06		15,000
2007/08	1.5.06 – 30.4.07		9,000
2008/09	1.5.07 – 30.4.08		10,500
2009/10	1.5.08 – 30.6.09	£(16,000 + 950 – 12,000)	4,950
			59,450

The overlap profits are the profits from 1 September 2004 to 5 April 2005 (taxed in 2004/05 and in 2005/06) and those from 1 May 2005 to 31 August 2005 (taxed in 2005/06 and 2006/07).

	£
1.9.04 – 5.4.05 £8,000 × 7/8	7,000
1.5.05 – 31.8.05 £15,000 × 4/12	5,000
Total overlap profits	12,000

2   The loss-making period ends in 2009/10, so the year of the loss is 2009/10.

	2008/09 £	2009/10 £
Total income	18,000	18,000
Less loss relief against general income	(7,000)	(18,000)
Net income	11,000	0
Less personal allowance	(6,475)	(6,475)
Taxable income	4,525	0

In 2009/10, £6,475 of the loss has been wasted because that amount of income would have been covered by the personal allowance. If Janet just claims loss relief against general income, there is nothing she can do about this waste of loss relief or the personal allowance.

3

	£
Income	19,500
Less loss relief against general income	(19,500)
Net income	0
Capital gains	11,000
Less loss relief: lower of £(27,000 – 19,500) = £7,500 (note 1) and £(11,000 – 5,000) = £6,000 (note 2)	(6,000)
	5,000
Less annual exempt amount (restricted)	(5,000)
	0

Note 1   This equals the loss left after the loss relief against general income claim

Note 2   This equals the gains left after losses b/fwd but ignoring the annual exempt amount.

A trading loss of £(7,500 – 6,000) = £1,500 is carried forward. Sibyl's personal allowance and £(10,100 – 5,000) = £5,100 of her capital gains tax annual exempt amount are wasted. Her capital losses brought forward of £5,000 are carried forward to 2010/11. Although we deducted this £5,000 in working out how much trading loss we were allowed to use in the claim, we do not actually use any of the £5,000 unless there are gains remaining in excess of the annual exemption.

Chapter 15
CORPORATION TAX

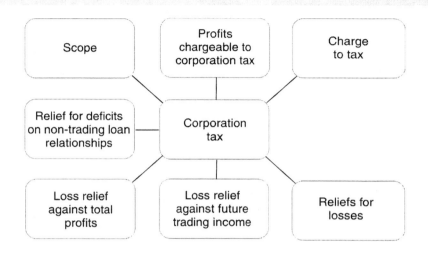

Introduction

Corporation tax is the tax on profits paid by public or private limited companies. Many of the principles you see here will be already familiar from your studies of personal and business taxation.

Your objectives

In this chapter you will learn about the following.

(a) The scope of corporation tax; chargeable entities; chargeable income

(b) Chargeable accounting periods for corporation tax

(c) How to compute profits chargeable to corporation tax for the chargeable accounting period

(d) The financial year(s) relevant to a chargeable accounting period

(e) The rate(s) of corporation tax which apply

(f) How to compute the corporation tax liability

(g) How to compute the corporation tax liability for periods longer or shorter than twelve months

(h) The loss reliefs available

(i) How to compute corporation tax repayable following a loss relief claim

1 THE SCOPE OF CORPORATION TAX

1.1 Companies

Companies must pay corporation tax on their **profits chargeable to corporation tax** for each **accounting period**. We look at the meaning of these terms below.

Definition

A **'company'** is any corporate body (limited or unlimited) or unincorporated association, eg sports club.

1.2 Accounting periods

Corporation tax is chargeable in respect of accounting periods. It is important to understand the difference between an accounting period and a period of account.

Definition

A **period of account** is any period for which a company prepares accounts; usually this will be 12 months in length but it may be longer or shorter than this.

Definition

An **accounting period** is the period for which corporation tax is charged and cannot exceed 12 months. Special rules determine when an accounting period starts and ends.

An accounting period starts when a company starts to trade, or otherwise becomes liable to corporation tax, or immediately after the previous accounting period finishes. An accounting period finishes on the earliest of:

- 12 months after its start
- the end of the company's period of account
- the commencement of the company's winding up
- the company's ceasing to be resident in the UK
- the company's ceasing to be liable to corporation tax

If a company has a period of account exceeding 12 months (a long period), it is split into two accounting periods: the first 12 months and the remainder. For example, if a company prepares accounts for the sixteen months to 30 April 2009, the two accounting periods for which the company will pay corporation tax will be the twelve months to 31 December 2008 and the four months to 30 April 2009.

1.3 Financial year

The rates of corporation tax are fixed for financial years.

Definition

> **A financial year runs from 1 April to the following 31 March and is identified by the calendar year in which it begins**. For example, the year ended 31 March 2010 is the Financial year 2009 (FY 2009). This should not be confused with a tax year, which runs from 6 April to the following 5 April.

1.4 Residence of companies

A company incorporated in the UK is resident in the UK. A company incorporated abroad is resident in the UK if its central management and control are exercised here. Central management and control are usually treated as exercised where the board of directors meet.

2 PROFITS CHARGEABLE TO CORPORATION TAX

2.1 Proforma computation

A company may have both income and gains. As a general rule income arises from receipts which are expected to recur regularly (such as the profits from a trade) whereas chargeable gains arise on the sale of capital assets which have been owned for several years (such as the sale of a factory used in the trade).

A company pays corporation tax on its profits chargeable to corporation tax (PCTCT). A company may receive income from various sources. All income received must be classified according to the nature of the income as different computational rules apply to different types of income. The main types of income for a company are:

- Profits of a trade
- Profits of a property business
- Investment income
- Miscellaneous income

A company's profits chargeable to corporation tax are arrived at by aggregating its various sources of income and its chargeable gains and then deducting gift aid donations. Here is a pro forma computation. All items are explained later in this chapter.

	£
Trading profits	X
Investment income	X
Foreign income	X
Miscellaneous income	X
Property business profits	X
Chargeable gains	X
Total profits	X
Less gift aid donations	(X)
Profits chargeable to corporation tax (PCTCT) for an accounting period	X

Dividends received from UK resident companies are usually exempt and so not included in the profits chargeable to corporation tax.

3 TRADING INCOME

3.1 Adjustment of profits

The trading income of companies is derived from the net profit figure in the accounts, just as for individuals, adjusted as follows.

	£	£
Net profit per accounts		X
Add expenditure not allowed for taxation purposes		X
		X
Less: income not taxable as trading income	X	
expenditure not charged in the accounts but allowable for the purposes of taxation	X	
capital allowances	X	
		(X)
Trading income		X

The adjustment of profits computation for companies broadly follows that for computing business profits subject to income tax. There are, however, some minor differences. There is no disallowance for 'private use' for companies; instead the director or employee will be taxed on the benefit received.

Gift aid donations are added back in the calculation of adjusted profit. They are treated instead as a deduction from total profits.

Investment income including rents is deducted from net profit in arriving at trading income but brought in again further down in the computation (see below).

3.2 Pre-trading expenditure

Pre-trading expenditure incurred by the company within the 7 years before trade commences is treated as an allowable expense incurred on the first day of trading provided it would have been allowable had the company been trading when the expense was actually incurred.

3.3 Capital allowances

The calculation of capital allowances follows income tax principles.

For companies, however, there is never any reduction of allowances to take account of any private use of an asset. The director or employee suffers a taxable benefit instead. As shown above capital allowances must be deducted in arriving at taxable trading income.

A company's accounting period can never exceed 12 months. If the period of account is longer than 12 months it is divided into two; one for the first 12 months and one for the balance. The capital allowances computation must be carried out for each period separately.

4 PROPERTY BUSINESS INCOME

Rental income is deducted in arriving at trading income but brought in again further down in the computation as property business income.

The calculation of property business income follows income tax principles.

The income tax rules for property businesses were set out earlier in this Text. In summary all UK rental activities are treated as a single source of income calculated in the same way as trading income.

However there are certain differences for companies:

(a) **Property business losses** are:

- first set off against non-property business income and gains of the company for the current period; and any excess is

- carried forward for set off against future income (of all descriptions).

(b) Interest paid by a company on a loan to buy or improve property is not a property business expense. The loan relationship rules apply instead (see below).

5 LOAN RELATIONSHIPS (INTEREST INCOME)

5.1 General principle

If a company borrows or lends money, including issuing or investing in debentures or buying gilts, it has a loan relationship. This can be a creditor relationship (where the company lends or invests money) or a debtor relationship (where the company borrows money or issues securities).

5.2 Treatment of trading loan relationships

If the company is a party to a loan relationship for trade purposes, any debits – ie interest paid or other debt costs – charged through its accounts are allowed as a trading expense and are therefore deductible in computing trading income.

Similarly if any credits – ie interest income or other debt returns – arise on a trading loan these are treated as a trading receipt and are taxable as trading income. This is not likely to arise unless the trade is one of money lending.

5.3   Treatment of non-trading loan relationships

If a loan relationship is not one to which the company is a party for trade purposes any debits or credits must be pooled. A net credit on the pool is chargeable as interest income.

Interest charged on underpaid tax is allowable and interest received on overpaid tax is assessable under the rules for non-trading loan relationships.

5.4   Accounting methods

Debits and credits must be brought into account using the UK generally accepted accounting practice (GAAP) or using the International Accounting Standards (IAS). This will usually be the **accruals basis**.

5.5   Incidental costs of loan finance

Under the loan relationship rules expenses ('debits') are allowed if incurred directly:

    (a)   to bring a loan relationship into existence

    (b)   entering into or giving effect to any related transactions

    (c)   making payment under a loan relationship or related transactions or

    (d)   taking steps to ensure the receipt of payments under the loan relationship or related transaction.

A related transaction means 'any disposal or acquisition (in whole or in part) of rights or liabilities under the relationship, including any arising from a security issue in relation to the money debt in question'.

The above categories of incidental costs are also allowable even if the company does not enter into the loan relationship (ie abortive costs). Costs directly incurred in varying the terms of a loan relationship are also allowed.

5.6   Other matters

It is not only the interest costs of borrowing that are allowable or taxable. The capital costs are treated similarly. Thus if a company issues a loan at a discount and repays it eventually at par, the capital cost is usually allowed on redemption (if the accruals basis is adopted).

6   MISCELLANEOUS INCOME

Patent royalties received which do not relate to the trade are taxed as miscellaneous income. Patent royalties which relate to the trade are included in trading income normally on an accruals basis.

7 CHARGEABLE GAINS

7.1 Introduction

Companies do not pay capital gains tax. Instead their chargeable gains are included in the profits chargeable to corporation tax. A company's capital gains or allowable losses are computed in a similar way to individuals but with a few major differences:

- There is relief for inflation called the indexation allowance

- No annual exempt amount is available

- Different matching rules for shares apply if the shareholder is a company.

8 GIFT AID DONATIONS

Gift aid donations are deductible in computing PCTCT.

Almost all donations of money to charity can be made under the **gift aid scheme** whether they are one off donations or are regular donations. **Gift aid donations are paid gross.**

Donations to local charities which are incurred wholly and exclusively for the purposes of a trade are deducted in the calculation of the tax adjusted trading profits.

9 LONG PERIODS OF ACCOUNT

As we saw above, if a company has a long period of account exceeding 12 months, it is split into two accounting periods: the first 12 months and the remainder.

Where the period of account differs from the corporation tax accounting periods, profits are **allocated to the relevant periods** as follows:

- **Trading income** before capital allowances is apportioned on a **time basis.**

- **Capital allowances** and balancing charges are **calculated for each accounting period.**

- **Other income is allocated to the period to which it relates** (eg rents to the period when accrued). Miscellaneous income, however, is apportioned on a time basis.

- **Chargeable gains and losses** are allocated to the **period in which they are realised.**

- **Gift aid donations** are deducted in the accounting **period in which they are paid.**

NOTES

> **Activity 1** (10 minutes)
>
> Xenon Ltd makes up an 18 month set of accounts to 30 September 2010 with the following results.
>
> | | £ |
> |---|---|
> | Trading profits | 180,000 |
> | Property income | |
> | 18 months @ £500 accruing per month | 9,000 |
> | Capital gain (1 August 2010 disposal) | 250,000 |
> | Less: Gift aid donation (paid 31 March 2010) | (50,000) |
> | | 389,000 |
>
> What are the profits chargeable to corporation tax for each of the accounting periods based on the above accounts?

10 CHARGE TO CORPORATION TAX

10.1 'Profits'

Although we tax PCTCT another figure needs to be calculated ('profits') to determine the rate of corporation tax to use to tax PCTCT.

'Profits' means profits chargeable to corporation tax plus the grossed-up amount of dividends received from UK and non-UK companies. The exception to this rule is any dividends received from a company which is a 51% or more subsidiary of the receiving company or from a company of which the recipient company is a 51% or more subsidiary of the paying company: these dividends are completely ignored for corporation tax purposes.

The grossed-up amount of dividends is the dividend received multiplied by 100/90. You may see the grossed up amount of dividend received referred to as **franked investment income (FII)**.

10.2 The full rate

The rates of corporation tax are fixed for financial years. The full rate of corporation tax is 28% for FY 2009 and FY 2008 (FY 2007 30%), and applies to companies with 'profits' of £1,500,000 or more. A company with PCTCT of, say, £2 million, will pay £560,000 corporation tax.

10.3 The small companies' rate (SCR)

The SCR of corporation tax of 21% for FY 2009 and FY 2008 (FY 2007 20%) applies to the profits chargeable to corporation tax of UK resident companies whose 'profits' are not more than £300,000.

Activity 2	(5 minutes)

B Ltd had the following results for the year ended 31 March 2010

	£
Trading profits	42,000
Dividend received 1 May 2009	9,000

Compute the corporation tax payable.

10.4 Marginal relief

Small companies' marginal relief applies where the 'profits' of an accounting period of a UK resident company are over £300,000 but under £1,500,000.

We first calculate the corporation tax at the full rate and then deduct:

$(M - P) \times I/P \times$ marginal relief fraction

where M = upper limit (currently £1,500,000)
       P = 'profits' (see above)
       I = PCTCT

The marginal relief fraction is 7/400 for FY 2009 and FY 2008 (FY 2007 1/40).

This information is given in the rates and allowances section of the exam paper.

EXAMPLE

Lenox Ltd has the following results for the year ended 31 March 2010.

	£
PCTCT	296,000
Dividend received 1 December 2009	12,600

Calculate the corporation tax liability.

	£
PCTCT	296,000
Dividend plus tax credit £12,600 × 100/90	14,000
'Profits'	310,000

'Profits' are above £300,000 but below £1,500,000, so marginal relief applies.

	£
Corporation tax on PCTCT £296,000 × 28%	82,880
Less small companies' marginal relief	
£(1,500,000 – 310,000) × 296,000/310,000 × 7/400	(19,885)
	62,995

In exam questions you often need to be aware that there is a **marginal rate of 29.75 %** which applies to any PCTCT that lies in between the small companies' limits.

This is calculated as follows:

	£			£
Upper limit	1,500,000	@	28%	420,000
Lower limit	(300,000)	@	21%	(63,000)
Difference	1,200,000			357,000

$$\frac{357,000}{1,200,000} = 29.75\%$$

Effectively the band of profits (here £1,200,000) falling between the upper and lower limits are taxed at a rate of 29.75%

EXAMPLE

Effective marginal rate of tax

A Ltd has PCTCT of £350,000 for the year ended 31 March 2010. Its corporation tax liability is

	£
£350,000 × 28%	98,000
Less small companies' marginal relief	
£(1,500,000 – 350,000) × $^7/_{400}$	(20,125)
	77,875

This is the same as calculating tax at 21% × £300,000 + 29.75% × £50,000 = £63,000 + £14,875 = £77,875.

Consequently tax is charged at an effective rate of 29.75% on PCTCT that exceeds the small companies' lower limit.

Note that although there is an effective corporation tax charge of 29.75%, this rate of tax is never used in actually calculating corporation tax. The rate is just an effective marginal rate that you must be aware of. It will be particularly important when considering loss relief and group relief .

The marginal rate of corporation tax for FY 2007 was 32.5%

10.5 Accounting period in more than one Financial Year

An accounting period **may fall within more than one Financial Year. If the rates and limits for corporation tax are the same in both Financial Years, tax can be computed for the accounting period as if it fell within one Financial Year.**

However, **if the rates and/or limits for corporation tax are different in the Financial Years, PCTCT and 'profits' are time apportioned between the Financial Years.** This will be the case where a company is a small company (or marginal relief company) with an accounting period partly in FY 2007 and partly in FY 2008. **It is also necessary to adjust the upper and lower limits.**

EXAMPLE

Wentworth Ltd makes up its accounts to 31 December each year. For the year to 31 December 2008, it has PCTCT of £174,000. It receives a dividend of £5,400 on 1 December 2008.

The corporation tax payable by Wentworth Ltd is calculated as follows.

	£
PCTCT	174,000
Dividend plus tax credit £5,400 × 100/90	6,000
'Profits'	180,000

	FY 2007 *3 months* *to 31.3.08* £	*FY 2008* *9 months* *to 31.12.08* £
PCTCT (3:9)	43,500	130,500
'Profits' (3:9)	45,000	135,000
Lower limit:		
£300,000 × 3/12	75,000	
£300,000 × 9/12		225,000

Small companies rate applies in both FYs

FY 2007 £43,500 × 20%	8,700	
FY 2008 £130,500 × 21%		27,405
Total corporation tax payable		
£(8,700 + 27,405)		£36,105

Activity 3   **(20 minutes)**

Elliot Ltd has the following results for the year to 30 September 2008.

	£
PCTCT	360,000
Dividend received 15 July 2008	8,100

Calculate the corporation tax payable to Elliot Ltd.

10.6 Short accounting periods

The upper and lower limits which are used to be determine tax rates are pro-rated on a time basis if an accounting period lasts for less than 12 months.

EXAMPLE

Ink Ltd prepared accounts for the six months to 31 March 2010. Profits chargeable to corporation tax for the period were £200,000. No dividends were received. Calculate the corporation tax payable for the period.

Upper limit £1,500,000 × 6/12 = £750,000

Lower limit £300,000 × 6/12 = £150,000

As 'profits' fall between the limits small companies' marginal relief applies.

	£
Corporation tax (FY 09)	
£200,000 × 28%	56,000
Less small companies' marginal relief	
7/400 × (£750,000 – £200,000)	(9,625)
Corporation tax	46,375

10.7 Long periods of account

Remember that an accounting period cannot be more than 12 months long. If the period of account exceeds 12 months it must be split into two accounting periods, the first of 12 months and the second of the balance.

EXAMPLE

Xenon Ltd in the previous chapter made up an 18 month set of accounts to 30 September 2010.

The 18 month period of account is divided into:

Year ending 31 March 2010
6 months to 30 September 2010

Results were allocated:

	Y/e 31.3.10 £	6m to 30.9.10 £
Trading profits 12:6	120,000	60,000
Property income	6,000	3,000
Capital gain (1.8.10)		250,000
Less Gift aid donation (31.3.10)	(50,000)	
PCTCT	76,000	313,000

Assuming Xenon Ltd received FII of £27,000 on 31 August 2010 calculate the corporation tax payable for each accounting period. Assume the rates of corporation tax for FY 2009 apply in FY 2010.

	Y/e 31.3.10 £	6m to 30.9.10 £
PCTCT	76,000	313,000
FII	0	27,000
Profits	76,000	340,000
Small companies lower limit	300,000	150,000
Small companies upper limit	1,500,000	750,000
	Small company	*Marginal relief*
CT payable		
£76,000 × 21%	15,960	
£313,000 × 28%		87,640
Less marginal relief £(750,000 – 340,000) × 313,000/340,000 × 7/400		(6,605)
		81,035
Total corporation tax payable £(15,960 + 81,035)		96,995

11   TRADING LOSSES

In summary, the following reliefs are available for trading losses incurred by a company.

  (a)   **Set-off against current profits**
  (b)   **Carry back against earlier profits**
  (c)   **Carry forward against future trading profits**

Reliefs (a) and (b) must be claimed, and are given in the order shown. Relief (c) is given automatically for any loss for which the other reliefs are not claimed.

12   CARRY FORWARD TRADE LOSS RELIEF

A company must set off a trading loss against income from the same trade in future accounting periods (unless it has been otherwise relieved; see below). **Relief is against the first available profits.**

EXAMPLE

A Ltd has the following results for the three years to 31 March 2010.

	Year ended		
	31.3.08	31.3.09	31.3.10
	£	£	£
Trading profit/(loss)	(8,550)	3,000	6,000
Property income	0	1,000	1,000
Gift aid donation	300	1,400	1,700

Calculate the profits chargeable to corporation tax for all three years showing any losses available to carry forward at 1 April 2010.

	Year ended		
	31.3.08	31.3.09	31.3.10
	£	£	£
Trading profits	0	3,000	6,000
Less: carry forward loss relief		(3,000)	(5,550)
	0	0	450
Property income	0	1,000	1,000
Less: Gift aid donation	0	(1,000)	(1,450)
PCTCT	0	0	0
Unrelieved gift aid donation	300	400	250

Note that the trading loss carried forward is set only against the trading profit in future years. It cannot be set against the property income.

The gift aid donations that become unrelieved remain unrelieved as they cannot be carried forward.

Loss memorandum

	£
Loss for y/e 31.3.08	8,550
Less used y/e 31.3.09	(3,000)
Loss carried forward at 1.4.09	5,550
Less used y/e 31.3.10	(5,550)
Loss carried forward at 1.4.10	0

13 TRADE LOSS RELIEF AGAINST TOTAL PROFITS

13.1 Current year relief

A company may claim to set a trading loss incurred in an accounting period against total profits before deducting gift aid donations of the same accounting period.

13.2 Carry back relief

Such a loss may then be carried back and set against total profits before deducting gift aid donations of an accounting period falling wholly or partly within the 12 months of the start of the period in which the loss was incurred.

For accounting periods ending between 24 November 2008 and 23 November 2010, the carryback period is extended to 36 months, subject to maximum relief of £50,000 outside the usual 12 month carryback period.

Any possible loss relief claim for the period of the loss must be made before any excess loss can be carried back to a previous period. Any carryback is to more recent periods before earlier periods. Relief for earlier losses is given before relief for later losses.

Any loss remaining unrelieved after any loss relief claims against total profits is carried forward to set against future profits of the same trade.

Activity 4   **(20 minutes)**

Helix Ltd has the following results.

	30.9.06	30.9.07	Year ended 30.9.08	30.9.09
		£	£	£
Trading profit/(loss)	22,500	30,500	20,000	(85,000)
Bank interest	500	500	500	500
Chargeable gains	0	0	0	4,000
Gift Aid donation	250	250	250	250

Show the PCTCT for all the years affected assuming that loss relief against total profits is claimed.

Any loss remaining unrelieved after any loss relief claims against total profits is carried forward to set against future profits of the same trade.

If a period falls partly outside the 12 (or 36) months, loss relief is limited to the proportion of the period's profits (before gift aid donations) equal to the proportion of the period which falls within the 12 (or 36) months.

EXAMPLE

Tallis Ltd started trading on 1 April 2006 and had the following results for the five accounting periods to 31 July 2009.

	Y/e 30.4.06	Y/e 30.4.07	3 months to 31.7.07	Y/e 31.7.08	Y/e 31.7.09
	£	£	£	£	£
Trading profit (loss)	20,000	4,000	12,000	15,000	(60,000)
Building society interest	1,000	1,000	400	1,000	1,800
Gift aid donations	600	600	500	0	0

Show the profits chargeable to corporation tax for all years. Assume loss relief is claimed against total profits where possible.

	Y/e 30.4.06	Y/e 30.4.07	3 months to 31.7.07	Y/e 31.7.08	Y/e 31.7.09
	£	£	£	£	£
Trading profit	20,000	4,000	12,000	15,000	0
Interest income	1,000	1,000	400	1,000	1,800
	21,000	5,000	12,400	16,000	1,800
Less current period loss relief					(1,800)
	21,000	5,000	12,400	16,000	0
Less carry back loss relief	(15,750)	(5,000)	(12,400)	(16,000)	
	5,250	0	0	0	0
Less gift aid donations	(600)				0
PCTCT	4,650	0	0	0	0
Unrelieved gift aid donations	0	600	500	0	0

Loss memorandum	£
Loss incurred in y/e 31.7.09	60,000
Less used y/e 31.7.09	(1,800)
Less used y/e 31.7.08	(16,000)
Less used 3 months to 31.7.07	(12,400)
Less used y/e 30.4.07	(5,000)
Less used y/e 30.4.06 9/12 × £21,000	(15,750)
C/f	9,050

Notes

1   The loss can be carried back to set against profits of the previous **36 months**. This means profits in the y/e 30.4.06 must be time apportioned by multiplying by 9/12.

2   The £50,000 maximum does not apply because the loss relieved beyond the 12 month carryback period is £(12,400 + 5,000 + £15,750) = £33,150.

3   Losses remaining after the loss relief claims against total profits are carried forward to set against future trading profits.

If the loss making period is a short period of account, the £50,000 limit is restricted. For example, if the loss making period is 9 months in length, the maximum carryback relief will be £(50,000 × 9/12) = £37,500.

13.3   Claims

A claim for relief against current or prior period profits must be made within four years of the end of the accounting period in which the loss arose. Any claim must be for the *whole* loss (to the extent that profits are available to relieve it). The loss can however be reduced by not claiming full capital allowances, so that higher capital allowances are given (on higher tax written down values) in future years.

13.4 Interaction with losses brought forward

A trading loss carried back is relieved after any trading losses brought forward have been offset.

EXAMPLE

Chile Ltd has the following results.

	Year ended		
	30.9.08	30.9.09	30.9.10
	£	£	£
Trading profit/(loss)	21,000	(20,000)	40,000
Bank interest	1,000	1,500	500
Chargeable gains	0	2,000	0
Gift Aid donations	500	500	500

Chile Ltd had a trading loss of £16,000 carried forward at 1 October 2007.

Show the PCTCT for all the years affected assuming that loss relief against total profits is claimed.

The loss of the year to 30.9.09 is relieved against current year profits and against profits of the previous twelve months. The trading loss brought forward at 1 October 2007 is relieved in the year ended 30 September 2008 before the loss brought back.

	Year ended		
	30.9.08	30.9.09	30.9.10
	£	£	£
Trading profit	21,000	0	40,000
Less carry forward loss relief	(16,000)	0	(10,500)
	5,000	0	29,500
Investment income	1,000	1,500	500
Chargeable gains	0	2,000	0
	6,000	3,500	30,000
Less current period loss relief	0	(3,500)	0
	6,000	0	30,000
Less carry back loss relief	(6,000)	0	0
	0	0	30,000
Less gift aid donation	0	0	(500)
PCTCT	0	0	29,500
Unrelieved gift aid donations	500	500	

Loss memorandum	£
Loss brought forward at 1 October 2007	16,000
Less used y/e 30.9.08	(16,000)
	0
Loss incurred in y/e 30.9.09	20,000
Less used: y/e 30.9.09	(3,500)
y/e 30.9.08	(6,000)
	10,500
Less used: y/e 30.9.10	(10,500)
C/f	Nil

13.5 Terminal trade loss relief

For trading losses incurred in the twelve months up to the cessation of trade the carry back period is extended from twelve months to three years, later years first. There is no maximum loss relief.

EXAMPLE

Brazil Ltd had the following results for the accounting periods up to the cessation of trade on 30 September 2009.

	Y/e 30.9.06 £	Y/e 30.9.07 £	Y/e 30.9.08 £	Y/e 30.9.09 £
Trading profits	60,000	40,000	15,000	(180,000)
Gains	0	10,000	0	6,000
Rental income	12,000	12,000	12,000	12,000

You are required to show how the losses are relieved assuming the maximum use is made of loss relief against total profits.

	Y/e 30.9.06 £	Y/e 30.9.07 £	Y/e 30.9.08 £	Y/e 30.9.09 £
Trading profits	60,000	40,000	15,000	0
Rental income	12,000	12,000	12,000	12,000
Gains	0	10,000	0	6,000
	72,000	62,000	27,000	18,000
Less current period loss relief Y/e 30.9.09				(18,000)
				0
Less carry back loss relief	(72,000)	(62,000)	(27,000)	
PCTCT	0	0	0	0

Chapter roundup

- Companies pay corporation tax on their profits chargeable to corporation tax(PCTCT).

- An accounting period cannot exceed 12 months in length so long period of account must be split into two accounting periods. The first accounting period is always twelve months in length.

- Tax rates are set for financial years.

- A company is UK resident if it is incorporated in the UK or if it is incorporated abroad and its central management and control are exercised in the UK.

- PCTCT comprises the company's income and chargeable gains, less gift aid donations. It does not include dividends received from other UK resident companies.

- Income includes trading income, property income, income from non-trading loan relationships (interest) and miscellaneous income.

- The adjustment of profits computation for companies broadly follows that for computing business profits subject to income tax. There are, however, some minor differences.

- Chargeable gains for companies are computed in broadly the same way as for individuals.

- Gift aid donations are paid gross by a company and deducted when computing PCTCT.

- A company pays corporation tax on its profits chargeable to corporation tax (PCTCT).

- 'Profits' is PCTCT plus franked investment income (FII).

- Companies may be taxed at the small companies' rate (SCR) or obtain marginal relief, depending on their 'profits'.

- The marginal rate of corporation tax between the small companies' limits is 29.75%. The marginal tax rate is an effective rate; is it never actually used in working out corporation tax.

- The upper and lower limits which are used to determine tax rates are pro-rated on a time basis if an accounting period last for less than 12 months.

- The upper and lower limits which are used to determine tax rates are divided by the total number of associated companies. Broadly, associated companies are worldwide trading companies under common control.

- Trading losses may be relieved against current total profits, against total profits of earlier periods or against future trading income.

- Trading losses carried forward can only be set against future trading profits arising from the same trade.

NOTES

- Loss relief against total profits is given before gift aid donations. Gift aid donations remain unrelieved.

- Loss relief against total profits may be given against current period profits and against profits of the previous 12 months. For accounting periods ending between 24 November 2008 and 23 November 2010, this is extended to 36 months, subject to a maximum relief of £50,000 outside the usual 12 month carryback period.

- A claim for current period loss relief can be made without claim for carryback. However, if a loss is to be carried back a claim for current period relief must have been made first.

- Trading losses in the last 12 months of trading can be carried back and set against profits of the previous 36 months.

Quick quiz

1   When does an accounting period end?

2   What is the difference between a period of account and an accounting period?

3   Should interest paid on a trading loan be adjusted in the trading income computations?

4   How are trading profits (before capital allowances) of a long period of account divided between accounting periods?

5   Which companies are entitled to the small companies' rate of corporation tax?

6   What is the marginal relief formula?

7   Against what profits may trading losses carried forward be set?

8   To what extent may losses be carried back?

Answers to Quick quiz

1   An accounting period ends on the earliest of:

    (a)   12 months after its start

    (b)   the end of the company's period of account

    (c)   the commencement of the company's winding up

    (d)   the company ceasing to be resident in the UK

    (e)   the company ceasing to be liable to corporation tax

2   A period of account is the period for which a company prepares accounts. An accounting period is the period for which corporation tax is charged. If a company prepares annual accounts the two will coincide.

3   Interest paid on a trading loan should not be adjusted in the trading income computation as it is an allowable expense, computed on the accruals basis.

4   Trading income (before capital allowances) is apportioned on a time basis.

5   Companies are entitled to the small companies' rate of corporation tax if they have profits of up to £300,000.

6   $(M - P) \times I/P \times$ marginal relief fraction.

7   Profits from the same trade.

8   A loss may be carried back and set against total profits (before deducting gift aid donations) of the prior 12 months (36 months for accounting periods ending between 24 November 2008 and 23 November 2010 limited to £50,000 outside the usual 12 month carryback period). A loss arising on the final 12 months of trading can be carried back to set against profits arising in the previous 36 months without limit. The loss carried back is the trading loss left unrelieved after a claim against total profits (before deducting gift aid donations) of the loss making AP has been made.

Answers to Activities

1   The 18 month period of account is divided into:

Year ending 31 March 2010

6 months to 30 September 2010

Results are allocated:

	Y/e 31.3.10 £	6m to 30.9.10 £
Trading profits 12:6	120,000	60,000
Property Income		
12 × £500	6,000	
6 × £500		3,000
Capital gain (1.8.10)		250,000
Less: Gift aid donation (31.3.10)	(50,000)	
PCTCT (profits chargeable to corporation tax)	76,000	313,000

2

	£
Trading profits	42,000
Dividend plus tax credit £9,000 × 100/90	10,000
'Profits' (less than £300,000 limit)	52,000
Corporation tax payable	
£42,000 × 21%	£8,820

3

	£
PCTCT	360,000
Add: FII £8,100 × 100/90	9,000
'Profits'	369,000

	FY 2007 6 months to 31.3.08 £	FY 2008 6 months 30.9.08 £
PCTCT (6:6)	180,000	180,000
'Profits' (6:6)	184,500	184,500
Lower limit:		
£300,000 × 6/12	150,000	150,000
Upper limit:		
£1,500,000 × 6/12	750,000	750,000

Marginal relief applies in both FYs

FY 2007
£180,000 × 30% — 54,000
Less: marginal relief £(750,000 − 184,500) × $\frac{180,000}{184,500}$ × 1/40 — (13,793)

40,207

FY 2008
£180,000 × 28% — 504,000
Less: marginal relief £(750,000 − 184,500) × $\frac{180,000}{184,500}$ × 7/400 — (9,655)

40,745

Total corporation tax payable
£(40,027 + 40,745) — £80,952

4   The loss of the year to 30 September 2009 is relieved against current year profits and against profits of the previous 36 months.

	Year ended			
	30.9.06	30.9.07	30.9.08	30.9.09
	£	£	£	£
Trading profit	22,500	30,500	20,000	0
Investment income	500	500	500	500
Chargeable gains	0	0	0	4,000
	23,000	31,000	20,500	4,500
Less current period loss relief	0	0	0	(4,500)
	23,000	31,000	20,500	0
Less carry back loss relief	(19,000)	(31,000)	(20,500)	0
	4,000	0	0	0
Less gift aid donation	(250)	0	0	0
PCTCT	3,750	0	0	0
Unrelieved gift aid donation		250	250	250

Loss memorandum	£
Loss incurred in y/e 30.9.09	85,000
Less used: y/e 30.9.09	(4,500)
y/e 30.9.08	(20,500)
y/e 30.9.07	(31,000)
y/e 30.9.06	(19,000)
(max)	
Loss available to carry forward	10,000

The maximum loss carried back to year ending 30.9.06 is £(50,000 – 31,000) = £19,000.

Part B: Taxation (Finance Act 2009)

Chapter 16
CORPORATION TAX ADMINISTRATION

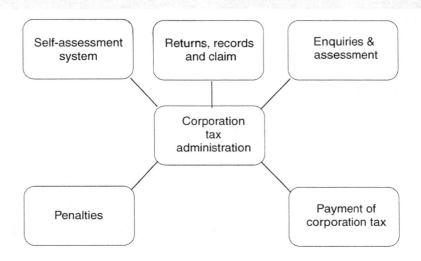

Introduction

This chapter covers two relatively small areas of corporation tax. The self assessment system and the payments system, apply to all companies, regardless of status.

Your objectives

In this chapter you will lean about the following.

    (a)   The self assessment administration system

    (b)   Payment of corporation tax

1 THE SELF ASSESSMENT SYSTEM

1.1 Introduction

The self assessment system relies upon the company completing and filing a tax return and paying the tax due. The system is enforced by a system of penalties for failure to comply within the set time limits, and by interest for late payment of tax.

Dormant companies and companies which have not yet started to trade may not be required to complete tax returns. Such companies have a duty to notify HMRC when they should be brought within the self assessment system.

1.2 Notification of first accounting period

A company must notify HMRC of the beginning of its first accounting period (ie usually when it starts to trade) and the beginning of any subsequent period that does not immediately follow the end of a previous accounting period. The notice must be in the prescribed form and submitted within three months of the relevant date.

1.3 Notification of chargeability

A company that does not receive a notice requiring a return to be filed must, if it is chargeable to tax, **notify HMRC within twelve months of the end of the accounting period.**

2 RETURNS, RECORDS AND CLAIMS

2.1 Returns

A company's tax return (CT600 version 2) must include a self assessment of any tax payable.

An obligation to file a return arises only when the company receives a notice requiring a return. A return is required for each accounting period ending during or at the end of the period specified in the notice requiring a return. A company also has to file a return for certain other periods which are not accounting periods (eg for a period when the company is dormant).

A notice to file a return may also require other information, accounts and reports. For a UK resident company the requirement to deliver accounts normally extends only to the accounts required under the Companies Act.

A return is due on or before the filing date. This is normally the later of:

(a) **12 months after the end of the period to which the return relates;**

(b) **three months from the date on which the notice requiring the return was made.**

The relevant period of account is that in which the accounting period to which the return relates ends.

> **Activity 1**   **(10 minutes)**
>
> A Ltd prepares accounts for the eighteen months to 30 June 2009. A notice requiring a return for the period ended 30 June 2009 was issued to A Ltd on 1 September 2009. State the periods for which A Ltd must file a tax return and the filing dates.

2.2   Amending a return

A company may amend a return within twelve months of the filing date.

HMRC may amend a return to correct obvious errors, or anything else that an officer has reason to believe is incorrect in the light of information available, within nine months of the day the return was filed, or if the correction is to an amended return, within nine months of the filing of an amendment. The company may amend its return so as to reject the correction. If the time limit for amendments has expired, the company may reject the correction by giving notice within three months.

2.3   Records

Companies must keep records until the latest of:

    (a)   six years from the end of the accounting period;

    (b)   the date any enquiries are completed;

    (c)   the date after which enquiries may not be commenced.

All business records and accounts, including contracts and receipts, must be kept or information showing that the company has prepared a complete and correct tax return.

If a return is demanded more than six years after the end of the accounting period, any records or information which the company still has must be kept until the later of the end of any enquiry and the expiry of the right to start an enquiry.

2.4   Claims

Wherever possible claims must be made on a tax return or on an amendment to it and must be quantified at the time the return is made.

If a company believes that it has paid excessive tax, for example as a result of an error in its tax return, a claim may be made within four years from the end of the accounting period. An appeal against a decision on such a claim must be made within 30 days. A claim may not be made if the return was made in accordance with a generally accepted practice which prevailed at the time.

Other claims must be made by four years after the end of the accounting period, unless a different time limit is specified.

If HMRC amend a self assessment or issue a discovery assessment then the company has a further period to make, vary or withdraw a claim (unless the claim is irrevocable) even if this is outside the normal time limit. The period is one year from the end of the accounting period in which the amendment or assessment was made, or one year from the end of the accounting period in which the enquiry was closed if the amendment is the result of an enquiry. The relief is limited where there has been fraudulent or negligent conduct by the company or its agent.

3 ENQUIRIES AND ASSESSMENTS

3.1 Enquiries

Opening an enquiry

A return or an amendment need not be accepted at face value by HMRC. **They may enquire into it, provided that they first give written notice that they are going to enquire.** The notice must be given by a year after the later of:

(a) Where the return is filed by the due filing date, the due filing date (most group companies) or the actual filing date (other companies)

(b) Where the return is filed late, the 31 January, 30 April, 31 July or 31 October next following the actual date of delivery of the return or amendment.

Only one enquiry may be made in respect of any one return or amendment.

During an enquiry

If a notice of an enquiry has been given, HMRC may demand that the company **produce documents** for inspection and copying. However, documents relating to an appeal need not be produced and the company may appeal against a notice requiring documents to be produced.

HMRC may amend a self assessment at any time during an enquiry if they believe there might otherwise be a loss of tax. The company may appeal against such an amendment within 30 days. The company may itself make amendments during an enquiry under the normal rules for amendments. No effect will be given to such amendments during the enquiry but they may be taken into account in the enquiry.

Closing an enquiry

An enquiry ends when HMRC give notice that it has been completed and notify what they believe to be the correct amount of tax payable. Before that time, the company may ask the Tribunal to order HMRC to notify the completion of its enquiry by a specified date. Such a direction will be given unless HMRC can demonstrate that they have reasonable grounds for continuing the enquiry.

Enquiries relating to a company are closed by the issuing of a closure notice in the same way as for income tax enquiries.

3.2 Determinations

If a return is not delivered by the filing date, HMRC may issue a determination of the tax payable within the four years from the filing date. This is treated as a self assessment and there is no appeal against it. However, it is automatically replaced by any self assessment made by the company by the later of four years from the filing date and 12 months from the determination.

3.3 Discovery assessments

If HMRC believe that not enough tax has been assessed for an accounting period they can make a discovery assessment to collect the extra tax. However, when a tax return has been delivered this power is limited as outlined below.

No discovery assessment can be made on account of an error or mistake as to the basis on which the tax liability ought to be computed, if the basis generally prevailing at the time when the return was made was applied.

A discovery assessment can only be made if either:

(a) the loss of tax is due to **deliberate or careless understatement** by the company or by someone acting on its behalf; or

(b) **HMRC could not reasonably be expected to have been aware of the loss of tax, given the information so far supplied to them,** when their right to start an enquiry expired or when they notified the company that an enquiry had finished. The information supplied must be sufficiently detailed to draw HMRC's attention to contentious matters such as the use of a valuation or estimate.

The time limit for raising a discovery assessment is four years from the end of the accounting period but this is extended to 6 years if there has been careless understatement and 20 years if there has been deliberate understatement. The company may appeal against a discovery assessment within 30 days of issue.

4 PAYMENT OF CORPORATION TAX AND INTEREST

4.1 Payment dates – small and medium companies

Corporation tax is due for payment by small and medium sized companies **nine months and one day after the end of the accounting period.** For example, if a company has an accounting period ending on 31 December 2009, the corporation tax for the period is payable on 1 October 2010.

4.2 Payment dates – large companies

Large companies must pay their corporation tax in instalments. **Broadly, a large company is any company that pays corporation tax at the full rate.**

Instalments are due on the 14th day of the month, starting in the seventh month. Provided that the accounting period is twelve months long subsequent instalments are due in the tenth month during the accounting period and in the first and fourth months after the end of the accounting period.

If an accounting period is less than twelve months long subsequent instalments are due at three monthly intervals but with the final payment being due in the fourth month of the next accounting period.

4.3 Example: quarterly instalments

X Ltd is a large company with a 31 December accounting year end. Instalments of corporation tax will be due to be paid by X Ltd on:

- 14 July and 14 October in the accounting period;
- 14 January and 14 April after the accounting period ends

Thus for the year ended 31 December 2009 instalment payments are due on 14 July 2009, 14 October 2009, 14 January 2010 and 14 April 2010.

4.4 Calculating the instalments

Instalments are based on the estimated corporation tax liability for the current period (not the previous period). **A company is required to estimate its corporation tax liability before the end of the accounting period, and must revise its estimate each quarter.** It is extremely important for companies to forecast their tax liabilities accurately. Large companies whose directors are poor at estimating may find their companies incurring significant interest charges.

The amount of each instalment is computed by:

(a) **working out 3 × CT/n** where CT is the amount of the estimated corporation tax liability payable in instalments for the period and n is the number of months in the period

(b) **allocating the smaller of that amount and the total estimated corporation tax liability to the first instalment**

(c) **repeating the process for later instalments until the amount allocated is equal to the corporation tax liability.**

If the company has an accounting period of 12 months, there will be four instalments and each instalment will be 25% of the estimated amount due.

The position is slightly more complicated if the company has an accounting period of less than 12 months, as is shown in the following question.

> **Activity 2**   **(10 minutes)**
>
> A large company has a CT liability of £880,000 for the eight month period to 30 September 2009. Accounts had previously always been prepared to 31 January. Show when the CT liability is due for payment.

Companies can have instalments repaid if they later conclude the instalments ought not to have been paid.

4.5 Exceptions

A company is not required to pay instalments in the first year that it is 'large', unless its profits exceed £10 million. The £10 million limit is reduced proportionately if there are associated companies. For this purpose only, a company will be regarded as an associated company where it was an associated company at the **start** of an accounting period. (This differs from the normal approach in CT where being an associated company for any part of the AP affects the thresholds of both companies for the whole of the AP).

Any company whose liability does not exceed £10,000 need not pay by instalments.

4.6   Interest on late or overpaid tax

Interest runs from the due date on over/underpaid instalments. The position is looked at cumulatively after the due date for each instalment. HMRC calculate the interest position after the company submits its corporation tax return.

Small and medium companies are charged interest if they pay their corporation tax after the due date, and will receive interest if they overpay their tax or pay it early.

Interest paid/received on late payments or over payments of corporation tax is dealt with as investment income as interest paid/received on a non-trading loan relationship. However, at the moment, the rate of interest on overpaid tax is 0%.

5   PENALTIES

5.1   Notification of first accounting period

Failure to notify the first accounting period will mean a **maximum penalty of £3,000.**

5.2   Notification of chargeability

The common penalty regime for late notification of chargeability discussed earlier in this Text applies for corporation tax.

5.3   Late filing penalties

There is a £100 penalty for a failure to submit a return on time, rising to £200 if the delay exceeds three months. These penalties become £500 and £1,000 respectively when a return was late (or never submitted) for each of the preceding two accounting periods.

An additional tax geared penalty is applied if a return is more than six months late. The penalty is 10% of the tax unpaid six months after the return was due if the total delay is up to 12 months, and 20% of that tax if the return is over 12 months late.

There is a tax geared penalty for a fraudulent or negligent return and for failing to correct an innocent error without unreasonable delay. The maximum penalty is equal to the tax that would have been lost had the return been accepted as correct. HMRC can mitigate this penalty. If a company is liable to more than one tax geared penalty, the total penalty is limited to the maximum single penalty that could be charged.

5.4   Failure to keep records

Failure to keep records can lead to a **penalty of up to £3,000** for each accounting period affected. However, this penalty does not apply when the only records which have not been kept are ones which could only have been needed for the purposes of claims, elections or notices not included in the return.

5.5 Failure to produce documents during an enquiry

If HMRC demand documents, but the company does not produce them, there is a **penalty of £50**. There is also a **daily penalty**, which applies for each day from the day after the imposition of the £50 penalty until the documents are produced. The daily penalty may be imposed by HMRC, in which case it is £30. If, however, HMRC ask the Tribunal to impose the penalty, it is £150.

5.6 Errors in returns

The common penalty regime for making errors in tax returns discussed earlier in this Text applies for corporation tax.

Chapter roundup

- A company that does not receive a notice requiring a return to be filed must, if it is chargeable to tax, notify HMRC within twelve months of the end of the accounting period.

- A company must, in general, file a CT600 tax return within twelve months of the end of an accounting period.

- HMRC can enquire into returns.

- In general, corporation tax is due nine months and one day after the end of an accounting period, but large companies must pay their corporation tax in four quarterly instalments.

- Penalties may be levied for failure to notify the first accounting period, failure to notify chargeability, the late filing of returns, failure to keep records, failure to produce documents during an enquiry and errors in returns.

Quick quiz

1   What are the fixed penalties for failure to deliver a corporation tax return on time?

2   When must HMRC give notice to a non-group company that it is going to start an enquiry if the return was filed by the due filing date?

3   _____ companies must pay quarterly instalments of their corporation tax liability. Fill in the blank.

4   State the due dates for the payment of quarterly instalments of corporation tax for a 12 month accounting period.

5   What is the penalty if a company fails to keep records?

    A   £1,000

    B   £2,000

    C   £3,000

    D   £4,000

Answers to Quick quiz

1   There is a £100 penalty for failure to submit a return on time rising to £200 if the delay exceeds three months. These penalties increase to £500 and £1,000 respectively when a return was late for each of the preceding two accounting periods.`

2   Notice must be given by one year after the actual filing date.

3   'Large' companies, ie companies that pay corporation tax at the full rate.

4   14th day of:

    (a)   7th month in AP
    (b)   10th month in AP
    (c)   1st month after AP ends
    (d)   4th month after AP ends

5   C. £3,000 for each accounting period affected.

Answers to Activities

1   The company must file a return for the two accounting periods ending in the period specified in the notice requiring a return. The first accounting period is the twelve months to 31 December 2008 and the second is the six months to 30 June 2009. The filing date is twelve months after the end of the relevant period of account, 30 June 2010.

2   £880,000 must be paid in instalments.

The amount of each instalment is $3 \times \dfrac{£880,000}{8} = £330,000$

The due dates are:

	£
14 August 2009	330,000
14 November 2009	330,000
14 January 2010	220,000 (balance)

NOTES

Chapter 17
CAPITAL GAINS TAX

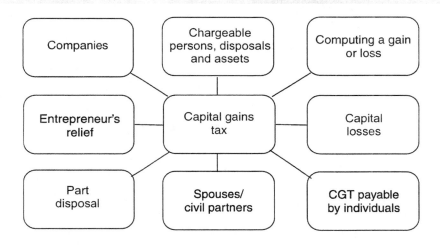

Introduction

Individuals, companies and partnerships are all liable to capital gains tax, which is effectively a tax on the profits made by virtue of selling an asset. There are many exemptions, however; for example, CGT is not payable on the sale of one's only or major home. As with other taxes there are reliefs for losses. This chapter gives you an overview of the basic principles of capital gains tax.

Your objectives

In this chapter you will learn about the following.

- (a) Chargeable persons, chargeable disposals and chargeable assets
- (b) The key elements of a personal capital gains tax computation
- (c) Computations of gains and losses
- (d) The relief for losses
- (e) The circumstances when market value is the transfer value
- (f) The basis of 'no gain no loss' transfers
- (g) How to compute the gain on an asset only part disposed of
- (h) Entrepreneurs' relief
- (i) Chargeable gains for companies

BPP LEARNING MEDIA

NOTES

1 CHARGEABLE PERSONS, DISPOSALS AND ASSETS

Definition

> For a chargeable gain to arise there must be:
>
> - A chargeable person; and
> - A chargeable disposal; and
> - A chargeable asset
>
> otherwise no charge to tax occurs.

1.1 Chargeable persons

The following are chargeable persons.

- **Individuals**
- **Partnership**
- **Companies**

1.2 Chargeable disposals

The following are chargeable disposals.

- **Sales of assets or parts of assets**
- **Gifts of assets or parts of assets**
- **The loss or destruction of assets**

A chargeable disposal occurs on the date of the contract (where there is one, whether written or oral), or the date of a conditional contract becoming unconditional. This may differ from the date of transfer of the asset. However, when a capital sum is received for example on the loss or destruction of an asset, the disposal takes place on the day the sum is received.

Where a disposal involves an acquisition by someone else, the date of acquisition for that person is the same as the date of disposal.

Transfers of assets on death are exempt disposals.

1.3 Chargeable assets

All forms of property, wherever in the world they are situated, are chargeable assets unless they are specifically designated as exempt.

1.4 Exempt assets

The following are exempt assets.

- **Motor vehicles** suitable for private use
- **National Savings and Investments certificates** and **premium bonds**
- Foreign currency for private use
- Decorations for bravery where awarded, not purchased
- Damages for personal or professional injury
- **Gilt-edged securities (treasury stock)**

336

- **Qualifying corporate bonds (QCBs)**
- **Certain chattels**
- Debts (except debts on a security)
- Investments held in individual savings accounts

If an asset is an exempt asset any gain is not taxable and any loss is not allowable.

2 COMPUTING A GAIN OR LOSS

2.1 Basic calculation

A gain (or an allowable loss) is generally calculated as follows.

	£
Disposal consideration	45,000
Less incidental costs of disposal	(400)
Net proceeds	44,600
Less allowable costs	(21,000)
Gain	23,600

Usually the disposal consideration is the proceeds of sale of the asset, but a disposal is deemed to take place at market value:

- Where the disposal is **not a bargain at arm's length**
- Where the disposal is made for a **consideration which cannot be valued**
- Where the disposal is by way of a **gift**.

Special valuation rules apply for shares.

Incidental costs of disposal may include:

- Valuation fees
- Estate agency fees
- Advertising costs
- Legal costs.

Allowable costs include:

- The original cost of acquisition
- Incidental costs of acquisition
- Capital expenditure incurred in enhancing the asset.

Enhancement expenditure is capital expenditure which enhances the value of the asset and is reflected in the state or nature of the asset at the time of disposal, or expenditure incurred in establishing, preserving or defending title to, or a right over, the asset. Excluded from this category are:

- Costs of repairs and maintenance
- Costs of insurance
- Any expenditure deductible from trading profits
- Any expenditure met by public funds (for example council grants).

> **Activity 1** (10 minutes)
>
> Joanne bought a piece of land as an investment for £20,000. The legal costs of purchase were £250.
>
> Joanne sold the land on 12 December 2009 for £35,000. She incurred estate agency fees of £700 and legal costs of £500 on the sale.
>
> Calculate Joanne's gain on sale.

3 THE ANNUAL EXEMPT AMOUNT

There is an annual exempt amount for each tax year. For each individual for 2009/10 it is £10,100. The annual exempt amount is deducted from the chargeable gains for the year after the deductions of losses and other reliefs.

Thus if Susie has chargeable gains for 2009/10 of £15,500 her taxable gains are £15,500 − £10,100 = £5,400.

4 CAPITAL LOSSES

4.1 Allowable losses of the same year

Allowable capital losses arising in a tax year are deducted from gains arising in the same tax year.

Any loss which cannot be set off is carried forward to set against future gains. Losses must be used as soon as possible (but see below).

4.2 Allowable losses brought forward

Allowable losses brought forward are only set off to reduce current year gains less current year allowable losses to the annual exempt amount. No set-off is made if net chargeable gains for the current year do not exceed the annual exempt amount.

EXAMPLE

(a) George has gains for 2009/10 of £11,000 and allowable losses of £6,000. As the losses are *current year losses* they must be fully relieved against the £11,000 of gains to produce net gains of £5,000 despite the fact that net gains are below the annual exemption.

(b) Bob has gains of £14,000 for 2009/10 and allowable losses brought forward of £6,000. Bob restricts his loss relief to £3,900 so as to leave net gains of £(14,000 − 3,900) = £10,100, which will be exactly covered by his annual exemption for 2009/10. The remaining £2,100 of losses will be carried forward to 2010/11.

(c) Tom has gains of £10,000 for 2009/10 and losses brought forward from 2008/09 of £4,000. He will leapfrog 2009/10 and carry forward all of his losses to 2010/11. His gains of £10,000 are covered by his annual exemption for 2009/10.

5   CGT PAYABLE BY INDIVIDUALS

Taxable gains are chargeable to capital gains tax at the rate of 18%.

EXAMPLE

Lucinda sold the following assets in 2009/10:

	Proceeds £	Cost £
Plot of land	100,000	80,000
Painting	40,000	15,000
Shares in XYZ plc	50,000	68,000

Calculate the CGT payable by Lucinda.

	£	£
Land		
Proceeds	100,000	
Less: cost	(80,000)	
Gain		20,000
Painting		
Proceeds	40,000	
Less: cost	(15,000)	
Gain		25,000
Shares		
Proceeds	50,000	
Less: cost	(68,000)	
Loss		(18,000)
Net gains		27,000
Less: annual exemption		(10,100)
Taxable gains		16,900
CGT @ 18% on £16,900		3,042

6   TRANSFERS BETWEEN SPOUSES/CIVIL PARTNERS

Spouses and civil partners are taxed as separate individuals. Each has his own annual exemption, and losses of one spouse or civil partner cannot be set against gains of the other spouse or civil partner.

Disposals between spouses or civil partners living together give rise to no gain no loss, whatever actual price (if any) was charged by the transferor. **This means that there is no chargeable gain or allowable loss, and the transferee takes over the transferor's cost.**

7 PART DISPOSALS

The disposal of part of a chargeable asset is a chargeable event. The chargeable gain (or allowable loss) is computed by deducting a fraction of the original cost of the whole asset from the disposal value. The balance of the cost is carried forward until the eventual disposal of the asset.

The fraction is:

$$\text{Cost} \times \frac{A}{A+B} = \frac{\text{value of the part disposed of}}{\text{value of the part disposed of} + \text{market value of the remainder}}$$

In this fraction, A is the proceeds *before* deducting incidental costs of disposal.

The part disposal fraction should not be applied indiscriminately. Any expenditure incurred wholly in respect of a particular part of an asset should be treated as an allowable deduction in full for that part and not apportioned. An example of this is incidental selling expenses, which are wholly attributable to the part disposed of.

EXAMPLE

Mr Heal owns a 4 hectare plot of land which originally cost him £150,000. He sold one hectare in July 2009 for £60,000. The incidental costs of sales were £3,000. The market value of the 3 hectares remaining is estimated to be £180,000. What is the gain on the sale of the one hectare?

The amount of the indexed cost attributable to the part sold is

$$\frac{60,000}{60,000+180,000} \times £150,000 = £37,500$$

	£
Proceeds	60,000
Less: disposal cost	(3,000)
Net proceed of sale	57,000
Less cost (see above)	(37,500)
Gain	19,500

8 ENTREPRENEURS' RELIEF

8.1 How the relief works

Entrepreneurs' relief is available to reduce the gains on a material disposal of business assets. Relief is given by reducing the eligible gains by $^4/_9$. This leaves $^5/_9 \times$ gains chargeable, which gives an effective rate (if no annual exemption is available) of 10% ($^5/_9 \times 18\% = 10\%$).

Where there is a material disposal of business assets which results in both gains and losses, losses are netted off against gains before entrepreneurs' relief is applied. Losses on assets not qualifying for entrepreneurs' relief and the annual exemption are deducted after the application of entrepreneurs' relief.

8.2 Example

Simon sells his business, all the assets of which qualify for entrepreneurs' relief, in September 2009. The gains arising are £200,000. He has no other chargeable disposals in the year.

The CGT payable on his disposal is:

	£
Gains	200,000
Less: reduction in gains $^4/_9 \times$ £200,000	(88,889)
Gains remaining in charge	111,111
Less: annual exemption	(10,100)
Taxable gains	101,011
CGT @ 18%	18,182

Note that if the annual exemption had not been available, the CGT payable would have been £111,111 x 18% = £20,000 ie an effective rate of 10%.

8.3 Lifetime limit

There is a limit of £1 million of gains on which entrepreneurs' relief can be claimed. This is a lifetime amount starting **from 6 April 2008.**

> **Activity 2** **(10 minutes)**
>
> Maureen sells her shareholding which qualifies for entrepreneurs' relief, in January 2010, realising a gain of £900,000. She has already used her annual exemption for 2009/10. Maureen had already made a claim for entrepreneurs' relief in 2008/09 in respect of gains totalling £300,000.
>
> Calculate the CGT payable by Maureen on her disposal in 2009/10.

8.4 Conditions

Entrepreneurs' relief is available where there is a **material disposal of business assets**.

A **material disposal of business assets** is:

- a disposal of the **whole or part of a business** which has been **owned by the individual** throughout the period of **one year** ending with the date of the disposal

- a disposal of **one or more assets in use for the purposes of a business at** the time at which the business **ceases to be carried on** provided that:

  - the business was owned by the individual throughout **the period of one year** ending with the date on which the business ceases to be carried on; **and**

  - the date of cessation is within **three years** ending with the date of the disposal.

- a disposal of **shares or securities of a company where** the company is the individual's **personal company**; the company is either a **trading company** or **holding company of a trading group**; the individual is an **officer or employee** of the company (or a group company) and these conditions are met either:

  - throughout the period of **one year** ending with the date of the disposal; **or**

  - throughout the period of **one year** ending with the date on which the company (or group) **ceases to be a trading company (or trading group)** and that date is within the period of **three years** ending with the date of the disposal.

For the first category to apply, there has be a **disposal of the whole or part of the business as a going concern,** not just a disposal of individual assets. A business includes one carried on as a partnership of which the individual is a partner. The business must be a **trade, profession or vocation** conducted on a **commercial basis with a view to the realisation of profits.**

For both the first and second category, relief is only available on relevant business assets. These are assets used for the purposes of the business and cannot include shares and securities or assets held as investments.

In relation to the third category, a **personal company** in relation to an individual is one where:

- the individual holds at least 5% of the ordinary share capital; and

- the individual can exercise at least 5% of the voting rights in the company by virtue of that holding of shares.

EXAMPLE

Robbie started in business as a manufacturer of widgets in July 2001. He acquired a freehold workshop for £80,000 in May 2002. He used the workshop in his business. In August 2006, Robbie invested £40,000 of his business profits in shares in an investment company. He bought a machine for use in his business in January 2009 at a cost of £30,000.

In November 2009, Robbie sold his business to a larger competitor. The sale proceeds were apportioned to capital assets as follows:

	£
Goodwill	50,000
Workshop	125,000
Shares	80,500
Machine	32,000

Calculate Robbie's CGT payable on the disposal, assuming that he does not have any other chargeable assets.

	£	£
Proceeds of goodwill	50,000	
Less: cost	(nil)	50,000
Proceeds of workshop	125,000	
Less: cost	(80,000)	45,000
Proceeds of machine (N1)	32,000	
Less: cost	(30,000)	2,000
Gains qualifying for entrepreneurs' relief		97,000
Less: reduction is gains $^4/_9 \times £97,000$		(43,111)
Gains remaining in charge		53,889
Proceeds of shares (N2)	80,500	
Less: cost	(40,000)	40,500
Chargeable gains		94,389
Less: annual exemption		(10,100)
Taxable gains		84,289
CGT @ 18%		15,172

Notes

1. The gain on the machine is eligible for entrepreneurs' relief even though it has not been owned for one year. The condition is that the individual has owned the business for one year.

2. The gain on the shares is not eligible for entrepreneurs' relief because it is not a relevant business asset.

8.5 Claim

An individual must claim entrepreneurs' relief: it is not automatic. The claim deadline is the first anniversary of 31 January following the end of the tax year of disposal. For a 2009/10 disposal, the taxpayer must claim by 31 January 2012.

9 COMPANIES

Companies do not pay capital gains tax. Instead their chargeable gains are included in the profits chargeable to corporation tax. A company's capital gains or allowable losses are computed in a similar way to individuals but with a few major differences:

- There is relief for inflation called the indexation allowance
- **No annual exemption** is available
- Different matching rules for shares apply if the shareholder is a company.

9.1 Indexation allowance

The purpose of having an indexation allowance is to remove the inflation element of a gain from taxation.

Companies are entitled to indexation allowance from the date of acquisition until the date of disposal of an asset. It is based on the movement in the Retail Price Index (RPI) between those two dates.

For example, if J Ltd bought a painting on 2 January 1987 and sold it on 19 November 2009 the indexation allowance is available from January 1987 until November 2009.

The indexation factor is:

$$\frac{\text{RPI for month of disposal} - \text{RPI for month of acquisition}}{\text{RPI for month of acquisition}}$$

The calculation is expressed as a decimal and is rounded to three decimal places.

Indexation allowance is available on the allowable cost of the asset from the **date of acquisition** (including incidental costs of acquisition). **It is also available on enhancement expenditure from the month in which such expenditure becomes due and payable. Indexation allowance is not available on the costs of disposal.**

EXAMPLE

An asset is acquired by a company on 15 February 1983 (RPI = 83.0) at a cost of £5,000. Enhancement expenditure of £2,000 is incurred on 10 April 1984 (RPI = 88.6). The asset is sold for £25,500 on 20 December 2009 (RPI = 207.2). Incidental costs of sale are £500. Calculate the chargeable gain arising.

The indexation allowance is available until December 2009 and is computed as follows.

	£
$\dfrac{207.2 - 83.0}{83.0} = 1.496 \times £5,000$	7,480
$\dfrac{207.2 - 88.6}{88.6} = 1.339 \times £2,000$	2,678
	10,158

The computation of the chargeable gain is as follows.

	£
Proceeds	25,500
Less incidental costs of sale	(500)
Net proceeds	25,000
Less allowable costs £(5,000 + 2,000)	(7,000)
Unindexed gain	18,000
Less indexation allowance (see above)	(10,158)
Indexed gain	7,842

Indexation allowance cannot create or increase an allowable loss. If there is a gain before the indexation allowance, the allowance can reduce that gain to zero but no further. If there is a loss before the indexation allowance, there is no indexation allowance.

If the indexation allowance calculation gives a negative figure, treat the indexation as nil: do not add to the unindexed gain.

Chapter roundup

- A gain is chargeable if there is a chargeable disposal of a chargeable asset by a chargeable person.

- Capital gains are chargeable on individuals and companies.

- CGT applies primarily to persons resident or ordinarily resident in the UK.

- A gain or loss is computed by taking the proceeds and deducting the cost. Incidental costs of acquisition and disposal may be deducted together with any enhancement expenditure reflected in the state and nature of the asset at the date of disposal.

- An individual is entitled to an annual exemption for each tax year.

- Losses are set off against gains of the same year and any excess carried forward. Brought forward losses are only set off to reduce net gains down to the amount of the annual exemption.

- Individuals pay CGT on gains arising in a tax year at 18%.

- Disposals between spouses or members of a civil partnership are made on a no gain no loss basis and do not give rise to a chargeable gain or allowable loss.

- On a part disposal, the cost must be apportioned between the part disposed of and the part retained.

- Entrepreneurs' relief applies on the disposal of a business and certain funding company shares. It reduces the rate of CGT from 18% to 10%.

- Chargeable gains for companies are computed in broadly the same way as for individuals, but indexation allowance applies and there is no annual exemption.

- The indexation allowance gives relief for the inflation element of a gain.

Quick quiz

1 Give some examples of chargeable disposals.

2 To what extent must allowable losses be set against chargeable gains?

3 At what rate or rates do individuals pay CGT?

4 What is enhancement expenditure?

5 10 acres of land are sold for £15,000 out of 25 acres. Original cost in 1999 was £9,000. Costs of sales are £2,000. Rest of land valued at £30,000. What is the total amount deductible from proceeds?

Answers to Quick quiz

1 The following are chargeable disposals

- Sales of assets or parts of assets
- Gifts of assets or parts of assets
- Receipts of capital sums following the loss or destruction of an asset

2 Current year losses must be set off against gains in full, even if this reduces net gains below the annual exempt amount. Losses brought forward are set off to bring down untapered gains to the level of the annual exempt amount.

3 Individuals pay CGT at the rate of 18%.

4 Enhancement expenditure is capital expenditure enhancing the value of the asset and reflected in the state/nature of the asset at disposal, or expenditure incurred in establishing, preserving or defending title to asset.

5 $\dfrac{15,000}{15,000 + 30,000} \times £9,000 = £3,000 + £2,000$ (costs of disposal) = £5,000

Answers to Activities

1

	£
Proceeds of sale	35,000
Less costs of disposal £(700 + 500)	(1,200)
	33,800
Less costs of acquisitions £(20,000 + 250)	(20,250)
Gain	13,550

2

	£
Gains	900,000
Less: reduction in gains £(1,000,000 (max) − 300,000) = £700,000 × $^4/_9$	(311,111)
Taxable gain	588,889
CGT @ 18%	106,000

Using the effective rate of tax on the gain, the CGT payable is:

	£
£700,000 × 10%	70,000
£200,000 × 18%	36,000
CGT payable	106,000

Tax Rates and Allowances

TAX RATES AND ALLOWANCES (FINANCE ACT 2009)

A   INCOME TAX

1   *Rates*

	2008/09		2009/10	
	£	%	£	%
Starting rate (savings income)	1 – 2,320	10	1 – 2,440	10
Basic rate	2,321 – 34,800	20	2,441 – 37,400	20
Higher rate	34,801 and above	40	37,401 and above	40

Dividend income in both the starting rate and the basic rate bands is taxed at 10%. Dividend income within the higher rate band is taxed at 32.5%.

2   *Personal allowance*

	2008/09	2009/10
	£	£
Personal allowance	6,035	6,475

3   *Cars – taxable percentage 2009/10*

The taxable percentage is 15% for petrol engine cars with a baseline CO_2 emissions figure of 135g/km or less. A lower rate of 10% applies to petrol cars with CO_2 emissions of 120 grams per kilometre or less.

4   *Car fuel charge – 2009/10*

Set figure £16,900

5   *Authorised mileage rates (AMR) 2009/10 rates*

The rates for the maximum tax free mileage allowances for 2009/10 are as follows:

Car mileage rates★

First 10,000 miles	40p per mile
Over 10,000 miles	25p per mile

Bicycles	*Motor cycles*
20p per mile	24p per mile
Passenger payments	5p per mile

★ For NIC purposes, a rate of 40p applies irrespective of mileage.

6   *Capital allowances*

Plant and machinery

Main pool –	First Year Allowance	40%
Main pool –	Writing Down Allowance	20%
Special rate pool		10%

Motor cars

CO_2 emissions up to 110 grams per kilometre	100%
CO_2 emissions between 111 and 160 grams per kilometre	20%
CO_2 emissions over 160 grams per kilometre	10%

Annual investment allowance	£50,000

Industrial buildings

Writing-down allowance	2%

B   CORPORATION TAX

1   *Rates*

Financial year	2008	2009
Small companies rate	21%	21%
Full rate	28%	28%
	£	£
Lower limit	300,000	300,000
Upper limit	1,500,000	1,500,000
Taper relief fraction		
Small companies rate	7/400	7/400

2   *Marginal relief*

$$(M - P) \times I/P \times \text{Marginal relief fraction}$$

C   RATES OF INTEREST

Official rate of interest: 4.75% (assumed)

Rate of interest on unpaid tax: 2.5% (assumed)

Rate of interest on overpaid tax: 0.0% (assumed)

D   CAPITAL GAINS TAX

Annual exemption (individuals)

	£
2008/09	9,600
2009/10	10,100
Rate of tax for individuals	18%
Entrepreneurs' relief	
Lifetime limit	£1,000,000
Reducing fraction	4/9

Appendix:
Edexcel Guidelines

Edexcel Guidelines for the BTEC Higher Nationals in Business

This book is designed to be of value to anyone who is studying finance, whether as a subject in its own right or as a module forming part of any business-related degree or diploma.

However, it provides complete coverage of the topics listed in the Edexcel Guidelines for Units 11 (Financial Systems and Auditing) and 12 (Taxation), of the BTEC Higher Nationals in Business (revised 2010). We include the Edexcel Guidelines here for your reference, mapped to the topics covered in this book.

Edexcel Guidelines
Unit 11 Financial Systems and Auditing

Description of the Unit

In this unit learners will develop skills to evaluate the accounting systems of a business, using both computerised and manual records, and apply fundamental concepts. Learners will also analyse the management control systems of a business and evaluate their effectiveness, particularly in terms of controls and safeguards against error and fraud.

This unit will also enable learners to develop audit skills by contributing to the planning and performance of an audit and the preparation of an audit report.

Summary of learning outcomes

To achieve this unit a learner must:

1   Understand the importance of keeping effective **accounting systems** within a business

2   Be able to analyse the **management control systems** of a business

3   Be able to contribute to the **planning and conduct of an audit assignment**

4   Be able to prepare **audit reports**.

Content

Chapter coverage

1 Accounting systems

Accounting records: books of prime entry (daybooks), accounts and ledgers (sales, purchases, nominal/general), trial balance, final accounts — 1

Fundamental accounting concepts: accruals, prudence, consistency, going concern, materiality, business entity — 4

Accounting systems: Manual and computerised, effect of business size and structure — 3

2 Management control systems

Business risk: types eg operational, financial, compliance; identification of risk and responsibility for risk management, influences on corporate governance (eg Cadbury Code) — 2

Control: control systems and procedures within the business eg segregation of duties, authorisation — 2

Fraud: types, implications, detection — 2

3 Planning and conduct of an audit assignment

Regulatory environment: legal duties and status of auditors, liability of auditors, auditing standards and guidelines — 3, 7

Role of the auditor: internal and external audit and the relationship between the two, responsibilities of management as opposed to auditors — 3

Audit planning: scope, materiality, risk — 4

Audit testing: systems based (compliance) and substantive testing, sampling methods eg random, stratified, systematic; confidence intervals — 5, 6

Records: audit files and working papers, checklists and programmes, flowcharts and questionnaires — 5

4 Audit reports

Statutory reports: purpose, content (opinion of auditor), qualified and unqualified, types of qualification — 7

Management letters: purpose and content — 7

Outcomes and assessment criteria

The learning outcomes and the criteria used to assess them are shown in the table below.

Outcomes	Assessment criteria
	To achieve each outcome a learner must demonstrate the ability to:
LO 1 Understand the importance of keeping effective accounting systems within a business	1.1 explain the purpose and use of the different accounting records 1.2 assess the importance and meaning of the fundamental accounting concepts 1.3 evaluate the factors which influence the nature and structure of accounting systems
LO2 Be able to analyse the management control systems of a business	2.1 identify the different components of business risk 2.2 analyse the control systems in place in a business 2.3 evaluate the risk of fraud within a business suggesting methods for detection
LO3 Be able to contribute to the planning and conduct of an audit assignment	3.1 plan an audit with reference to scope, materiality andrisk 3.2 identify and use appropriate audit tests 3.3 record the audit process in an appropriate manner
LO4 Be able to prepare audit reports	4.1 prepare a draft audit report 4.2 draft suitable management letters in relation to a statutory audit.

EDEXCEL GUIDELINES
UNIT 12 TAXATION

Description of the Unit

This unit aims to give learners an understanding of the taxation of individuals and limited companies in the United Kingdom.

Learners will understand the need for taxation and may already be familiar with the calculation and collection of income tax through the Pay as You Earn system applied to employees.

The unit introduces learners to the UK tax environment and explores the administration and collection of taxation in the UK and the duties of the tax practitioner.

The unit gives learners the skills needed to understand and compute the calculation of income tax for both individuals and businesses Learners will then consider the liability for and computation of corporation tax and capital gains tax.

Summary of learning outcomes

To achieve this unit a learner must:

1   Understand the duties and responsibilities of the **tax practitioner in the UK tax environment**

2   Be able to calculate **personal tax liabilities** for individuals and partnerships

3   Be able to calculate **corporation tax liabilities** for companies

4   Be able to calculate **capital gains tax payable** for individuals and businesses.

Chapter coverage

1 Tax practitioner and the UK tax environment

UK tax environment: purpose and types of taxation (income tax, corporation tax, capital gains tax, inheritance tax), different methods of collection, tax legislation   8

Tax practitioner: dealing with HM Revenue and Customs advising clients, calculating liabilities, implications for non-payment, respecting confidentiality, seeking advice when needed   8

2 Personal tax liabilities

Sources of income: income from employment including benefits in kind; income from self employment eg sole trader or partnership; income from investments   9, 10, 11

Tax computations: relevant and allowable expenses, charges on income, payments to charities, tax free allowances, tax rates and payment dates   9

Tax of the self-employed: bases of assessment, adjustment of profits and losses eg disallowed expenditure, tax losses, capital expenditure and allowances   13, 14

Documentation: tax returns, P60, P45, P11D   10, 12

3 Corporation tax liabilities

Bases of assessment: scope of corporation tax, accounting periods and chargeable profits, due dates   15

Computation: adjusted profits, treatment of losses, corporation tax rates, capital expenditure and allowances, treatment of income tax deductions   15

4 Capital gains tax payable

Incidence and administration of CGT: chargeable persons/assets/disposals, basis of assessment, payment dates   17

Computation: layout of computation, allowable expenditure indexation allowance and taper relief, dealing with losses, allowances, rates   17

Outcomes and assessment criteria
The learning outcomes and the criteria used to assess them are shown in the table below.

Outcomes		Assessment criteria
		To achieve each outcome a learner must demonstrate the ability to:
1	Understand the duties and responsibilities of the **tax practitioner and the UK tax environment**	1.1 describe the UK tax environment
		1.2 analyse the role and responsibilities of the tax practitioner
		1.3 explain the tax obligations of tax payers or their agents and the implications of non-compliance
2	Be able to calculate **personal tax liabilities** for individuals and partnerships	2.1 calculate relevant income, expenses and allowances
		2.2 calculate taxable amounts and tax payable for employed and self employed individuals and payment dates
		2.3 complete relevant documentation and tax returns
3	Be able to calculate **corporation tax liabilities** for companies	3.1 calculate chargeable profits
		3.2 calculate tax liabilities and due payment dates
		3.3 explain how income tax deductions are dealt with
4	Be able to calculate the **capital gains tax payable** for individuals and companies	4.1 identify chargeable assets
		4.2 calculate capital gains and losses
		4.3 calculate capital gains tax payable.

Index

Accommodation, 174
Accountability, 37
Accounting date, 280
Accounting packages, 4
Accounting period, 302
Accounting records
   adequate, 20
   statutory requirements, 20
Accounting suite, 4
Adjustment of profits, 231
Adverse opinion, 125
Age allowance, 160
Allowable deductions, 185
Altering cheques, 29
Analysis of errors, 106
Annual exemption, 338
Annual Investment Allowance (AIA), 247
Appropriations, 238
Around the computer, 101
Assets made available for private use, 181
Assurance engagement, 39
Audit committee, 37
Audit documentation, 72
Audit evidence, 92
Audit interrogation software, 99
Audit risk, 60
Audit sampling, 102
Audit trails, 101
Auditors' opinion, 121
Auditors' report, 44, 122
Authorised mileage allowance, 179
Authority of ISAs, 49
Awards for long service, 183

Badges of trade, 230
Balancing charges and allowances, 254
Beneficial loans, 179
Betting and gaming winnings, 156
Bicycles, 184
Blind person's allowance, 161
Block selection, 105
Budget, 145
Bulletins, 48
Business expenses, 173
Business interest, 159
Business risk, 20

Cadbury Committee, 36
Capital allowances, 186, 204, 243, 305
Capital gains tax (CGT)
   annual exemption, 338
   capital losses, 338
   chargeable asset, 336
   chargeable disposal, 336
   chargeable person, 336

enhancement expenditure, 337
   exempt asset, 336
   gifts, 337
   tax payable, 339
Capital receipts, 237
Carry forward trade loss relief
   (corporation tax), 313
Cars, 176
Charge on income, 157
Chargeable assets, 336
Chargeable disposals, 336
Chargeable gains, 307, 336
Chargeable persons, 336
Charges on income, 157
Childcare, 184
Civil partners, 162
Claims, 215, 327
Collusion with external parties, 28
Companies Act 1985, 116
Company, 302
Components, 153
Computer assisted audit tecniques
   (CAATs), 99
Computer software, 245
Confidentiality, 76
Connected person, 242
Control
   activities, 25
   environment, 25
   monitoring, 26
   risk, 63
Controlling of CAATs, 101
Copyright royalties, 157
Corporate governance, 36
Corporation tax, 302
Costs of registering patents and trade
   marks, 237
Current audit files, 76

Decision support systems, 100
Deductible expenditure, 235
Definition of an audit, 44
Design of the sample, 103
Detection risk, 63
Determinations, 220, 328
Disclaimer of opinion, 125, 127
Discovery assessments, 220, 329
Dispensation, 195
Dividends, 156, 203
Donations, 238
Duties, 47

Earnings, 170
Embedded audit facilities, 100
Emphasis of matter, 124
Employment and self employment, 171

Enquiries, 328
Enquiries into returns, 219
Entertaining, 234
Entertainment, 183
Entrepreneurs' relief, 340
Error, 27, 102
Evaluation of sample results, 106
Excluded employees, 172
Exempt benefits, 183
Exempt income, 156
Expectations gap, 45
Expected error, 105
Expression of opinion, 121
External audit, 51
External auditors, 46
Extra-statutory concessions, 144

Failing to record all sales, 29
Final year, 278
Finance Acts, 145
Financial Aspects of Corporate
    Governance, 46
Financial statement assertions, 94
Financial year, 303
Fire regulations, 245
First tax year, 276
Fiscal year, 152
Flowcharts, 78
Franked investment income (FII), 308
Fraud, 27, 51
Fuel, 178
Functional authority, 14
Furnished holiday lettings, 207

General earnings, 170
Ghost employees, 28
Gift aid donations, 161, 307
Gifts, 156, 234
Gifts of goods, 183
Going concern, 124
Goods for own use, 239
Government securities, 203
Greenbury Committee, 36

Hampel Committee, 36
Haphazard selection, 105
Higgs Report, 36
Hire purchase, 263
HM Revenue and Customs, 143
Hotel, 265

Impaired trade receivables, 234
Income from land and buildings, 204
Income taxed at source, 146

Indexation allowance, 343
Industrial buildings, 268
Inflating expense claims, 29
Information system, 25
Inherent risk, 61
Inheritance tax (IHT), 147
Instalments, 329
Institute of Internal Auditors, 50
Integral features, 256
Interest, 202
    on loans for purchase by a partner of
        plant or machinery, 158
    on loans for purchase by an employee of
        plant or machinery, 158
    on loans for purchase of an interest in a
        partnership, 158
    on loans for purchase of shares in an
        employee-controlled company, 158
Interest on late paid tax, 218, 331
Internal audit, 46, 50
Internal Control Evaluation
    Questionnaires (ICEQs), 84
Internal Control Questionnaires (ICQs),
    84
Internal control system, 22, 38
International Standards on Auditing
    (ISAs), 48
Investment in a co-operative, 158
IR35, 189
ISA 200 *Objective and general principles
    governing an audit of financial statements*,
    44, 60
ISA 260 *Communication of audit matters
    with those charged with governance*, 132
ISA 320 Audit materiality, 66
ISA 500 *Audit evidence*, 92
ISA 700 Auditor's report on financial
    statements, 117
ISA *audit documentation*, 72
Issuing false credit notes, 29

Joint property, 162
Judgmental sampling, 106

Knowledge-based systems, 100

Lease charges for expensive cars, 235
Leased assets, 263
Legal and professional charges, 239
Liability, 131, 186
Liability in tort, 131
Liability under contract law, 129
Limitation on scope, 126
Limited liability partnerships, 295
Line authority, 14

Loan finance, 236
Loan relationships, 305
Long life assets, 256
Loss relief (income tax)
    Carry forward loss relief, 282
    Early trade losses relief, 287
    Terminal trade loss relief, 289
    Trade loss relief against general
       income, 283
    Trade losses, 281
    Trading losses relieved against capital
       gains, 284
Losses, 281
Low emission car, 248
Lower paid employment, 172
Luncheon vouchers, 174

Management fraud, 31
Material misstatement, 66
Materiality, 65
Minor children, 163
Miscasting of the payroll, 28
Miscellaneous income, 306
Mobile phone, 185
Modifications, 123
Module, 6
Motor cars, 258

Narrative notes, 77
National Savings and Investments
    (NS&I), 203
National Savings Certificates, 156
Negligence, 130
Net income, 153
Non-executive directors, 37
Non-sampling risk, 102
Non-savings income, 163
Non-statistical sampling, 103
Non-statutory audits, 46
Notification of chargeability, 326

Objectives of internal audit, 50
Official rate, 179
Opinion paragraph, 119
Overlap profits., 278

P11D dispensation, 173
Parallel simulation, 100
Part disposals, 340
Partnership investment income, 295
Partnerships, 291
PAYE settlement agreements, 195
Payment of corporation tax, 329

Payment of income tax and capital gains
    tax, 215
Payments on account, 216
Payroll deduction scheme, 185
Penalties, 195, 221, 331
Period of account, 302
Permanent audit files, 76
Personal allowance, 160
Personal incidental expenses, 173
Personal service companies, 189
Personal tax computation, 152
Plant and machinery, 243
Population, 103
Post-cessation receipts, 241
Postponement of payment of tax, 220
Practice Notes, 48
Premium bond prizes, 156
Premium bonds, 203
Premiums on leases, 205
Pre-trading expenditure, 235, 304
Private medical insurance premiums, 185
Private use assets, 257
Profits, 308
Profits chargeable to corporation tax
    (PCTCT), 303
Projected population error, 107
Property business income, 305

Qualified opinion, 125
Qualifying loans, 181

Random selection, 105
Real Estate Investment Trusts (REITs),
    206
Records, 327
Recovery of overpaid tax, 215
Redundancy, 236
Reliability of audit evidence, 95
Removal expenses, 184
Renewals, 236
Renewals basis, 204
Rent a room scheme, 207
Repayment supplement, 218
Reporting fraud to management, 31
Reports by exception, 116
Residence of companies, 303
Residual charge, 183
Returns, 326
Risk assessment process, 24
Risk-based approach, 60
Role of the auditors, 44
Round the computer, 101

Safety requirements for sports ground, 245
Sample size, 104
Sampling risk, 102, 104
Sampling units, 102
SAS 100 *Objective and general principles governing an audit of financial statements*, 44
SAS 530 *Audit sampling and other means of testing*, 102
Savings certificates, 203
Savings income, 155, 202
Scholarships, 156, 183
Scope of external audit, 46
Scope paragraph, 118
Second tax year, 276
Segregation of duties, 33
Selection by value, 106
Selection of the sample, 105
Self-assessment, 214
Sequence sampling, 106
Short life asset, 262
Significant uncertainty, 124
Simulation, 100
Small companies marginal relief, 309
Small companies rate (SCR), 308
Social security benefits, 156
Special rate pool, 255
Specific employment income, 170
Specimen management letter, 134
Spouses, 162
Staff authority, 14
Staff parties, 185
Staff suggestion schemes, 183
Standardised working papers, 72
Statement of Auditing Standards SAS 100 *Objective and general principles governing an audit of financial statements*, 44
Statement of auditor's responsibility, 118
Statement of management's responsibility, 118
Statements of practice, 144
Statements of responsibility, 121
Statistical sampling, 103, 106
Statute, 144
Statutory Instruments, 144
Statutory mileage allowances, 179
Stealing assets, 29
Stealing unclaimed wages, 28
Stock dividends, 156
Subscriptions, 238
Subscriptions to professional bodies, 185
Substantive procedures, 64, 92, 94
Successions, 263
Sufficient appropriate audit evidence, 92
Surcharges, 217
Systematic selection, 105

Tax Bulletin, 144
Tax credit, 203
Tax law, 144
Tax liability, 153
Tax payable, 153
Tax returns, 212
Tax year, 145, 152
Taxable benefits, 172
Taxes, 144
Tax-free investments, 202
Teeming and lading, 28
Test data, 99
Tests of control, 92, 93
Tests of controls, 58
The accountant's role, 16
The AGM, 37
The board, 37
Thermal insulation, 245
Third parties interested in reports to directors or management, 133
Third tax year, 278
Through the computer, 102
Tolerable error, 102, 104
Total income, 153
Trade loss relief against total profits, 314
Trading stock on cessation, 241
Transfers between spouses/civil partners, 339
Travel expenses, 186
True and fair, 20, 116, 117
Turnbull Committee, 36

UK property business, 204
Uncertainty, 124
Unpaid remuneration, 234
Unqualified report, 116

Vans, 178
Vouchers, 174

Walk-through, 58
Wear and tear allowance, 204
Wholly and exclusively for the purposes of the trade, 233
Work related training, 184
Working papers, 72
Workplace nursery, 184
Writing down allowance (WDA), 249, 267

Year of assessment, 152

NOTES

Review Form – Business Essentials – Finance: Auditing and Financial Systems and Taxation (07/10)

BPP Learning Media always appreciates feedback from the students who use our books. We would be very grateful if you would take the time to complete this feedback form, and return it to the address below.

Name: _____   Address: _____

_____

_____

How have you used this Course Book?
(Tick one box only)

☐ Home study (book only)

☐ On a course: college _____

☐ Other _____

Why did you decide to purchase this Course Book? *(Tick one box only)*

☐ Have used BPP Learning Media books in the past

☐ Recommendation by friend/colleague

☐ Recommendation by a lecturer at college

☐ Saw advertising

☐ Other _____

During the past six months do you recall seeing/receiving any of the following?
(Tick as many boxes as are relevant)

☐ Our advertisement

☐ Our brochure with a letter through the post

Your ratings, comments and suggestions would be appreciated on the following areas

	Very useful	Useful	Not useful
Introductory pages	☐	☐	☐
Topic coverage	☐	☐	☐
Summary diagrams	☐	☐	☐
Chapter roundups	☐	☐	☐
Quick quizzes	☐	☐	☐
Activities	☐	☐	☐
Discussion points	☐	☐	☐

	Excellent	Good	Adequate	Poor
Overall opinion of this Course Book	☐	☐	☐	☐

Do you intend to continue using BPP Learning Media Business Essentials Course Books?   ☐ Yes   ☐ No

Please note any further comments and suggestions/errors on the reverse of this page.

Please return this form to: Pippa Riley, BPP Learning Media Ltd, FREEPOST, London, W12 8BR

Review Form (continued)

Please note any further comments and suggestions/errors below